Alexander Stewart

Twixt Ben Nevis and Glencoe

The Natural History, Legends and Folk-Lore of the West Highlands

Alexander Stewart

Twixt Ben Nevis and Glencoe
The Natural History, Legends and Folk-Lore of the West Highlands

ISBN/EAN: 9783337154868

Printed in Europe, USA, Canada, Australia, Japan

Cover: Foto ©Andreas Hilbeck / pixelio.de

More available books at **www.hansebooks.com**

NETHER LOCHABER:

BY

Rev. ALEXANDER STEWART, LL.D.,

With Beautiful Woodcut Frontispiece by Whymper.

Crown 8vo, Cloth, 10s. 6d.

OPINIONS OF THE PRESS.

"'Nether Lochaber' has been styled a phenomenon in the literary world. No other writer is at all equal to him on his native heath. He has imitators, just as Dickens and Carlyle have imitators, but as one star differeth from another star in glory, so do 'Nether Lochaber's' imitators. He is the centre sun, and all other Highland naturalists revolve round him. The truth is, that we fail to appreciate the influence and wonderful scope of his knowledge in matters terrestrial and celestial, because we have him amongst us. 'Nether Lochaber' was the first public writer to popularise science."—*Oban Times.*

"We lay 'Nether Lochaber' aside with much reluctance, for a more enjoyable book we have not read for many a day. The delicious breeze of the sea and the heather stirs its every page, and the whole bears the mark of a rare literary grace and elegance."—*Whitehall Review.*

"This is a delightful book, worthy to be ranked with White's History of Selborne, full of accurate yet amusing descriptions of the habits of beasts, birds, and fishes, intermingled with Highland folk-lore, and overflowing with quiet humour."—*N. B. Mail.*

"Such a book as 'Nether Lochaber,' by the Rev. ALEXANDER STEWART, belongs to the best class of the lighter literature of natural history—a class in which we have already so many good books. The author has a pleasant knack of mingling observations on the scenery and the productions of the Western Highlands with scraps of folk-lore, popular legends, and sporting reminiscences. . . . There is something for every one, for the naturalist, the historian, the angler, the artist, and the collector of old Highland traditions. . . . A more delightful book for those of kindred tastes than 'Nether Lochaber' it is difficult to conceive."—*The Argus.*

"From beginning to end it has not a single dreary page."—*Newcastle W. Chronicle.*

"To lovers of quaint customs, curious legends, and odd bits of natural history, this book will be welcome, being purely the result of personal observation and close intercourse with the people of the West Highlands, amongst whom the writer has long lived and laboured, written, too, with that *entrain* with which a busy man throws himself into the favourite occupation of his leisure hours."—*Spectator.*

"*Ad aperturam libri* we see that it is a veritable book, constructed on sound principles, and this means that it is both substantial and beautiful—the kind of book one likes to see in a drawing-room or to give to a friend. The contents deserved such excellent setting at the printer's hands, for 'Nether Lochaber' is a delightful book."—*Elgin Courant.*

WILLIAM PATERSON, EDINBURGH.

'TWIXT BEN NEVIS AND GLENCOE.

"There is a pleasure in the pathless woods,
There is a rapture on the lonely shore,
There is society where none intrudes,
By the deep Sea, and music in its roar :
I love not Man the less, but Nature more,
From these our interviews, in which I steal
From all I may be, or have been before,
To mingle with the Universe, and feel
What I can ne'er express, yet cannot all conceal."
Childe Harold's Pilgrimage.

From a Negative by Ramsay, Bridge of Allan.

THE

NATURAL HISTORY, LEGENDS, AND FOLK-LORE OF THE WEST HIGHLANDS.

BY

The Rev. ALEXANDER STEWART, LL.D., F.S.A. Scot.;
AUTHOR OF "NETHER LOCHABER."

EDINBURGH:
WILLIAM PATERSON.
MDCCCLXXXV.

EDINBURGH : BURNESS AND COMPANY, PRINTERS TO HER MAJESTY.

IN GRATEFUL ACKNOWLEDGMENT OF MANY KINDNESSES,

THIS VOLUME IS INSCRIBED

TO

The Rev. ROBERT HERBERT STORY, D.D., F.S.A. Scot.;
MINISTER OF ROSENEATH,

BY

HIS OBLIGED AND AFFECTIONATE FRIEND

THE AUTHOR.

"*Author.* Grant that I should write with sense and spirit a few scenes, unlaboured and loosely put together, but which had sufficient interest in them to amuse in one corner the pain of body; in another to relieve anxiety of mind; in a third place, to unwrinkle a brow bent with the furrows of daily toil; in another, to fill the place of bad thoughts, or to suggest better; in yet another, to induce an idler to study the history of his country; in all, save where the perusal interrupted the discharge of serious duties, to furnish harmless amusement,—might not the author of such a work, however inartificially executed, plead for his errors and negligences the excuse of the slave, who, about to be punished for having spread the false report of a victory, saved himself by exclaiming—'Am I to blame, O Athenians, who have given you one happy day?'"—*Cuthbert Clutterbuck* (*Introductory Epistle to* "*The Fortunes of Nigel.*")

CONTENTS.

CHAPTER I.

Rats!—Rat Incantations—The Rat in *Hamlet*—Burns—*Punch*—*Probatum est* Recipe for cure of Abdominal Pain, ... 1

CHAPTER II.

Monument to the Great Brae-Lochaber Bard "Ian Lom"—The Murder of Keppoch—Montrose—Battle of Inverlochy, . . . 11

CHAPTER III.

Haymaking—Madame de Sévigné—Haymaking in 1388—Big Stags—Antlers—Gigantic Cephalopod—*Kraken* of Scandinavian Story, 19

CHAPTER IV.

Mild February—Birds in the Love Season—The Starry Heavens—Meteors—Rabies—Its origin—How communicated—Extinction, 26

CHAPTER V.

Unfavourable Harvest—Patience and Resignation of Highlanders under adverse circumstances—Tunny captured at Corran Ferry—Its characteristics—Tunny Steaks, ... 34

CHAPTER VI.

Popular Superstitions—The Water-Bull—His Bridle, 39

CHAPTER VII.

Winter Solstice—Homer—"A fire when it cheerily blazes"—Bird-Catchers—Their character—Greenfinch—Crossbill—Chaffinch—Blackbirds sent to America, ... 46

CONTENTS.

CHAPTER VIII.

The Macdonells of Glengarry—Sale of the Estate—Creagan-an-Fhithich—The last Family Bard—"Blind Allan," . . . 53

CHAPTER IX.

Weather Prophets and Prophecies—Beauty of the West Highlands in early Summer—"Pedometric" Spring Temperature—Story of a Song-Thrush—A mid-May Idyl, ... 58

CHAPTER X.

A Hebridean Correspondent—A Box and its Contents—A Skeleton—A rare Cetacean—*Delphinus Delphis*—The Sacred Fish of the Ancients—*Bec d'Oie* or "Goose-bill" of the French—Its Food, . 66

CHAPTER XI.

Ramble among the Hills—Encounter with an aged Parishioner—Song of the Smuggling Times—A version in Herd's Collection—Which is the Original? 74

CHAPTER XII.

Pets—"Merdo," a pet Billy-Goat—His Habits—Antipathy between Goats and Rats—Goat's Hoof, Horns, &c. . . . 82

CHAPTER XIII.

Hedgehogs—Frank Buckland—Hedgehog Pets—Hedgehogs combative—Excellent to eat—New Year Festivities—Story of Pyrrhus the Epiret—An Evening with Christopher North—Professor Blackie—"Songs of Religion and Life"—*Sancte Socrates, ora pro nobis*, . 89

CHAPTER XIV.

A Wintry March—God made the Country, Man made the Town—Spanish Mackerel—An Owl making a mistake—Dog and Hedgehog—Intelligent Collies—Interchange of News, ... 99

CHAPTER XV.

Cold Spring—An Arab Proverb—An old "Piobaireachd"—Its Origin and Date—Words attached to—Translation—A strange Charm or Talisman—Paralysis and Palsy proper, ... 105

CONTENTS.

CHAPTER XVI.

Glen Tarbert—*Lyche-Gate* of Church at Strontian—Hedgehog—Contribution to the Natural History of, ... 113

CHAPTER XVII.

Letter from the Hebrides—Curious old Song—Translated into English, 119

CHAPTER XVIII.

Sea-Fowl seeking shelter—Coming Storms—A Fieldfare in sad plight—Surgical Operation—"Sobieski" wrongously suspected—The Nightingale in Scotland, ... 124

CHAPTER XIX.

Wild-Birds and Meteorological Forecasts—Stewart of Appin and the Marquis of Tweeddale—A Christening—Miss Knight and Dr. Johnson, ... 132

CHAPTER XX.

Great Grey Shrike—Its Habits—Stormy Petrel—Terrible force of Mountain Squalls, ... 139

CHAPTER XXI.

The Throstle-Cock—Substantial Breakfast—St. Valentine's Day—The Paston Letters—How to lead a Stubborn Pig the way you would have her to go, ... 147

CHAPTER XXII.

Primroses—The Primrose in Gaelic Poetry—Translation—The little Auk or Rotch—Skuas—Their habits, ... 157

CHAPTER XXIII.

A Crooked Sixpence—A Luckpenny, or Coin of Grace—Popular Superstition—Weasel-skin Purse—Sealskin Purse—Fresh Herrings amongst the Heather, ... 166

CHAPTER XXIV.

The Crozier of St. Fillan—Its Gaelic name *Cuigreach*—Etymology and meaning of term—East Indian Hoopoe—*Upupa Longirostris*—Arrival of Cuckoo, ... 174

CHAPTER XXV.

Folk-lore from the Hebrides—An Incantation of Increase—A Confabulation in Glencoe—Periphrases as to Death and Dying—A Daughter of Allan Dall, the Bard of Glengarry, ... 181

CHAPTER XXVI.

A "Slide" on a Frozen Stretch of River in an Upland Glen—Amazement of Black-faced Sheep at the Performance—"Lassie" also astonished—All Quadrupeds have a horror of Ice—Intelligence of "Lassie"—Finds the Cows unaided in a Midnight Storm—Age at which Dogs cease to be useful—Famous Dogs, ... 187

CHAPTER XXVII.

Cold January—Pet Days—Rainfall—Highlander's standard in gauging a Fall of Snow—Anecdote of Alasdair Macdonald, the Ardnamurchan Bard—Shoemaking—Shoes sent home unblackened, . 196

CHAPTER XXVIII.

Safe from East and North-East Storms under the Lee of Ben Nevis—Story of a Ballad of the Maritime Highlands—A Fragment—Translation, ... 204

CHAPTER XXIX.

Demons of the Dust-Cloud and Spindrift—Gaelic Rhyme—Demons sometimes visible in form of Lambent Flame—Wit-Word Combats—Meaning of a Gaelic Phrase, ... 212

CHAPTER XXX.

Splendid Wild-Bird Season—Sea-fowl at Work—Following in the wake of Steamers—Sharpness of Eye, ... 217

CONTENTS.

CHAPTER XXXI.

Puss-Moth Caterpillar—The Astronomy of Buddhist Priests—Galileo—Chinese Encylopædia in 5020 Volumes! 222

CHAPTER XXXII.

The Pearl Mussel in Highland Rivers and Streams—Story of a Pearl belonging to Stewart of Appin—*Byssus* of *Mya Margaritifera* a Specific in Affections of the Eye—Pearls in the Common Mussel—Mussel sometimes poisonous, ... 228

CHAPTER XXXIII.

Weather Prognosticators sometimes "out in their reckoning"—Magnificent Double Rainbow over Glencoe—Cats—A One-Eared Cat a Treasure—How it came about—Rival Rhymes—Cat's Whiskers, 231

CHAPTER XXXIV.

Meteorological Observatory to be erected on Ben Nevis—Electric discharges on top—Curious Story, ... 241

CHAPTER XXXV.

Comfortable condition of the People at Term-time—The old Quern Hand-mill or *Bràth*—The *Cnotag* or *Eòrnachan*, the Knockin'-Stane or Pot-Barley Preparer—Knockin'-Stane Stick and Sword Combat, 249

CHAPTER XXXVI.

November Meteor Showers—Occultation of Stars—Superstition—Old-Wife Herbalist—How a Cow was rescued from the effects of the Evil Eye—Virtue of an Oatmeal Bannock—Fox caught sleeping—Badgers, ... 258

CHAPTER XXXVII.

Intense Cold—Bird-Pensioners in frost and snow—Their tameness—Fond of Scraps of Flesh and picking Bones—Stupidity of Cochin-China Cock—Cochin-Chinas and Bantams—Ninth Ode of First Book of Horace done into English, ... 265

CONTENTS.

CHAPTER XXXVIII.

Old Gaelic Rhyme, Meaning of—Golden Eagle at Kelvingrove Museum, Glasgow—Golden Eagle on the wing—Circling *Sguir-na-Ciche* of Glencoe—The Epithet *Chrysaëtos* first applied to it by Aristotle—Its predominant Colour—Professor Geddes of Aberdeen—His *Problem of the Homeric Poems*, ... 273

CHAPTER XXXIX.

Meteors—Professor Blackie—Homer—The Descent as a Meteor of Pallas Minerva—A sparkling swift-descending Fireball Meteor ought to be called a *Minervalite*—The "*Dreag*" of the Gaels—An exploding *Dreag* in 1746—The great Meteor Shower of 1866, . . . 285

CHAPTER XL.

Cold out of Season—Its effects on the Nidification of Birds—The Golden Eagle in the Hebrides and on the Mainland—Letter about Golden Eagle from Kintail—Story of an Eagle from Loch Lomond—Ben Lomond and Ben Nevis—Best View of the latter from Ardgour and Banavie, ... 296

CHAPTER XLI.

Storm—Stormy Petrel—Rare Birds—Red-necked Phalarope—Wild-Bird Notes from Mull and Stranraer—Antique Silver Brooch found on the top of Benvere, in Appin—Appin an old Hunting-Ground of the Stuart Kings, ... 303

CHAPTER XLII.

Mild Winter—A *Crubhan-Cait*—Wild-Flowers—Birds singing—Bats abroad—An Egg in a Sparrow's Nest at New-Year Time, . . 310

CHAPTER XLIII.

The Cuckoo on February 10th—Willie Drummond, Pearl Fisher and Herbalist, ... 316

CHAPTER XLIV.

April Drought—Early Nesting Birds—Survival of the Fittest—Rival Song-Thrushes singing at Midnight—Ian Mac Roanuill Oig of Glencoe—Singing Mice, ... 324

CONTENTS.

CHAPTER XLV.

Heavy Snowfall in April—Snow at Culloden Moor on the day of the Battle, 16th April 1746—Flora Macdonald, ... 330

CHAPTER XLVI.

Sailing on Loch Leven—Mackerel—Porpoises—*Argus* in the *Odyssey*—"*Lassie*"—Age of Dogs—Dame Juliana Berners—Lassie's Grave, 336

CHAPTER XLVII.

A Visit to the Oval Brochs of the Island of Luing—Their Position and Dimensions—The Hiding Craigs near Easdale, ... 345

CHAPTER XLVIII.

Pied Swallows—1882 remarkable for Albinoism and Abnormal Colouring in Birds—Kestrel neatly plucking a Partridge Poult, that it might be the more easily carried against the wind, ... 354

CHAPTER XLIX.

Stormy October—Birds taking shelter—Superstition—The Oxeye Tit a Bird of good omen, ... 359

CHAPTER L.

Meteorology and Weather Forecasts—Ornithology in aid of, 367

CHAPTER LI.

Cold and Stormy Winter—Transit of Venus—Dr. Tait, Archbishop of Canterbury, ... 372

CHAPTER LII.

Winter in the Country—Wild-Fowl—Flock of "Hooper" Swans (*Anus cygnus*, Linn.)—Wild-Swan Notes—Letter from Perthshire—The Eagle—Fox—Curious Egg—Alpine Hares on the Low Lands a sign of severe Winter, ... 379

'TWIXT BEN NEVIS AND GLENCOE.

CHAPTER I.

Rats!—Rat Incantations—The Rat in *Hamlet*—Burns—*Punch*— *Probatum est* Recipe for cure of Abdominal Pain.

Why, of all living animal plagues, rats should in popular superstition be considered the most amenable to good advice and expostulation, if couched in rhyme—the most readily frightened and easily driven away from any particular locality by the mere force of a doggerel incantation—is a puzzle we have long pondered over, without arriving at anything like a satisfactory solution. A belief in the efficacy of this mode of getting quit of rats seems to have been common from very early times. *Giraldus Cambrensis*, who lived in the twelfth century, and wrote a "History of the World," tells of a certain district in the south of England so plagued with rats in his day, that they could only be expelled by a powerful incantation specially composed for the occasion by no less a mediator than the austere and holy Saint Yvor. Rats seem to have had no special or distinctive name of their own at this time, for the chronicler is content to speak of them simply as *Mures majores*, or bigger mice, by which there can be no question rats are meant. In many countries, even at the present day, it is believed among the vulgar that rats, when they become annoyingly troublesome, can be very easily disposed of in this way, if the thing is gone about in proper form; and nowhere, perhaps, is this very curious superstition more common than in the Highlands of Scotland. In speaking of it, indeed, you generally find the people treat the subject with a certain degree of jocular levity, as if they would have you understand that they believe it no more than you do; but this is only a common trick, frequently resorted to in such matters, in order to throw the inquirer off his guard, for though they pretend to laugh at many other superstitions, as well as at this particular one of rat incantation, they yet make no scruple to practise them in all seriousness when they think a fitting occasion has arrived. A clergyman of considerable standing in the West Highlands once told us that he was tutor when quite a young man in the family of Maclachlan of Rahoy, in Morven. One morning that gentleman—one of the most respectable men in the county—came in from an examination of his stack-yard and barn, and complained grievously of the multitude of rats that had recently so increased about the place as to have become a pest so destructive and annoying, that some decided steps must instantly be taken to get rid of them. "You, sir," he exclaimed, turning to the tutor, who was then but a divinity student or parson in embryo—"You, sir, a scholar, and something, as I believe, of a poet too, might surely help us in this emergency. Why not compose an *Aoir* or incantatory rhyme to drive the rats away? If you succeed in ridding us of this pest, or even diminishing it to any appreciable extent, you shall have a horse and saddle to ride about on wherever you like for the rest of the season." The prospect of a horse and saddle to ride on such terms was not to be resisted, and the incantation was forthwith composed in excellent Gaelic, and said or sung in due form at the barn door and stackyard corners. Curiously enough, as our informant assured us, not only did the rats shortly afterwards totally disappear, but they actually reappeared in great numbers in the opposite district of Sunart, whither in the spell or incantation they had been directed to betake themselves. Our friend, the author of the incantation, laughed, as a matter of course, at the whole affair, but the disappearance at the time of the rats from Morven was by hundreds attributed to the cunning and power of the spell, and to nothing else. It is curious that in such spells the absolute destruction of the rats was never wished for; the spell, if it was to be efficacious, must distinctly assign them some other place of residence, generally separated from the home whence they were being expelled by a mountain chain, a lake or running stream, or arm of the sea. The following rat-spell, picked up quite accidentally the other day, must suffice for the present. Standing in our kitchen, we were growling over the rat-eaten and very *holey* state of a sack of meal that had just come in from Ballachulish Pier, where it had been stored for only a single night, when an old man in the neighbourhood came in, who joined us in heartily abusing the Ballachulish Pier rats, from whose depredations he also had suffered somewhat on a recent occasion. The circumstance easily led to a long talk on the natural history of rats and rat-spells, and our friend repeated the following as a well-known rat incantation that had been completely successful in a case of the kind some time during the last century. The author was a farmer of the name of Livingstone, in the Island of Lismore, and the spell-driven rats swam across the ferry at Port Appin, taking up their residence with Mr. Downie, the then proprietor, who was very soon nearly eaten out of house and home by the chisel-toothed invaders. It is no doubt a colony of their descendants that now makes Ballachulish Pier about the last place in the world to leave a sack of meal at, even for the shortest night in the year. Here is the Lismore rat-spell, or

Aor Nan Radan.

Mìle marbhaisg ort, a radain!
A shlaidearc nam badan arbhair;
Cha leòr leat sop ach an làn sguab dheth,
Dh-fàg thu 'm bualadh dhomh nêo-tharbhach.
Rinn thu gradan de'm chuid còrna,
A mhéirlich gur mòr do cháil dheth;
Na'n robh do cheann agam air innean,
'Smise nach tilleadh mo làmh dhiot!

Cha d'fhàg thu mulan anus san iolainn
Nach do mhil thu 's nach do mhab thu,
Cha d'fhàg thu poca 'san t'sabhal,
Nach do tholl thu 's nach do shlaid thu;
Mo thruaighe mi aig àm 'cuir coirce
An t'seann lairdhonn bi 'bochd da-rireamh;
Mhic an Radain 's mór do pheacadh,
Mar a chreach thu de gach nì mi!

Ach èirich a laochain a's dean imric,
Imich th'ar a chaol gu séolta,
Thu fein 's do chuid daoine uile

> Falbhaibh gu builleach mar chomhla'
> Air Michail 'sair Bride mìn,
> Eirich, imich as mo thìr!

The Gaelic is uncommonly good, and there is a touch of humour in the whole that is very difficult to catch and reproduce in a translation; but we have ventured upon the following version, which we warn the reader, in order to prevent future quarrel on the subject, is more of a paraphrase than a metaphrase :—

A Rat-Expelling Incantation.

A thousand ills befall thee, greedy rat!
   Expertest thief that ever yet was born!
In barn and stack-yard, *maugre* trap and cat,
   Sad is the state of all my stock of corn;
Nor does a handful serve thee, shameless thief,
Unblushing rogue, thou claimest the whole sheaf!

My barley thou hast millered into meal,
   Chaff and small dust together close commingled;
Thou spoilest more than ever thou canst steal;
   Hadst thou but any shame, thine ears had long since tingled;
I wish I had thy head upon a stithy,
I'd rap it with the biggest hammer in the smithy!

Nor corn in sheaf, nor barley snugly stacked,
   Could serve thy turn; but all my garner'd grain,
In well-filled sacks is next by thee attacked,
   And all yspoiled, thou thief of fertile brain.
And all my sacks are nibbled too, and holed,—
A sight most aggravating to behold.

Alas, for all my seed corn in the spring!
   Alas, for all thy keep, my good brown mare!
But take advice, and leave me, rat; and bring
   All thy companions with thee; else beware
My malison shall fall withouten fail
On thee and thine, from whisker-tip to tail!

So rat be warned; away! across the Ferry,
And in some quarter new be sleek and merry;
By good St. Michael, and by chaste St. Bride,
I charge thee, leave me ere the morning tide!

(*Exeunt Ratti* tumultuously, and best foot foremost.)

Why, as we have already remarked, rats should be considered more manageable in this sort of way than any other animals is a very great puzzle. We have thought over it much, and can make nothing of it. In the natural history of the animal, however, it is a fact that should not be overlooked, that a colony of rats are very often known, with or without an incantation —oftener, indeed, without than with—to leave a certain homestead, or entire district even, and take up new quarters sometimes at a great distance. Rats are proverbially said to leave an old rotten ship likely soon to founder by a sort of still unexplained instinct, and generally, we may be sure, they have good reasons, if we only knew them, for all their migrations. The puzzle is simply why they should be supposed to listen and be obedient to a mere human spell, if cunningly concocted and couched in rhyme. It is curious that a certain degree of humour and fun should so invariably be associated with the person and character of the rat rather than with that of mouse, or cat, or dog, or weasel, or other animal whatever. The scene in *Hamlet* would lose much of its grim humour and effectiveness, if it were not for the rat behind the arras, that at the sword's point of the Prince was

"Dead, for a ducat, dead!"

And the well-known scene in Burns' *Jolly Beggars*

would be poor and tame indeed if it were not for the prominency of the rats in the picture—

> "He ended; and the kebars sheuk
> Aboon the chorus roar;
> While frighted rattans backward leuk,
> And seek the benmost bore."

Nothing else, perhaps, could so vividly impress us with a full sense of the heartiness of the applause that followed the song of him who was a son of Mars, and had been in many wars. One of the best things that ever appeared in *Punch* was the

> " Still so gently o'er me *stealing* "

of one of these midnight depredators. The rat is unquestionably an animal of great intelligence, and almost more than vulpine cunning, as every one who has tried to trap or take them unawares must readily bear witness. To this extraordinary and really super-quadrupedal *nous* and intelligence is probably due the fact that their expulsion from any place by direct and violent means being well-nigh an impossibility, people fell into the belief that fair means might perhaps succeed, and hence, we take it, the expostulatory nature and wheedling tone of all the rat incantations that have ever come under our notice. Not in the " I'll make you," but in a " please go " sort of phrase, is the rat in these " spells " invariably addressed. Any one capable of composing a really efficacious rat-expelling incantation *in re* the Ballachulish Pier colony would, we make no doubt, be repaid by a large amount of genuine gratitude on the part of the pier-master and a numerous host of interested clients. In such a spell, however, we have to beg the incantator not to direct the rats to the Lochaber shore, where we have already quite as many of the whiskered marauders as we want or care about.

A few days ago we were witness to an almost instantaneous cure of a common ailment, the secret of which and *modus operandi* we make public for the benefit in all time coming of all whom it may concern. A man of middle age, who had been cutting peats all day, was on his return home in the evening taken ill with severe abdominal pains. Happening to be passing his door, we were called in to see him, and he certainly seemed to be in the greatest agony, so much so, that we feared it must be something much more serious than any mere colic. Brandy had been administered without effect, and all we could suggest in addition was the immediate application of hot fomentations. Before this could be done, however, an old woman in the neighbourhood came in, and at once undertook, if her advice was followed, to effect a cure. She was known as a sensible and most respectable woman, who had passed many years as a domestic servant in the south, and it was on all hands gladly agreed that she should try her skill, there being some consolation in the fact that, whatever she did or administered to the patient, he could hardly be made worse than he then was. We were going to leave as she was about to commence operations, but she begged of us to stay for a short time, and her manifest confidence in herself rendering us not a little curious as to the upshot of it all, we consented. She first asked the patient's daughter for a common smoothing iron, which having got, she placed not simply with its smooth face to the fire, as is usually done in laundry work, but bodily into the heart of the fire, heaping the peats above and around it, and blowing the fire, until in a few minutes it had attained a dull red heat. Filling a small wooden bicker or "cog" with cold water from the neighbouring stream, she took the iron from the fire, and dipped it, hissing and hot, some half-dozen times into the water, until it had attained a temperature considerably higher than mere tepidity, by which time the iron had of course, *pari passu*, again become cold. Filling a bowl, which might perhaps contain an English pint or thereby, with this water, hot and iron-impregnated, she made the patient drink it off at a draught, and it acted like a charm. The "Faculty" and uninitiated may smile incredulously as they read, but it is perfectly true, as we can vouch, that in less than five minutes the man was entirely and completely well, not a trace of pain remaining. So effectual was this very singular and simple cure, that within a quarter of an hour of the moment we first saw him in excruciating pain, he voluntarily put on his shoes and walked with us quite comfortably and calmly for fully half a mile on our way home. We visited the old lady next day, in order to find out, if we could, what she had to say as to the *rationale* of her cure. To all our inquiries she answered honestly and quietly that she really did not know how the hot-iron-impregnated water operated so beneficially in such cases. She only knew that she had often tried it in alleviation of severe abdominal pains, and never once knew it to fail. She first saw it used in a case of the kind by her whilom mistress, an old lady in Ayrshire, and the simplicity and ready application, as well as the invariable success attending the remedy, struck her so forcibly, that she treasured up the knowledge of it as something well worth remembering, and for many years had continued to practise it when occasion offered, as we saw. She made no secret or mystery of the matter, and we felt convinced of her perfect honesty, and of the efficacy of the remedy as it came under our own observation. These popular remedies in cases of human ailment, though no doubt frequently empirical and illusory, are nevertheless worthy, we think, of more attention and careful study on the part of our regular practitioners than they have hitherto deigned to bestow upon them.

CHAPTER II.

Monument to the Great Brae-Lochaber Bard "Ian Lom"—The Murder of Keppoch—Montrose—Battle of Inverlochy.

THROUGH the munificence and patriotism of Mr. Fraser Mackintosh of Drummond, M.P., a monument, no less substantial and enduring than beautiful and every way appropriate, has been erected over the grave of the celebrated Gaelic bard "Ian Lom," on *Dun Aingeal* in *Kill Choirread* of Brae-Lochaber. As a poet and satirist of a very high order, and as a steady and consistent Loyalist, in days when Loyalism was accounted a crime, "Ian Lom," whose proper name was John Macdonald, is from a certain point of view just as deserving of a monument as John Bunyan. Both were in extremes—the Puritan allegorist of England, and the uncompromising Catholic of Brae-Lochaber—but both were in the main honest men and true from their widely different standpoints, and equally deserve the tribute of our respect and regard in the always appropriate and fitting form of monumental commemoration.

The monument is ten feet in height, and placed upright, like the ancient stones of Scotland, of which, in style and outline, it is intentionally an imitation. The face is richly ornamented in relief. At the foot is a raised plate, with the following inscription in Gaelic :—

"'An so 'n Dun-Aingeal a'm Braigh-Lochabar,
Tha Bàrd na Ceapaich gu trom na chadal ;
'Se Ian Lom Mac Dhomhnuill b'ainm dha,
Ian Lom! ach theireadh cuid Ian Manntach."

The English of the lines is—

"Here in Dun-Aingeal, in the Braes of Lochaber,
The Bard of Keppoch is very sound asleep:
His name was John Mac Donald, John the Bare—
John the *Bare* and *Biting!* but by some called John the Stammerer."

Of the personal life and history of "Ian Lom" very little is known for certain. He was of the family of *Mac-ic-Raonuill*, or Macdonalds of Keppoch, and, living through the greater part of the reigns of Charles I. and II., died unmarried, a very old man, in the autumn of 1709. He was a man of considerable education, which we have heard accounted for by one likely to be well informed on such a matter, by the assertion that he had been for some years in training for the priesthood at the College of Valladolid, in Spain, when some unpardonable indiscretion caused his expulsion from that seminary, and his return to Scotland as a gentleman at large—a sort of hybrid nondescript, half clerical and half lay. His poetical powers are of a very high order, and he was unquestionably a man of very superior talents. He first became known beyond the borders of his native Lochaber by the active part he took in the punishment of the murderers of the heir of Keppoch. Of this atrocious crime the following account is given in a short life of the bard, written by our late amiable and excellent friend, the well-known Celtic scholar and *Seanachie*, the Rev. Dr. Macintyre, minister of Kilmonivaig :—

"The Keppoch massacre was perpetrated by the cousins of the young man about the year 1663. The poet had foreseen what really happened, and had done all he could to prevent it. He perceived that the minds of the people were alienated from the lawful heir in his absence; he and his brother being sent abroad to receive their education during their minority, and their affairs being entrusted to their cousins, who made the best use they could of the opportunity in establishing themselves by the power and authority thus acquired in the land. Although he could not prevent the fatal deed, he was not a silent witness. He stood single-handed in defence of the right. As he failed in his attempt to awaken the people to a sense of their duty, he addressed himself to the most potent neighbour and chieftain, Glengarry, who declined interfering with the affairs of a celebrated branch of the great *Clan Dughaill*, and there was no other that could have aided him with any prospect of success. Thus situated, our poet, firm in his resolution, and bold in the midst of dangers, was determined to have the murderers punished. In his ire at the reception he met from Glengarry, he invoked his muse, and began to praise Sir Alexander Macdonald of Sleat. Nothing can give us a better idea of the power of the Highland clans and of the state of the nation at this period than this event, which happened in a family and among a people by no means inconsiderable. Macdonald of Keppoch could bring out on emergency three hundred fighting men of his own people, as brave and as faithful as ever a chieftain called out or led to battle, that would have shed the last drop of their blood in his cause, and yet he had not an inch of land to bestow upon them. The Macdonald of Keppoch appeared at the head of his own men, although only a branch of the great clan. He might have got rights, as he had just claims to land for signal services, but 'would he care for titles given on sheepskin?' He claimed his rights and titles by the edge of the sword. The kingdom of Scotland, as well as other nations, often suffered from the calamities that have been consequent on minorities. The affairs of Keppoch must have been in the most disordered state, when a people, warlike and independent in spirit, were trusted to the care and left under the control of relations. Selfish and, as they proved, unworthy of their trust, the innocent, unsuspicious young men were sacrificed to the ambitious usurpations of base and cruel relatives. Our poet alone proved faithful, and after doing what he could, it was not safe for him to rest there. The cause he espoused was honourable, and he was never wanting in zeal Confiding in the justice of his cause and his own powers of persuasion (and no man better knew how to touch the spring that vibrated through the feelings of a high-spirited and disinterested chieftain), he succeeded. Being favourably received by Sir Alexander Macdonald, he concerted measures for punishing the murderers, which met his Lordship's approval, and indicated the judgment and sagacity of the faithful clansman. A person was sent to *North Uist* with a message to Archibald Macdonald (*An Ciaran Mabach*), a poet as well as a soldier, commissioning him to take a company of chosen men to the mainland, where he would meet with the Lochaber Bard, who would guide and instruct him in his future proceedings. The usurpers were seized and beheaded. They met with the punishment they so richly deserved; but the vengeance was taken in the most cruel manner, and the exultation and feelings of the man who acted so boldly and stood so firmly in the defence of the right have been too ostentatiously indulged in verses from which humanity recoils. How different from his melting strains, so full of sympathy and compassion for the innocent young men whose death he avenged! The atrocious deed has been palpably commemorated in a manner repugnant to humanity by '*Tobar nan Ceann*' in Glengarry."

In the wild and perturbed times in which he lived, Macdonald's talents and habits of life caused him to become a very prominent man indeed. To Montrose and *Alasdair Mac Cholla-Chiotaich*, as well as afterwards to Graham, Lord Viscount Dundee, and other leading Loyalists, he was well known, and by them all much trusted and employed on the most delicate political embassies. No man of his day knew the Highlands and its temper so thoroughly. While the most zealous and uncompromising of Royalists, he managed to be on good terms, outwardly at least, even with those most opposed to the cause to which he had, heart and soul, attached himself, his talents, his life, his all ; and was thus able, though constitutionally a coward and purposely a non-combatant as far as mere fighting was concerned, to render the King and his cause such services as made him a man of no small mark and note throughout the kingdom. In those wonderful campaigns which, true in every particular, yet read like Mediæval romances, in which Montrose made himself the talk and envy of every soldier in Europe, it is certain that he consulted " Ian Lom " at almost every step. A brief but characteristic note, which we have more than once seen and read, from the great Marquis to the Bard was in the possession of the late Rev. Dr. Macintyre, and is probably still preserved in the family as a very valuable and interesting relic, which in truth it is. It consists but of some half-dozen lines, but when we find the Marquis declaring himself under his own hand, from his " Camp near Kilsyth," Ian Lom's " very loving and trew (*sic*) friend to command," we may be pretty sure that the Brae-Lochaber Bard was a man of no small account and consequence in his day. Tradition gives " Ian Lom " the credit of being the person that at Fort-Augustus overtook Montrose and his army, and told them that Argyll and the Campbells were at Inverlochy, and was thus indirectly the cause of one of the completest victories ever gained by Montrose— and he had gained many,—a man of whom Scotland has more reason to be proud than any one else that we can think of within the limits of three consecutive centuries, except Walter Scott. Unrivalled in his day as a soldier, and almost faultless as a man, you will have some difficulty, if you try, in finding any one entitled for an instant, and on any claims whatever, to stand with the slightest pretensions to equality of stature beside the, perhaps, greatest man of his age— James Graham, Earl and Marquis of Montrose.

Of "Ian Lom's" poetry it is hardly possible to speak too highly. Rough, and rugged, and rude almost always, it yet hits the mark arrived at so unmistakeably that you cannot but applaud. The fact that his songs may be still heard from the lips of unlettered shepherds on the hillside of a summer morning, as well as from the more red and ripe and musical lips of the "lassie" at the washing-tub by the burn side in the summer evening, go where you may, from the extreme west to east or north, where Gaelic is spoken, is perhaps the best proof of the merits of poems which it is utterly impossible to make a non-Gaelic speaking reader understand, far less appreciate. His *Battle of Inverlochy*, of which he was a delighted spectator, and his *Murder of Keppoch*, every Highlander knows by heart. His terrible satire on *William and Mary*, his allusions to the DAUGHTER particularly, who could so unnaturally aid and abet in the dethronement and expulsion from his kingdom of her own *father*, must, in parts at least, be familiar to every reader of Gaelic poetry, while nothing can be more beautiful and pathetic than his threnody on the *Execution of Montrose*, ending as it does with a satiric string of such pungency and venom as is perhaps unequalled, search for its compeer where you may, in any language, ancient or modern. Indignantly and scornfully referring to Macleod of Assynt, who so shamefully betrayed the hero to his doom, he in the concluding stanza turns round, and, in the most withering and contemptuous language, compares the *reward* with the valuable life betrayed :—

> "Marbh-fhaisg ort a dhi-mheis,
> Nach ole a reic thu a'm firean,
> Air son na mine Litich,
> A's da thrian di goirt!"

He—that is, Macleod of Assynt—sold the life of the best and greatest man of his day for a cargo of meal from Leith, two-thirds of said meal, says the bard, in which he is corroborated by contemporary chroniclers, proving to be "rotten, weevily, worthless!" Our own favourite among all his poems is his address to Sir James Macdonald of Sleat's *birlinn* or galley, two verses of which cling to our memory from earliest childhood.

> "Dia na stiuir air na daraich,
> Dh' fhalbh air thùs an t'suil mhara,
> Seal mu'n tug e chiad bhoinne de 'n traghadh."
>
> "Cha be marcaich n' eich leimnich,
> A bhuigneadh geall rèis ort,
> 'N uair a thogadh tu bréid os ceann sàile!"

We wish we could translate them, but we cannot, and no one can, with anything like justice to the original. His *Marbhrann*, or elegy on the death of "Black Alasdair of Glengarry," is also a very beautiful and widely known poem, which old men and old women continue yet to sing with unspeakable point and pathos, when in the long and stormy winter nights the oil in the lamp has wasted and the wick burns but dimly. His song in praise of Sir Alexander Macdonald of Sleat is also very fine. His account in one verse of the heraldic bearings of the Macdonalds is inimitable. Not daring to attempt even a paraphrase, we can only direct the Gaelic reader's attention to the lines themselves:—

> "Be do shuaicheantas taitneach,
> Long, 's leoghan a's bradan,
> Air chuan liobhara 'n aigeil ;
> A chraobh fhìgeis gun ghaiseadh,
> A chuireadh fion di le pailteas ;
> Lamh dhearg ro na gaisgich 'nan tim !"

A plain prose literal translation is tame, but here it is:—

> "Thy well-known and well-beloved cognisance
> Was the graceful galley, the lion, and the salmon,
> All on a field of laughing ocean waves !
> With the unblemished wild fig-tree,
> That never failed in fruit of large-heartedness and generosity !
> And the Red Hand of the race that never blenched in combat !"

CHAPTER III.

Haymaking—Madame de Sévigné—Haymaking in 1388—Big Stags—Antlers—Gigantic Cephalopod—*Kraken* of Scandinavian Story.

It is told of Buffon, the celebrated naturalist, that when engaged on his great work he was in the habit of dressing himself in his very best, wearing all his orders and jewellery before sitting down to composition. The more elegantly he was dressed, the more easily and elegantly flowed his periods. Such was his notion; and those who knew him intimately went so far as to assert that this was true, and that if on any occasion he was worse or better dressed than ordinarily, they could readily detect and point out the page or pages written during that particular sitting. And, luckily for him, this taste for elegance and dress Buffon could well afford to gratify to the full, for he was Count de Buffon, Lord of Montbart, Marquis of Rougemont, and Intendant of the King's Gardens and Cabinets of Natural History. All naturalists, unfortunately, are not so happily circumstanced. Some of our readers, for instance, will perhaps be shocked to know, while others will very readily and sympathisingly believe the fact, that we have sat down to write this article in our shirt sleeves. Why? Merely because it is wise and well to make hay while the sun shines. One stone of hay well made is worth half a dozen of such sodden and swept-out stuff as you often see let down into your horse-rack of an early spring morning in every stable in the country. And irrespective of the propriety and profit of making hay in favourable weather, we like it, and would be sorry to exchange such a pleasant jolly labour in its season for all the elegance and *pernickitiness* of Buffon's dress, and all the comforts of his study, with all its velvet-cushioned sofas and its "too easy" chairs. We had rather have Madame de Sévigné along with us in haymaking than Monsieur Le Comte de Buffon, distinguished naturalist though he was. Do you know anything of Madame de Sévigné, good reader, the most amiable, cheeriest, and gayest of Frenchwomen, the most delightful of letter-writers? Pure, too, and spotless in a court as corrupt as it was brilliant, she was one of the very few that could touch pitch without being defiled. Of her many beautiful letters, one of the most charming is that on haymaking. It is written from the country to her cousin, Monsieur de Coulanges, telling him she has been obliged to dismiss Picard, her valet, and explaining the reason why. It is altogether so charming, *naïf*, and thoroughly Frenchwoman-like, that we make no apology for giving it in full. The translation, almost as good as the original, is by Leigh Hunt.

"THE ROCKS, 22*d July* 1671.

"I write, my dear cousin, over and above the stipulated fortnight communications, to advertise you that you will soon have the honour of seeing Picard; and as he is brother to the lackey of Madame de Coulanges, I must tell you the reason why. You know that Madame the Duchess de Chaulnes is at Vitry. She expects the Duke there in ten or twelve days with the Estates of Brittany. 'Well, and what then?' say you. I say that the Duchess is expecting the Duke with all the States, and that meanwhile she is at Vitry all alone, dying of *ennui*. 'And what,' return you, 'has this to do with Picard?' Why, look! she is dying of *ennui*, and I am her only consolation, and so you may readily conceive that I carry it with a high hand over Mademoiselle de Kerborgne and Kerqueoison. A pretty roundabout way of telling my story, I must confess, but it will bring us to the point. Well, then, as I am her only consolation, it follows that after I have been to see her, she will come to see me, when, of course, I shall wish her to find my garden in good order, and my walks in good order—those fine walks of which you are so fond. Still you are at a loss to conceive whither they are leading you now. Attend, then, if you please, to a little suggestion by the way. You are aware that haymaking is going forward! Well, I have no haymakers; I send into the neighbouring fields to press them into my service; there are none to be found, and so all my people are summoned to make hay instead. But do you know what haymaking is? I will tell you. Haymaking is the prettiest thing in the world. You play at turning grass over in a meadow; and as soon as you know how to do that, you know how to make hay. The whole house went merrily to the task; all but Picard. He said he would not go, that he was not engaged for such work, and that he would sooner betake himelf to Paris. Faith! didn't I get angry? It was the hundredth dis-service the silly fellow had done me. I saw he had neither heart nor zeal; in short, the measure of his offence was full. I took him at his word, was deaf as a rock to all entreaties in his behalf, and he has set off. It is fit that people be treated as they deserve. If you see him, don't welcome him, don't protect him, and don't blame me. Only look upon him as, of all servants in the world, the one least addicted to haymaking, and, therefore, the most unworthy of good treatment. This is the sum total of the affair. As for me, I am fond of straightforward histories that contain not a word too much. that never go wandering about and beginning again from remote points; and, accordingly, I think I may say without vanity that I hereby present you with a model of an agreeable narration."

Was there ever anything more charming? A nearly perfect prose idyl, in which the erring Picard, though really the hero of the story, is nevertheless, with admirable judgment and tact, allowed only to occupy a secondary and very subordinate position, while really occupying a forward place in the picture : so skilfully is the grouping effected that even his co-servitors, the laughing, willing haymakers, seem nearer to you than he. And, in truth, as Madame de Sévigné found it, haymaking in its season, under a bright sun and blue skies, is one of the most delightful of pastimes. With such weather as they were likely to have in the south-east of France on the 22d July, two hundred years ago, one need not wonder that she thoroughly enjoyed it. Even if she had not said so, we should conclude that at such a date, and in such a climate, it must have been the making of natural or meadow hay that created such a commotion in her household, and gave occasion for such a charming letter as we have quoted. We do not know, indeed, that rye-grass, or what are commonly called artificial grasses, were cultivated at that time. It is interesting to note that several centuries ago, as we daresay is still the case, the season of haymaking—*natural haymaking*, that is—on the borders of England and Scotland was about three weeks later than in France, adopting the date of Madame de Sévigné's letter as about the proper season, which we think we may, for besides being too shrewd and intelligent a lady to engage in such a work unseasonably, the difficulty of finding labourers willing to help for love or money, every one being probably busy with his own, seems to indicate pretty clearly that from the middle to the end of July was at that time, as it probably still is, the proper meadow-haymaking season in the department of Marne. Now, in the well-known ballad of the *Battle of Otterbourne*, a composition which, whatever date we agree to assign to it, is probably at least much older than Madame de Sévigné's time, it is said that when

> "The doughty Douglas boun' him to ride
> To Englande for to drive a prey,"

it was the haymaking season.

> "It fell upon *the Lammas tide*,
> *When husbandmen do win their hay.*"

In the Old Style Lammas falls upon the 12th August, and we know that the battle of Otterbourne was fought on the 15th August 1388, so that for the haymaking, the time for which in France was the last fortnight of July, the season on the Scottish Borders was "upon the Lammas tide," or about the middle of August—some three weeks, as we have said, later. Never, perhaps, even in Lochaber, was meadow haymaking so difficult to encompass satisfactorily as this season. Throughout the whole of August, and up to this date in September, it has been almost constantly wet; and when a dry day does come, or on a wet day the sun bursts out for a time through the clouds, we are all on the *qui vive*, up and doing, as if our all depended on it. Like Madame de Sévigné, we head our household, old and young, "merrily to the task," and the healthy appetite on such occasions of every one at dinner-time, and the sound sleep o' nights, prove that an active spell at haymaking is a good thing in more ways than one.

We have just been looking over some very interesting photographs of deer's heads and antlers. One is a photograph of the champion head of last season, shot in Kinloch Forest of Mamore, in our immediate neighbourhood. It is, in truth, a magnificent head, the grandest, perhaps, we ever saw, except one shot some years ago in Glengour. The other is the photograph of a head with curiously malformed antlers that was shot last year in the Duke of Portland's forest. We understand that a stag with singularly malformed antlers has recently been seen in Mr. Thistlethwayte's forest here, which we hope he may be able to get before the close of the season, to be added to his already very interesting and valuable collection of similar trophies. The other photographs are from across the Atlantic, from Newfoundland, representing such parts of the gigantic Cephalopod as the fishermen were able to show as trophies of their victory over the big-eyed, parrot-beaked monster in the memorable battle of Conception Bay, about a twelvemonth ago. The *Kraken* of Scandinavian story may not be such a mere myth after all, as the unbelievers have so long accounted it, when, on the inductive " *ex pede Herculem* " principle, it is authoritatively asserted that this Briareus-armed monster of the deep must have had a body proper quite 5 feet in diameter and some 50 or 60 feet in length. The portion of one of the arms now preserved in the Museum of St. John's, Newfoundland, is 19 feet in length, which, fairly estimating the part left attached to the body as of equal, or nearly equal, length, gives to the entire member a length of five-and-thirty or forty feet, its under surface, from its junction with the body to extremest tip, thickly studded with powerful sucking discs— truly formidable weapon ! With black piercing eyes "of intense ferocity," larger than the biggest gold-fish glass globe, and a hard and horny parrot beak "as big as a six gallon keg," that could crack a cocoa-nut as easily as if it were an empty egg-shell, add to which an inexhaustible supply of ink (*sepia*), of which it can eject gallons together at will to make turbid the sea, and thereby stupify and confuse its prey, and you have a marine monster as formidable as can be well imagined. Even with the fiercest shark an expert swimmer may have some chance; once within sweep of the arms of such a monster as this, absolutely none. We may state, as an additional proof for the existence of such monster Cephalopods in the North Atlantic, the fact that a ten-armed specimen, 7 feet in length and 5 feet in circumference, has recently been captured in a net in Logy Bay, N.F. Two of the arms in this animal, which has fortunately been preserved complete in all its points, are no less than 24 feet in length, armed with formidable sucking discs to their tips. When we meet with such a baby "cuttle" as this, what dimensions may not a centenarian Cephalopod arrive at? Fishes, and all sorts of marine animals, if they escape their natural enemies, are essentially long-lived; and a cuttle of this gigantic species once attaining its full growth, and safely arrived at the years of cephalopodal discretion, might well be supposed to live through the greater part of a century, or even longer. Full-grown and full-armed, such a monster could hardly meet with many enemies willing to venture, on any pretence whatever, within reach of his terrible disc-armed, cable-like tentaculæ of 50 feet in length, with the inward parrot-beak ready to act as the arms slowly contracted!

CHAPTER IV.

Mild February—Birds in the Love Season—The Starry Heavens—Meteors—Rabies—Its origin—How communicated—Extinction.

WITH the exception of one very wet and wild day, ushered in by a night of bright aurora—the first aurora of the season, by the way—February has thus far been exceptionally genial and mild, with more of bright sunshine within a single fortnight than could honestly be placed by any fair apportionment to the credit of the four preceding months together. Our wild-bird favourites are jubilant and joyous beyond measure, in full plumage, and already almost in full song, from earliest dawn to the fading of twilight into star-lit night, making wild-wood, copse, and hedgerow vocal with their exquisite melodies. Even the hoarse *caw* of the industrious rook, if not exactly "musical as is Apollo's lute," is yet very far from being unpleasant, and you feel as you listen that it has an honest, frank, and cheery ring about it, which tells you as plainly as plain can be that it is the very best note at the command of a rook over head and ears in love, and, except the small cares and anxieties ever attendant on the tender passion, as happy and comfortable, he would reply if you questioned him, as on any St. Valentine's day within his recollection. A bird in love is just as ridiculous as his more pretentious featherless brother-biped in similar circumstances, and that is saying a great deal; and of all bipeds a rook in love, and throughout the early honeymoon, is perhaps the most comical and amusing. No intelligent observer can watch them day by day at this season, as we do, without being forced, *nolens volens*, into many a loud laugh at the oddity of their proceedings, nor are valuable additions to one's stock of philosophy awanting on such occasions. The redbreast, too, pert and pertinacious as ever, is now in his glory, constantly pouring forth the liquid riches of his mellow song, which, probably because of the commonness of the bird, and for no better reason, fanciers do not, we think, half enough admire. And, look! emerging mouse-like from a crevice in the coping of yonder wall, the wren, hardiest and pluckiest of British birds, albeit the least, with *mens sana in corpore sano* legibly written in his every look and gesture, and a cheeriness that is perfectly contagious, as you listen, in every note of his mellifluously pure and clear and oft-repeated song. Of Earl Russell it was said, when he was plain Lord John, that he had cheek enough to undertake anything, were it even the command of the Channel Fleet, at a day's notice, or a lithotomical operation, if it came in his way, and a surgeon wasn't at the moment handy. Our wren, for cheekiness and pluck, is a bird of precisely similar feather. If the *Sylviadæ* had a fleet, he would at once volunteer as its admiral, and would, we make no doubt, prove a very Nelson on the quarter-deck, as he never fails to prove himself a Napoleon in copse and hedgerow. Never was there so much courage and *verve* in such a tiny Tom Thumb of a thing; young Lochinvar himself was not "so gallant in love and so dauntless in war." We always call him the Little Corporal—*Le Petit Corporal*, as the French soldiers so fondly styled him—who, prejudice apart, and when all is said and done, was beyond all question the greatest captain of modern times, as well as one of the greatest men otherwise the world has ever known. Most of our birds are now busy with the important labours of nidification. In some instances the nests are already finished, and the full complement of eggs laid. In another ten days, should the present fine weather continue, incubation will be general among our earlier spring nest-builders.

The student of the starry heavens cannot fail to be delighted with the magnificence of our present cloudless nights, with just that scarcely perceptible tinge of frostiness in the air which so adds to the brilliancy of star and planet. From early evening on to midnight the finest constellations in the heavens sweep by with slow and solemn march, to the heart's ear of the devout gazer—

> " For ever singing as they shine,
> The hand that made us is divine."

The gorgeous Orion, with glittering belt and sword, and grand "Cairngorm" of incalculable price and ruddy hue adorning his right shoulder; *Sirius*, the brightest of all the starry host, in the mouth of the Greater Dog; *Procyon* in the Lesser Dog; Castor and Pollux; Virgo, with bright *Spica* far down on the horizon, graced, too, at present by the presence of the planet Jupiter; the Lion, with front bold and erect, and brightest *Regulus*, beside whose lustre and sheen a million *Koh-i-noors*—mountains of light—rolled into one were but the merest diamond point, diminutive and dim; the Greater Bear, whose resplendent tail points down to the ruddy *Arcturus;* Andromeda, Perseus, and Pegasus, and Auriga, with the beautiful *Capella;* Taurus, with the Hyades and Pleiades, and matchless *Aldebaran;* Draco, the Northern Crown; Lyra, and "all the host of them," with other constellations and bright stars well worth the gazing at with reverent intelligence and knowing, so as to be able to recognise and name them in after years, are now visible throughout the evening and night, and claim the attention of every one who would not willingly be ranked with those of whom it is predicated, and with too much truth, that knowing not and caring nothing for these things, they are but "of the earth, earthy." There was a considerable and very pretty display of falling stars on the night of the 12th. The meteors came into visibility near the zenith, and for the most part had a south-easterly course, the principal stream passing through the large gateway of apparently blank space between *Sirius* and *Procyon,* and disappearing as they approached the horizon. None of these was of remarkable size. In our first paragraph we said that our only storm of this month was ushered in by a display of aurora. We should have remarked that, with this single exception, the whole of this winter has been altogether auroraless. Not for the quarter of a century during which we have nightly studied the heavens has there been a season so devoid of auroral phenomena as this has been. Why it should be so no one can tell, but the fact at least is worth the chronicling.

We have now to direct our reader's attention to

a very disagreeable subject—*horresco referens*—but which ought, nevertheless, to be steadily looked in the face, and, as far as possible, provided against by every wise precaution while it is yet time. We refer to the rapid and alarming spread of *rabies*, or dog-madness, within the last four months throughout the midland and northern counties of England. We are not aware that the horrid disease, altogether incurable, and in its every stage the most distressing and terrible to which man or animal can be subjected, has as yet crossed the borders; the isolated cases one reads about from time to time being only what may be looked for any season. In England, however, the scourge has spread to a most alarming extent, many human beings, as well as numbers of dogs, horses, sheep, and horned cattle, having died of it. It is remarkable that *all* animals seem equally liable to the attacks of this dreadful malady, for when it does not rise spontaneously—and it is a question not yet satisfactorily decided whether it ever does so originate even in dogs—the virus from a rabid animal has only to be anyhow injected into the blood of the healthy animal, and that animal, after a longer or shorter interval, becomes raving mad—a madness, alas, for which there is as yet no known cure!—and after some days of indescribable agony, dies a horrible and cruel death. No experiments, we believe, have ever been made with a view to ascertain whether fishes and reptiles can be inoculated with the rabid poison; probably not, though we make no doubt that the *Cetacea* and *Phocidæ*, at least—the whale and seal tribes—if duly inoculated, would prove just as susceptible to the disease as our terrestrial mammals. A common opinion is that dog-madness is greatly more prevalent in hot than in cold weather, that it is, in fact, entirely or in a great measure due to intense heat—the weather of the "dog-days;" but all the statistics that have been collected go to prove that the disease is confined to no particular season, and that, in our country at least, it is if anything rather more common in winter and spring than in summer and autumn. Another popular fallacy is that rabid dogs will not drink nor even look at water but with the utmost repugnance and horror. This, which is perfectly true of human beings suffering under this disease, is by no means true of dogs and other animals. The latter will not only attempt to drink, though they always seem to have the greatest difficulty in swallowing any, but when they come across a river or pond, will frequently wade in, and even lie down in it at length, as if to cool the raging fever of their blood, for *rabies*, though generally attended by much nervous suffering, is clearly enough of the nature of pure blood-poisoning. It is curious that dog-madness should be unknown, or at all events extremely rare, in such hot countries as Egypt, Constantinople, and its neighbourhood, South Africa, Syria, and South Sea Islands, where dogs swarm and run at large, for the most part ownerless and masterless, and feeding almost entirely on such offal and garbage as they pick up in their wanderings. In the extreme north, too, among the Esquimaux and Siberian dogs, rabies is, we believe, altogether unknown, It would thus seem to be mainly confined to the Temperate Zones. The serpent's poison, the reader is aware, is injected into the victim in a concentrated form, through the grooved and hollow fang, from a gland reservoir specially provided for the purpose. The rabies poison, on the contrary, is in the affected animal's saliva, and the virus is generally communicated by the teeth in the act of biting. We say generally, for it has been abundantly proved that the malady may be communicated, not only by the teeth in biting, but also by the nails of a dog and the claws of a cat, the only explanation in the latter case being that the disease, being attended by severe spasmodic contractions of the throat, and the mouth being full of a viscid, glairy saliva, wherein lurks the poison, the dog and cat, as is their habit, rubbing their paws along and around their muzzles for relief, some of the saliva sticks to their pads and claws, and thus, when the skin is abraded and blood drawn by a scratch, the dreadful poison is instantly communicated, and, the fell disease entering into the circulation, the victim is irrevocably doomed to several days, sooner or later, of excruciating agony, ending in the most terrible of all deaths. We have seen several instances of canine madness, and once a sad case of hydrophobia, as the disease in the human subject is properly termed, and the reader may well believe that we have no wish to see it in man or beast again. All who happen to be bitten or scratched, so that blood is drawn, by dog, cat, or other animal, should at once consult the nearest surgeon, who will do what in his judgment is best in the particular case. An application of *nitrous acid* to the injured part has, in the experience of many medical men of eminence, been found most efficacious in neutralising the virus. When a dog is observed to lose his appetite, and has a wild staring look; to be sullen and fidgety, and heedless of his master's orders and caresses; begins to eat straw, hair, and other such stuffs, frequently rubbing his mouth and nose with his paws, and constantly lapping at any liquid that comes in his way, though manifestly able to swallow little or none of it; when, after hiding in some corner and shunning observation for a time, he suddenly runs about excitedly, becomes quarrelsome, attempts to bite such animals as come in his way, and frequently howls rather than barks, that animal should instantly be shut up where he can do no harm to any other animal, or, best of all, should incontinently be shot, for in all such cases it is best to err on the safe side; and all other animals suspected to be under the influence of the mania should be similarly dealt with. The most effectual way of dealing with the *rinderpest* was found to be " stamping out;" let rabies be treated in the same way, for every attempt at successful treatment and cure is attended with danger, and is, besides, of no avail. Dog-madness has been known from very early times, there being some expressions in the Old Testament Scriptures that seem to refer to it. It is clearly enough spoken of by Aristotle, Pliny, and Horace, the first remarking that all animals *except man* are subject to its attacks. We have long known, from sad experience, how mistaken was the philosopher in making any such exception. The subject has not been examined with all the care and attention it unquestionably merits.

CHAPTER V.

Unfavourable Harvest—Patience and Resignation of Highlanders under adverse circumstances—Tunny captured at Corran Ferry—Its characteristics—Tunny Steaks.

WE fear that a respectable South-country shepherd's prophecy some weeks ago has little chance of fulfilment. He averred, with a grave, meteorological shake of the head, that, bad as was the weather then, we should have "a grand backend o' hairst." We have now entered upon the "backend o' hairst," and there are as yet little, or rather no signs of improvement. For more than a score of years, at least, our crops all over the West Coast have not been gathered so unsatisfactorily; and the worst of it is that there is much still to gather, which must be poor feeding stuff after all the rain it has got, come now what weather may. One would think that our small crofters, whose all may be said to depend on the favourableness or otherwise of the harvest, would, in such a season as this, grumble loudly, or at least wear an air of despondency and gloom; but this is not the case, nor have we ever known it to be the case, even in more disastrous times, when our Highlanders suffered long and severely, yet bore it all with admirable patience and resignation. In recently talking this matter over with one older and wiser than ourselves—one, too, who has had opportunities of studying the Celtic character such as are afforded to few—we were surprised to hear him attribute this uncomplaining patience in misfortune to a deep tinge of fatalism in the Celtic mind, a mere helpless acquiescence, so to speak, in the inevitable, indicative, he thought, of their Eastern origin. The suggestion is a curious one, and might be made the subject of a very interesting treatise. Meantime we had to differ from our learned friend, attributing, as we do, the patience and fortitude referred to, to something higher and holier than blind fatalism; to a pious acquiescence in, and resignation to, the Divine will: the cloud, to the Celtic eye of faith, invariably having its silver lining, the overcast sky its bow of promise. The Highlander, in such circumstances, calls not fatalism, but true piety, truer because of its unostentatiousness, to aid. He thinks and feels as the ancient prophet thought and felt when he exclaimed, "Although the fig-tree shall not blossom, nor fruit be in the vines; though the labour of the olive shall fail, and the fields shall yield no meat; the flock shall be cut off from the fold, and there shall be no herd in the stalls; yet will I rejoice in the Lord, I will joy in the God of my salvation!" Thus beautifully paraphrased in words that every Highlander has by heart,—

"Chaoidh ged nach toir crann fige blath,
'S nach fàs air fion-chrann meas;
Saoth'r a chroinn oladh ged a thréig,
'S fàs dèis gun bhi air slios;
Gach treud o'n mhainnir ged a bhuail,
Grad fhuathas 'nuair nach saoil;
Greigh ged nach fàg an t-Earrach cruaidh,
No bò air uachdar raoin;

> "Gidheadh 'san Triath bidh mise ait
> Is ni mi uaill 'na ghràdh
> Mor aoibhneas ni mi ann am Dhia;
> 'S e Dia mo shlaint' gu bràth!"

The English paraphrase is good—uncommonly good—one of the very best in the collection; but the Gaelic is splendid, with the true Hebraic ring about it from first to last. Earnestly and honestly sung, to such a beautiful and plaintive air as "*Pembroke*," for example, by a whole churchful of devout worshippers, with the heavy rain-drops pattering upon the window-panes the while, and the stooks in ragged rows still afield, as we recently heard it, the effect is as solemn and striking as can well be imagined.

A rare fish was recently run ashore just under the lighthouse at the narrows of Corran Ferry. Several whales were at the time passing in with the flood-tide, and it is thought that they must have hunted the stranger until he had no other way of escape than flinging himself bodily high and dry upon the beach. A gentleman who happened to be passing ran for an axe, and gave the animal its *coup de grace* as it flopped about and floundered upon the shingle. Owing to some stupidity—so rare, however, in our neighbourhood as to be in this case readily pardoned—we got no word of the matter till some days afterwards, when, unfortunately, before we could reach it, an unusually high tide and an equinoctial gale had carried off the fish no one knew whither. Our excellent friend Mr Macmillan of Aryhualan, who saw the fish, and examined it minutely, gave us such a clear and precise description of it as convinced us that we knew it; and drawing with his riding switch a rough outline of the fish on the puddled road, we were certain in the matter, and had no difficulty in at once, then and there, giving our verdict. It was the Tunny, the *Thynnus vulgaris* of ichthyologists, a common fish in the Mediterranean, but rare on the British coasts, and rarest of all in our north-western seas. It is a large fish; this specimen, we are assured, must have weighed nearly a ton. If we say that his weight in the gross was *half* a ton, we shall probably not be far wrong. If the people about only knew it, this fish was as good as a winter "mart" to any one taking the trouble to cut and cure it; and its head and viscera would have yielded some ten or a dozen gallons of the purest oil. The tunny is of the mackerel family, the *Scomberidæ*, its vast rotundity and thickness of body, and crescent-shaped tail, being its distinguishing characteristics. In the Mediterranean, from the Pillars of Hercules to the Hellespont, it is common; and the tunny fisheries at certain places are quite as important, if not more so, than our own herring fisheries in the North of Scotland and the Hebrides in their season. The flesh, if the term be allowable, of the tunny is excellent. Cut fresh in slices or steaks, it is, in the opinion of many, better than the best salmon. It is rich and succulent without being too rich, more like young beef than anything else that it can be compared with. A nobleman, whose many yachting cruises over the blue waves of the Mediterranean have made him intelligently conversant with its natural history, writes as follows in answer to a note of inquiry with which we took the liberty to trouble him :—"Your Corran fish was certainly a tunny; the description will fit no other fish that I know. Pity you did not get hold of him : a tunny broil is first-rate. I have eaten it a hundred times, and, properly done, it is a feast for priest or presbyter. Keep a good look-out, for there was probably a shoal of them; they rarely travel singly, and, if they are headed in shallow water, are easily driven ashore. Let me know if any more turn up, and I shall send you a recipe for tunny broil and all about the curing of them. If the tunny only took it into its head to become as plentiful in your lochs as in some parts of the Mediterranean, it would be a fortune to you all." Should any more tunnies really "turn up," the reader shall not fail to hear of it.

CHAPTER VI.

Popular Superstitions—The Water-Bull—His Bridle.

There is much in the popular superstition of the Highlands, even when it deals with the supernatural, that is perfectly harmless, and a great deal that is very beautiful and suggestive to the unprejudiced and thoughtful investigator; but its absurdities are endless, and so ridiculously silly at times, as to make one wonder how such transparent nonsense could find shelter within the pale of honest popular belief for a single hour. Some things are so perfectly childish, so certainly without any possibly conceivable *raison d'etre*, that you cannot conceive how any one out of petticoats and pinafore can listen to them with patience, far less repeat them with grave imperturbed visage and seriously avowed belief. It is, however, we suppose, of the very nature and essence of popular superstition, that amidst much that is harmless and beautiful, possible and poetical, there shall be a great deal that is at once ridiculously childish and absurdly impossible. What strikes us as a very absurd article of superstitious belief came under our notice for the first time only a day or two ago. The reader must know that the *Water Kelpy* of the south of Scotland is also a prominent character in Highland superstition. The kelpy, or *uirisg*, is generally represented as of the male sex; of a form rude, indeed, and grotesque, but, upon the whole, of human shape; cross and ill-tempered, delighting in forboding and witnessing calamity, but to be propitiated and readily attached to such as have the courage to treat him with confidence and kindness. In the south the kelpy is an inhabitant indifferently of rivers and lakes, while in the Highlands he is almost always associated with solitary rivers, where they wind their murmuring way through wild and uninhabited glens, or with those deep, dark, eddying cauldron pools that mountain torrents so frequently scoop out for themselves as they plunge and roar adown the steep in their mad and headlong gallop to the sea. Thus the kelpy of the south and the *uirisg* of the north are, upon the whole, identical; half human, half demoniac, to be shunned and avoided if possible; but, if accidentally encountered, to be conciliated and caressed, never to be openly challenged or defied. But while the waters of the south can only boast of their kelpy, those of the north are the habitation not only of the *uirisg*, but of the water-horse and water-bull (*An t'Each Uisge, 'san Tarbh Uisge*) as well. These last are painted on that tablet of the popular mind consecrated to superstition, as, upon the whole, of the same shape and form as the more kindly quadrupeds after whom they have been named, but larger, fiercer, and with an amount of " devilment " and cunning about them of which the latter fortunately manifest no trace. They are always fat and sleek, and so full of strength, and spirit, and life, that the neighing of the one and the bellowing of the other frequently awake the mountain echoes to their inmost recesses for miles and miles around. The habitation of the water-horse and water-bull is not the sluggish river or mountain torrent pool, which belong of right to the *uirisg* only, but the solitary inland lakes and dark mountain tarns rarely seen by other eyes than those of the red deer in his many wanderings, and of the eagle, as, on the lookout for prey, he gracefully circles round on tireless wings as far above the clouds as the clouds are above the mountain tops. Calves and foals are the result of occasional intercourse between these animals and their more civilised domestic congeners, such calves bearing unmistakeable proofs of their mixed descent in the unusual size and pendulousness of their ears, and the wide aquatic spread of their jet black hoofs; the foals in their clean limbs, large flashing eyes, red distended nostrils, and fiery spirit. The initiated still pretend to point out cattle with more or less of this questionable blood in them, in almost every drove of pure Highland cows and heifers you like to bring under their notice. The intercourse between these demon quadrupeds and the domestic breed is now necessarily rarer than in the olden times, when all the crofters of a hamlet sent their cattle and horses to summer sheiling grazings among the hills, where lakes and tarns, the dark, deep homes of the water-horse and water-bull, abounded. Even to this day, however, if a young heifer gives much trouble in the milking, and is recalcitrant and reluctant to have her head bound up in her stall, and her feet confined in the *buarach* or milking shackle, it may be gravely suspected that she has more or less of the old water-bull blood in her veins; while horses having the points already indicated, and much given to shying in the day-time without apparent cause, and a fondness when out at grass for wading through rivers and streams, and standing in listless meditative mood by the margin of pools, may be confidently set down as descendants in a nearer or remoter degree of some demon steed progenitor. The lakes of Llundavrá and Achtriachtan, in Glencoe, both in our immediate neighbourhood, were at one time celebrated for their water-bulls, while Loch Treig could at once boast of the magnificent eagles that made its encircling mountain clefts their favourite breeding-place, and of the largest, wildest, fiercest breed of water-horses in the world. Rarey, with some difficulty, managed to tame "Cruiser,"

"Impiger, iracundus, inexorabilis, acer,"

with all his devilry; suggest to a Lochaber or Rannoch Highlander that the same distinguished American hippothist could clap a saddle on one of the demon steeds of Loch Treig, as he issues in the grey dawn, snorting, from his crystal paved sub-lacustral stalls, and he would answer, with a look of mingled horror and awe, "Impossible!" The water-horse would tear him into a thousand pieces with his teeth, and trample and pound him into pulp with his jet black, iron-hard, though unshod hoofs!

The reader will now have a better idea of the absurdity of the following superstition. We were talking to an old woman about a man whom we both knew well, and who has been wonderfully successful in life; from very small beginnings having become a person of considerable substance in horses, cattle, and lands. We remarked that it was curious how everything he took in hand seemed to prosper with him. The old lady agreed with us, but observed that what he owed his success to wasn't so much of a mystery after all; that she and some others knew it, and had long known it. We earnestly begged for further enlightenment on the subject, and being somewhat of a favourite with the good old lady, she promised to gratify our curiosity, if we called on her in the evening, when she should be quite alone. We did call on her in the evening, and when we had shut the door and barred it at her request, she invited us to a seat by the ingle cheek, and in a low voice informed us that the secret of the success in life of the man about whom we had been speaking in the forenoon was that he possessed a water-horse bridle, *srian Eich-Uisge*. "A water-horse bridle!" we exclaimed, hiding, however, our astonishment and inclination to laugh outright under an assumed air of simple curiosity. "Where in the world did he get hold of such a thing?" "I can tell you all about it," she continued. "His granduncle, who was a drover, was once returning home from a cattle market at Pitlochry, in Perthshire. As he was coming through the Moor of Rannoch the night overtook him, but as it was in the autumn time, and the moon rose full and bright behind him, he continued his journey as easily as if it was the clear noonday; and he was, besides, perfectly acquainted with the way, having often travelled it at all seasons. With his stick in his hand, and his plaid over his shoulder, he walked along hastily, without stop or halt, till he reached *Lochanna Cuile,* where he sat down to refresh himself with some bread and cheese, and a bottle of milk he had got at a shepherd's house on the way; for *Dòmhnull Mòr Dròbhair,* as they called him, was a very sober man, and seldom drank whisky. As he sat on a stone by the side of the lake he saw something glittering in the moonlight, which, on taking it up, he found to be a horse-bridle. Dòmhnull Mòr carried the bridle home with him, and was surprised next morning to find that the bit and buckles were of pure silver, and the reins of a soft and beautifully speckled sort of leather, such as he had never seen before. What astonished him most was, that on touching the silver bit it felt so hot as to be unbearable. He was very much frightened as well as astonished, and now wished that he had let it lie where he found it. It was only when a 'wise woman' was sent for from a neighbouring glen that the truth became known. She declared it to be a water-horse's bridle, the bit of deep down, subterranean silver still retaining part of the heat which belonged to it in its primeval molten state. The reins, she said, were the skin of *Buarach-Baoibh,* a sort of magical serpents, dreadfully poisonous, that frequent such rivers and lakes as are inhabited by the kelpy and water-horse. The 'wise woman' directed the bridle to be hung up on a *cromag* or crook made of rowan tree, which, while permitting free escape for all its beneficial influences, would yet effectually check the radiation of any evil that might be inherent in it. This was done, and from that day forward Dòmhnull Mòr was fortunate and successful in all his undertakings. At his death, having no family of his own, he bequeathed the magic bridle to his grandnephew, the present owner; and this man has been prosperous just because of the possession of a water-horse 'bridle of luck.'" "But how," we asked, "do water-horses happen to have bridles? Who could ride or drive them? and if they can neither be driven or ridden, why should they have bridles?" "Thomas the Rhymer," the old lady replied, "or some other magician and prophet of the olden time now detained in Fairyland, is destined yet to reappear upon earth with some companions almost as powerful as himself; then shall the water-horses be bridled and saddled by a brave company of Scottishmen from Fairyland, some Highland, some Lowland, bridled and saddled, and fearlessly mounted; a great battle will be fought; all Englishmen and other foreigners will be driven out of the country; the crown will again revert to the rightful heirs, and Scotland once again become a free, independent, and happy kingdom!"

Such, in substance, is a very respectable old lady's account of a superstition which, on inquiry, we find to be known, and more or less believed in, everywhere. There is much in it, as we have said, that is puerile and absurd; but thoughtful students of such matters, accustomed to look under the surface of things, will, we daresay, also find in it not a little that is poetical and beautiful, and more instructively suggestive as a whole than is possible of detection to the mere cursory glance of uninitiated and careless outsiders.

CHAPTER VII.

Winter Solstice—Homer—"A fire when it cheerily blazes"—Bird-Catchers—Their character—Greenfinch—Crossbill—Chaffinch—Blackbirds sent to America.

As we approach the winter solstice, the weather is rapidly becoming colder and colder, and after the indispensable matutinal tub, the first plunge into which sets your teeth on edge, one begins to rummage his drawers in search of the thickest and warmest articles of clothing he can put on. A fire in your parlour is now indispensable; if one could afford it, a fire is always a good thing. Every room has, or ought to have, its grate, and every grate should decidedly have its fire, in such a humid climate as ours, not "once a week," but "all the year round." Homer is not only *facile princeps* "Father of Verse" and king of poets—one and indivisible, let the Germans yelp to the contrary as they may—but one of the wisest of men as well. The grand old *gaberlunzie* once landed on the island of Samos, so runs the story, cold and chill, from off a long-protracted sea voyage. He arrived at a house wherein happened that evening to be a feast in honour of the gods. Homer was hungry, as you may suppose, and, bard-like, thirsty too, you may be sure. But as he stood on the threshold, and viewed the company and goodly table groaning under its consecrated load, he made no mention of his joy at sight of meat and drink, but of a good, blazing fire, as being the best of good things, in unimpeachable Greek hexameters, which our good friend, Professor Blackie, has admirably rendered into English as follows :—

"Children bring glory to men; strong towers are the praise of a city;
Steeds are the pride of the plain; swift ships the boast of the ocean;
Riches adorn a house; and when kings in the Forum are seated,
Glad is the eye that beholds the purple pomp of their session;
*But of the family hall, the praise, and the pride, and the glory,
Boast and honour supreme, is a fire when it cheerily blazes!*"

Homer is right; and a fire, "when it cheerily blazes," is the antidote to a thousand domestic discomforts, and we beg all good housewives to remember the fact. Depend upon it that in presence of a tidy fireside and a bright and cheery fire the inevitable grumbling over such annoyances and discomforts as buttonless shirts, ill-cooked dinners, and other such domestic *désagréments*, will be reduced to a minimum, if it be not converted into such good-natured banter as leaves no clouds behind it. The popularity of a well-known song is mainly due, we take it, to the beauty and cheery suggestiveness of its refrain, that so happily celebrates the comforts and *agrèments* of the "bonnie blythe blink" of one's "ain fireside." Those conversant with vital statistics will bear us out in the assertion that fires, altogether irrespective of their moral and æsthetic aspects, are as necessary as food itself to robust health and longevity.

A peripatetic bird-catcher, with whom we have been long acquainted, a man, too, of much more intelligence and good sense than is usually met with in people of his class, brought us a curiosity a few days ago in the shape of a bird, the identity of which puzzled him extremely. He could make nothing of it, unless it was a male canary that had somehow escaped from captivity, and had devoted its freedom to the companionship and fortunes of a flock of chaffinches, out of which it was recaptured. We, too, were for the moment puzzled, but, on minute examination, the bird proved to be a greenfinch (*Loxia Chloris*, Linn.). The difficulty arose from its very unusual plumage. The head, neck, and all along one side was bright yellow, exactly like the yellow-hammer's spring plumage, while the other side was of a dull white, except the tips of the quill feathers, which were jet black. We should like to have kept it, but, as a curiosity, it was worth more money to the poor man than we could well afford to give for it; and it seemed sickly, besides, and not likely to live long in captivity, even if we had it. We have long since remarked that among birds pure *albinos*, which are by no means uncommon, and such as present any very marked colourings different from those generally obtaining in the order, are in captivity invariably sickly and short-lived. We may therefore conclude that instances of abnormal colouring in beasts and birds are to be attributed to some constitutional derangement, which first manifests itself in this way, and sooner or later causes death. This man had at least a hundred birds in cages slung around him, and was very proud of his load. To him the money value of the lot was perhaps £10 or £12, and that, of course, was no small consideration, but we really believe he liked the birds for their own sakes; for, while he sat in our kitchen, we noticed that he fed them very liberally, giving them at the same time a drink all round, and otherwise treating them with the greatest gentleness and affection. Two or three of the birds had been in his possession for years, and he assured us he wouldn't part with them for any money. They were splendid singers, and probably valuable from their docility as decoy or call birds. It was pleasant to notice that on being fed many of the birds began to sing merrily; nor did they cease when the man slung the cages on his shoulders, and took to the road, so weather-hardened that he seemed not to care a whit for the wind and rain that beat and battered him as he trudged along. The feathered captives in this instance were mostly linnets and goldfinches; and besides the oddly coloured greenfinch already mentioned, the only other bird that particularly attracted our attention was a *Crossbill* (*Loxia curviostra*, Linn.), which he told us he had captured shortly before in the neighbourhood of Ardverikie, in Badenoch. This last is so rare a bird on the West Coast, that, on turning to our commonplace book, we can find mention of only a single specimen that was shot many years ago somewhere about Tirindrish, in Brae-Lochaber, and which, through the kindness of the Rev. Mr. Fraser, now minister of Fearn, found its way as a stuffed specimen into our own collection. The reader will perhaps be slow to credit it, but we have good reason to believe that this particular birdcatcher, however it be with the rest of the fraternity, is worth upwards of a couple of hundred pounds, safely lodged in bank, every shilling of it made from

D

his profession of bird-catching. He is of course a perfectly steady and sober man, else the thing had been impossible; nor must we forget the fact that during what he emphatically called the "deid months o' the year," when bird-catching is impossible, or at all events unprofitable, he is a bird-trainer—training and teaching his linnets, siskins, and goldfinches to sing little airs, which he plays to them on the flute or Jew's harp, and to perform such pretty tricks and feats of cleverness as best illustrate the intelligence and docility of the feathered performers. For the best of these, he assured us, he sometimes got a guinea, and even more when he could produce a pair of about equal cleverness that could perform their tricks together, and warble their songs in concert. The best birds, he told us, are disposed of without difficulty at home, principally in the manufacturing districts, where well-to-do operative artisans never grudge the highest price for a perfectly healthy and well-trained bird. Within the last five years he has sold upwards of forty dozen linnets, green, gold, and chaffinches, mostly newly caught and untrained, to go to America and the colonies, where they command such high prices as handsomely repay all the trouble and expense of their capture and transportation. Considering the delicacy of these little beauties, the per-centage of deaths, even amongst those sent long voyages, is very small. Amongst those sent to America, for instance, the death-rate, he assured us, was under 20 per cent.; and, with more attention than is generally bestowed upon them on the voyage, he believed that, under skilful management, even this death-rate might be largely diminished.

One of this man's most successful overturns in recent years was the despatch last spring of five dozen coral-billed cock blackbirds by steamer from Liverpool to Philadelphia, where they all arrived safely except seven, and were readily sold at prices ranging from three to five dollars a piece, leaving him, after payment of all expenses, a clear profit of nearly two dollars per head, or something like twenty pounds sterling on the transaction. When overtaken, too, by a long tract of wet weather on his bird-catching perambulations through the country (bird-lime, you must now, is useless in the wet, nor can birds in rainy weather be readily lured to the vicinity of the clap-net), he can always employ his leisure time profitably in the manufacture of bird cages of all shapes and sizes, and neater cages than some of those made by him we have never seen. One word in conclusion in favour of bird-catchers as a class. Some of them are sorry wretches enough, out at elbows and out at heels, ragged and wretched-looking in the extreme, but you almost invariably find them intelligent and ready witted, with a delicacy and refinement of speech and manner which has always struck us as surprising, and which we can in nowise satisfactorily account for, except on the supposition that, passing so much of their time in solitude, and necessarily moving about quietly and cautiously, always on their guard, as it were, gives them the habit of using a subdued and gentle tone of speech, which is not only, as the poet avers, "a most excellent thing in woman," but, as a rule, in man as well; while the constant companionship of such gentle and pretty creatures as they make captive has doubtless its effect in making them kindly mannered, good-natured, and cheery. If you take the trouble to compare them, you will find that the bird-catcher is not only infinitely above every conceivable description of tramp, but a gentleman in word and deed, even when compared with the best class of travelling packmen, and the peripatetic vendors of stationery and small ware. We had rather, of course, that there were no bird-catchers; but bird-catchers know birds, and he who knows a bird knows more than the world wots of.

CHAPTER VIII.

The Macdonells of Glengarry—Sale of the Estate—Creagan-an-Fhithich—The last Family Bard—" Blind Allan."

THERE has recently been a discussion on the Macdonells of Glengarry, and the right still of the representative of the family to the title, though no longer owner of an acre of the ancient lordship. Such matters are of interest to any Highlander, and we beg leave to contribute the following anecdote to the subject. In the grey dawn of a November morning, many years ago, we were riding in a gig along with our good friend the late Rev. Dr. Macintyre, of Killmonivaig, from his manse to Fort-Augustus. In passing Invergarry we naturally began to speak of the old family, with whom Dr. Macintyre had been for many years on terms of close intimacy, and of the changed times since the Macdonells were all-powerful, and could well hold their own against all comers, from the heights of Knoydart to Killeanain on Loch Lochy. "I well remember," says Dr. Macintyre, "the day on which it was decided that the lands of Glengarry must be sold. I had been spending the night in the Castle, and was standing in the morning by the breakfast parlour fire when the door opened, and Glengarry entered in his Highland dress, as usual, and with a bundle of papers in his hand." "Mr. Macintyre," he quickly observed, "I regret to have to inform you that Glengarry must be sold, and I, your friend Glengarry, be Glengarry no longer!" "Is it *must?*" returned Mr. Macintyre; "is there no alternative?" "None, my good friend," continued the chief, "it is really *must*; within a few days Glengarry shall have passed to a stranger." "What must be must be," said Mr. Macintyre, "but, at all events, do not part with 'Creagan-an-fhithich,' the old Raven Rock, the watchword and gathering cry of your clan! With 'Creagan-an-fhithich' yours, you shall still be Glengarry, 'A dh'aindeoin co 'theireadhe,' gainsay it who may, and placing your back to that steadfast rock, you can exclaim with undaunted front, like James Fitz-James in your friend Scott's *Lady of the Lake*—

'Come one, come all, this rock shall fly
From its firm base as soon as I.'"

"It shall be done!" said Glengarry, with a proud toss of his head; "and to this day," continued Dr. Macintyre, "I believe that 'Creagan-an-fhithich' belongs to the representative of Glengarry, whoever he may be, and with the 'Raven Rock' the titles of Mac-Ic-Alasdair and Glengarry." Such was Dr. Macintyre's story to us; and whether the "Raven Rock" was really excepted from the sale or not, we may be certain that its retention was at least in contemplation.

On the same occasion Dr. Macintyre told us the following anecdote in illustration of Glengarry's amiability and frank and kindly manner:—"On that same morning," said the Doctor, "although his mind must have been disagreeably busied about his own affairs, he happened to notice, after we had been talking for a little, a bit of thread, or straw, or feather, or something of that kind in my hair. He stepped forwards, and, with a smiling ' By your leave, Mr. Macintyre,' took the offending waif from my head, and holding it up in his hand, remarked, ''S math an sgàthan sùil caraid' ('An excellent looking-glass is a true friend's eye'). Driving his carriage one day through the village of Fort-Augustus, he found a certain corner of the street unnecessarily obstructed by a plasterer's or mason's ladder, the owner standing on the topmost round, busily engaged in renovating a house front. Glengarry pulled up, and in a stern voice called out to the mason, ' C'ainm a th'ort a dhuine?' ('What is thy name, man?') The man looked down, displaying a face by no means prepossessing, and deeply pitted besides with the small-pox. ''Se Domhnull Grannd as ainm dhomh' ('Donald Grant is my name!'), pronouncing *Grannd*, however, like 'Granta,' for he was a north countryman. Glengarry looked at him for a moment, and, with a smile, observing, ' Air m' fhallain gu bhail thu granta da rireamh' ('By the vestments, but you are well named, for you are Donald *Ugly* in very truth),' drove leisurely past the obstruction." This Glengarry, Colonel Alexander Ranaldson Macdonell, was perhaps the last Highland chief that had a family bard, and provided abundantly for all his wants. This bard was the well-known Gaelic poet "Allan Dall," or Blind Allan. He was a Macdougall, and originally connected with the *Clan Iain* of Glencoe, a sept of the great family of Macdonald, and could thus the more readily attach himself to the family of Glengarry. Every one must know his excellent song to the chief who so liberally befriended him :—

" Faigh a nuas dhuinn am botal,
'S theid an deoch so mu'n cuairt ;
Lion barrach an copan,
Cum socrach a chuach !
Tosda Choirneil na féile,
Leis an eireadh gach buaidh,
Oighre Chnoideairt a bharraich,
'S Ghlinne Garaidh na thuath.

. . . .

"Co 'thairneadh ruit riobadh
Nuair a thig na bheil 'uat ?
Iarl *Antruim* a Eirinn
Leis an eireadh na sluaigh ;
Mac-Ic-Ailein nan geur-lann,
Dheanadh éuchd air a chuan,
Aig am bheil na fir ghleusda
'Dhol a reubadh nan stuadh ! "

Another Gaelic poet befriended by Glengarry was Ewen Maclachlan, "of Aberdeen," whom the big-hearted chief not only patronised as a lank, lean, kilted lad of promising talents, but was always glad to see at his table as an honoured guest in after years, when these talents had raised him to eminence and distinction. "Come," said Glengarry one morning to Maclachlan, who was at the Castle on a visit, "Come and let us call upon my bard, Allan Dall." They went, and on reaching the door of the bard's cottage, Maclachlan, bending and putting his head just within the lintel, exclaimed, "Am beil am bard dall a stigh, a chi gu gle shoilleir ? " ("Is the *blind* bard who is yet so clear-sighted in ? ") "Tha mi," readily answered Allan, " 'S cha neil dad air an t'saoghal a b'fhearr leam na sibhse fhaicinn, ge be co sibh!" ("Yes, I am in, and nothing in the world could so please me as to *see* you, whoever you may be!") With a loud burst of laughter, Glengarry and Maclachlan went in, and, with an occasional dram from the bard's bottle—a bottle which, by the liberality of the gallant chief, was but rarely allowed to run dry—listened for hours to his songs, anecdotes, and violin performances, for of Allan it might be asserted, as of Neil Gow himself, that he "played the fiddle weel," and, even more ardently than the Athole musician himself, "dearly lo'ed the whisky, O!"

Let us add, by way of note, that the Glengarry spoken of here throughout is the celebrated chief, Colonel Alexander Ranaldson Macdonell, who was killed on the rock of Inverscaddle in 1828. In leaping ashore from the West Highland steamer, which had been driven on the rock in a gale of wind, his foot slipped; he fell forward heavily on his head, and sustained such injuries as resulted in his death a few hours thereafter. This Glengarry took a very prominent part in the grand reception given by Scotland to George IV. on occasion of the royal visit in 1822. Scott, who knew him well, introduces him into his well-known ballad-song on the occasion—

> " But yonder come my canty Celts,
> With dirk and pistols at their belts,
> Thank God, we've still some plaids and kilts—
> Carle, now the King's come!

> " Lord, how the pibrochs groan and yell!
> *Macdonell's* ta'en the field himsell;
> Macleod comes branking o'er the fell—
> Carle, now the King's come."

CHAPTER IX.

Weather Prophets and Prophecies—Beauty of the West Highlands in early Summer—"Pedometric" Spring Temperature—Story of a Song-Thrush—A mid-May Idyl.

THE scientific meteorologist is always chary of venturing upon anything like positive weather forecasts, and when he does so venture, he is careful to give you the *data* on which his anticipated weather changes are founded. It is only the sea, we believe, that is generally spoken of as the "treacherous" element, but the meteorologist knows that all the elements are treacherous—treacherous, that is, in the sense that, to use an expressive old Scripture phrase, their "going forth," irregularities, and incessant changes are, as a rule, as utterly beyond human foresight as beyond human control. An ignorant non-scientific weather prophet may sometimes vaticinate correctly; out of many guesses it is impossible but that he shall sometimes be right, but this chance and happy-go-lucky system of prediction has long since, and deservedly, fallen into disfavour and disrepute. A very obvious method of arriving at a knowledge of truth is the ascertainment, first of all, of facts, and then reasoning upon these facts towards conclusions; and yet, obvious and simple as is the process, the world, strange to say, never thoroughly recognised or understood it, though it doubtless often unconsciously employed it, until, in the fulness of time, it was boldly enunciated and enforced by our own illustrious Bacon. Strictly adhering to this method of investigation, meteorologists tell us that from their observations of many years, a check, or retrogression rather, of a day or two's duration in the onward march of temperature over the British Islands may very confidently be looked for some time during the third week of April; and a second check, of somewhat longer duration, about the middle of the second week in May; and this year the forecast has been verified in a very remarkable manner. The 20th and 21st April were two decidedly cold days, with flying sleet showers, in a month otherwise almost unprecedentedly warm and genial, with such floods of sunshine, too, as April rarely knows. The second week of May has also been wet and cold, and however grateful to vegetation after so bright and uninterruptedly dry a spring, the check on the previously high and rapidly increasing temperature has been such as to show how valuable and carefully observed, and honestly recorded, are meteorological statistics towards an attempt at forecasting weather changes. The weather has now again become warm and bright, and never before, perhaps, in mid-May did the country appear so beautiful from every conceivable standpoint. The luxuriance of vegetable and floral life at so early a date is something astonishing. In garden and orchard the sight is magnificent. You have heard of trees bending under their load of fruit; at this moment they are actually bending under their load of blossoms, just as you have seen their boughs bent until they kissed the ground after a quiet and stormless fall of snow. Should the crop of fruit only equal even half the promised abundance, it will be such a crop as has rarely, if ever before, been gathered. And have you noticed the extraordinary abundance of wild-flowers this season? Primroses especially, wherever you turn your eyes, are as numerous —singly, clustered, and constellated—as to the telescopic eye are the stars in the midnight Milky Way; the hawthorn everywhere is one towering mass of scented, snow-white beauty, actually laughing in the sunlight, as if in response to the wild bee's grateful hum on and around it, while the very air seems surcharged as you never knew it before with the richest fragrance of flowers and the sweetest melodies of birds. On one point, at least, we are at this moment the most unanimous people in the world—the exceeding loveliness of the Western Highlands and Islands in such delightful seasons as this. One day, about a month ago, as we were talking to an old man, still lively and active, though upwards of fourscore years of age, he observed that for fifty years at least he had not known so "natural" a spring, so seasonable a season, as he termed it, as from mid-March to mid-April. His way of proving it was curious. "When I was a big boy, long-legged and clumsy (we translate his Gaelic literally), bare-headed and barefooted—for I was twenty years of age before I had a shoe on my foot or a bonnet on my head—I well recollect that in carting out the manure in the spring I had frequently, barefooted as I was, to jump now and again from off the top of the dung-heap; it had become so hot in the burning sun that I couldn't bear it. Dung-heaps in those days used to reek like so many kilns, sir!

Thinking of this the other day, I made a barefooted oe of mine stand in a manure heap that I remarked was reeking as it was being carried afield, and after a minute or two, he also found it so hot that he couldn't bear it; and from this I conclude that this is one of the real good old springs of my younger days; for if you try in ordinary years, you will find the dung-heap at the time of its removal not hot, but at the best clammy, no warmer than a spadeful of the soil around, and oftentimes as cold, or colder, than a puddle of black peat moss. Depend upon it, sir, that when manure has to be put upon the land in spring otherwise than hot and steaming, the season is not of the good old sort." A method this of pedometrically ascertaining the maximum and minimum of spring temperatures probably unknown to our friends of the Meteorological Society.

A remarkable instance of affectionate intelligence in wild-bird life was brought under our notice a few days ago. A boy, idling through the woods near us, set a horse-hair noose, in which, by-and-by, to his no small delight, he found that a song-thrush had firmly entangled itself by one of its legs. It was a great prize, and the boy carried it home as proud as proud could be. The capture was made in the morning, and in the course of the afternoon the boy's mother told us about it, begging us to come and persuade the boy to let it go, as they had no proper way of keeping it; and, indeed, as neither herself nor the boy, she assured us, knew exactly what kind of bird it was, they were uncertain if it was worth the keeping, even if they could abundantly and comfortably provide for all its wants. It was a song-thrush (*Turdus musicus*), a female, which the boy had meantime provided for in the best way he could by putting it into a roomy reticule basket, hung on a nail near the open window. When we had sufficiently examined the bird, the mother drew our attention to the fact that there was at that moment another bird very like it perched on an elder-tree branch right opposite the house, about eight or ten yards away. "Yes!" eagerly exclaimed the boy, a very intelligent little fellow, "and it followed me home all the way from the wood." Glancing in the direction indicated, and seeing the bird, we understood the thing at once. It was the captive's mate, the cock song-thrush, that, when he could do nothing else for her, had faithfully followed his partner to the scene of her captivity, and there he sat with speckled breast touching the branch on which he perched, disconsolate and sad, chirping querulously in little broken notes, that said as plainly as plain could be, that, cruelly deprived of the partner of his love, May, even with its sunshine, its verdure, and its flowers, had no more joys for him. Taking the basket in our hand, we took it outside, and hung it against the eave of the cottage, and retiring with the boy and his mother to a little distance, we stood quietly watching for what might happen. After a little while the captive, revived and emboldened by finding herself in the open air, ventured, in a scarcely audible whisper, to respond to her mate's chirping—it was the first time she had done so since her capture—and his joy was unbounded. First springing to the topmost spray of the elder tree, he trilled out two or three rapid notes of his usual song, and then, descending in a graceful curve, he alighted on the basket lid, through a hole in which the head and neck of the captive were now thrust forth. It was now that a most touching scene took place. After billing and cooing with the captive for a time in the most affectionate manner, preening and stroking her head and neck with his bill, all the while fluttering his wings and uttering a low, and to us scarcely audible, undersong or *crònan*, clearly of encouragement to the captive, and an assurance of his unalterable love, and, as such, understood by her, you may be sure; after indulging for a little while in these demonstrations of affectionate solicitude, the cock bird suddenly assumed a totally different attitude. Gathering up his drooping wings, and assuming his compactest and erectest position, he began vigorously to peck and pull away at the edges of the hole on the basket-lid, endeavouring with all his ingenuity and strength to enlarge it, so as to facilitate the captive's escape! And if he had only been allowed plenty of time, we do not know but he might have succeeded, for the throstle cock is a strong bird, and with his horny, compressed bill he can both strike hard and home, and pull with a force and strength of purchase astonishing in a bird of his size. It was a most touching and beautiful sight, and even the boy was so impressed with it that he at once agreed to the liberation of the prisoner, that he had vowed and determined only a few minutes before to have and to hold as his pet while it lived. The poor widowed mother had her apron more than once at her eyes, partly affected by the bird scene, and partly from maternal pride that her boy had evinced so much feeling and heart. With a view of testing the gallant cock bird's affection and intelligence a little further, we now suggested that the boy and ourselves should carry the basket to the wood, and liberate the prisoner as nearly as possible on the spot where she had been captured. Giving the basket to the boy to carry, we set him off before us, while we followed at a little distance, the better to watch and note the doings of the cock bird. No sooner were we fairly away from the cottage than he followed, as we were sure he would, sweeping occasionally close past the boy, and uttering short, abrupt, swallow-like chirps, as if to assure his mate—who had now drawn back her head into the basket—that he was still near her, and that his motto, even unto death, was "Faithful and true." In this way we marched along, until we reached the primrose-carpeted glade in which she had been noosed. As we sat down to open the many strings, with many intricate knots—for it was the boy that had tied them—by which the basket-lid was secured, so that we might set the captive at liberty, the cock bird alighted on a hazel bough so near us, that we might have reached him from where we sat, if not with an ordinary walking-stick, at least with the shortest of fishing-rods. He uttered not now a chirp, nor moved, but sat and watched with his large intelligent hazel eyes, which seemed to beam with hopeful eagerness, as if he half divined what we were about to do, and wondered why we could be so long about it! The captive was at length liberated—freed!—dashing away as soon as the basket-lid was raised with a wild scream of mingled terror and joy, and he followed like an arrow from a bow, the pair instantly disappearing from our sight behind a clump of birch trees that crowned a knoll before us. It was, upon the whole, we take it, an excellent lesson for the boy, and one which he is never likely altogether to forget; nor was it without its significance to the widowed mother and ourselves. We are not rich, but very much the contrary, yet would we give the brightest and newest brace of sovereigns that our friends the Fort-William bankers could hand over to us in exchange for two of their notes, if we knew and could tell, fairly and fully, all that passed between the whilom captive songthrush and her mate on that evening, after they found themselves at leisure to converse,—all they felt and all they thought and said, for birds *can* feel, and think, and speak intelligibly enough amongst themselves, gainsay it who may.

CHAPTER X.

A Hebridean Correspondent—A Box and its Contents—A Skeleton—A rare Cetacean—*Delphinus Delphis*—The Sacred Fish of the Ancients—*Bec d'Oie* or "Goose-bill" of the French—Its Food.

THAT it is right and proper to give every one his due—*suum cuique tribuere*—is an old Greek and Latin adage, as obvious and trite as it is honest and true; an adage, indeed, to be met with in some form or other in all languages, but in no language in such an emphatic form as in English, which teaches that fair-play and his righteous due is to be accorded even to the great enemy of mankind. For our own part, all our life long we have been ready to acknowledge favours received, and to remember them; and if in after years our benefactor should, as sometimes happens, find such fault in us, or we such fault in him, as brought a cloud over the hitherto fair prospect, we have tried, and so trying, have always succeeded in finding the edges of said cloud silver-fringed or golden. Upon the whole, however, all our prospects of this kind have been, and we rejoice to say still remain, unclouded, a readiness to oblige, and to receive, and at once heartily acknowledge obligations, being an ethereal atmosphere, in which one can always breathe freely, and in which clouds, mists, or noxious exhalations of any kind can hardly have existence. To come to the point and "the particular," as Jeremy Taylor has it, we once for all hereby acknowledge and proclaim to all whom it may concern, that to our good friend, Mr. A. A. Carmichael, of Uist, we are, and for many years have been, largely indebted for natural history and antiquarian kindnesses of great value; and if our "Nether Lochaber" column is interesting, a great deal of the praise and commendation which accrues to us as writer and demonstrator should go, each his fair and full share, to our many excellent correspondents, amongst whom Mr. Carmichael, in his own particular line, stands very high—the first amongst the foremost.

With all this prefacing, the reader doubtless expects something unusual to follow, nor shall the reader be disappointed. Coming from Fort-William the other evening, by steamer "Mountaineer," when about to land, we had shaken hands with and bade goodbye to our always polite and excellent friend, Captain Maccallum, the piermaster accosted us with the information that there was a box for us in the office. Said box, of narrow and elongated, gun-case-like form, was at our request at once produced, brought by omnibus to Ballachulish Ferry, and thence in our own conveyance home. It couldn't be grouse, we knew, in mid-May, nor would such a length of box be necessary for a salmon, and we could meantime only guess that it might be some natural history curiosity or other from our friend, Mr. T. B. Snowie, of the northern capital. On getting it home, we only wish you saw the eagerness and all-a-tiptoe expectation with which our household, particularly our "woman-kind," as the *Antiquary* has it, surrounded the box, as we, with coat off, and hammer and chisel in hand, proceeded to the no easy task of taking off the lid, and bringing the contents into the golden light of the western sunset. First came into view the occipital hemisphere of a skull or *cranium* of such human-like phrenological development, that our servant girl, who stood intensely curious and all agape beside us, screamed with affright, and the solemnly declared averment that it was the skeleton of a child, or, when we pointed out to her its size and the firm contexture of its bones, even of an adult. The ladies beside us didn't exactly scream nor fall into hysterics—we are not much given to nonsense of that kind in Lochaber —but they stood with bated breath, with an expression of face so puzzled and dumfoundered, that, as we lifted the skeleton from its coffin, and held it forth before the gaze of our awe-struck audience, the whole affair was so comically solemn and serious, that we burst into a shout of laughter that made the roof ring again. This partly broke the spell, but a neighbouring drover, to whom we had given a ride from the Ferry, and who in his day has sold many a thousand pounds worth of wide-horned West Highlanders at Falkirk, still stood in front of us in such manifest perplexity of mind—such dubiety of opinion as to what the skeleton might be—that at that moment he would have let the best bargain in stirks in all Lochaber slip through his nerveless fingers like so much running water. By next morning's post came a letter from our aforesaid correspondent in Uist, Mr. Carmichael, which we cannot do better perhaps than transcribe at length—

" CREAGORRY, OUTER HEBRIDES, 11*th May* 1875.

" REV. DEAR SIR,—I send for your inspection the skeleton of a *Saurian.* My knowledge of zoology is not sufficiently good to enable me to quote the scientific name; nor have I a comprehensive work on this particular branch of natural history at hand to consult. However, what I lack in these respects you possess, and I doubt not that the world will have another of your beautiful and brilliant descriptions of animal life.

"The skeleton was found at Airdmore, Barra, about three weeks ago. Those who discovered it incidentally mentioned it to me, and I at once sent a man to secure it; and I have now much pleasure in sending it to you for examination. When discovered, the skeleton lay a few feet beyond the tide-mark (*Os cionn tàir an làin*), and was as cleanly dissected then as you now see it. The remains of the blood had not yet become hard, nor had the articulation of the ribs become stiff, thus evidencing that the dissecting operators—crabs, fish, and sea-birds, probably—had only recently finished their anatomical labours.

"How this animal found its way to Barra, and whether it arrived there dead or alive, are simply matters of conjecture upon which I can throw no light.—With kindest regards, yours very faithfully, ALEX. A. CARMICHAEL."

And now for a verbal description of our skeleton—very unsatisfactory, of course, as all verbal descriptions of such matters must be. It is exactly four feet one inch in length; it is not complete, for all the caudal vertebræ are wanting. Making a fair allowance of at least two feet for these, the length of the living animal may be set down as upwards of six feet. It must have been an immensely strong animal, the size, contexture, and articulation of the bones showing that in its proper element, which we at once decided must be the sea, river, or lake, it must have been at once active and powerful. The skull is strongly built and large, with the jaws curiously prolonged into a flattened platypal or duck-bill-like beak. In our specimen the lower jaw is wanting, but we may state that along its edges the upper jaw is furnished with a row of equal, or nearly equal, ivory white teeth, fifty-four in number, and allowing an equal number for the lower jaw, the animal could boast of a set of teeth of 108 or more—all of them teeth not intended for grinding or mastication, but steel-trap-like, for laying hold, and keeping hold when got, of slippery prey. And what now, the reader will ask, have you made of it? Whose skeleton is it? Well, we are neither a Cuvier nor an Owen, but a single forenoon's careful study satisfied us that it was neither a Saurian reptile nor a fish of any kind. That Mr. Carmichael should have dubbed it a Saurian was the most natural thing in the world, for the elongated beak or snout, and the formidable dentition, have a most suspicious Saurian look about them, very likely to deceive any one unaccustomed to such studies. And if it wasn't a Saurian, it was still clearer that it couldn't be a fish. We finally decided that the animal was a *Cetacean*, of the order *Delphinidæ*, and that this particular species was the *Delphinus Delphis*, or Dolphin proper. Dead or alive, it is rare on our British shores, its proper home being in tropical and sub-tropical seas. It is a Mammal, bringing forth its young—generally one, and never more than two, at a birth—and suckling them at its breast like all the Cetaceans. This is the true dolphin—the *Hieros Ichthys*, or sacred fish of the ancients, the identical animal that, along with some companions—so charmed were they with the incomparable music of his lyre—bore the Lesbian Arion through many a league of sea safely to land; a fable having its origin, probably, in the fact that the smaller Cetaceæ, at least, are by no means insensible to the charms of music, vocal or instrumental. Porpoises may be arrested in their course, as they tumble along, by a judicious strain of loud whistling, almost as readily as seals, and we recollect that several years ago a whole "school" of porpoises used to collect from all parts of the loch around a yacht that was anchored for some days in our bay, when, on a fine evening after gun-fire, the men on board formed themselves into an impromptu band, and played on several wind instruments so well, that we, with better instructed ears, probably, than the porpoises, were also attracted to the beach to listen to the music. No other animal of the deep was held in such veneration by the ancient Greeks as the dolphin. With the Tritons it was represented appropriately enough as in constant attendance upon Neptune. It was in a special manner—though why it would be difficult to say—sacred to Apollo, whose celebrated shrine at *Delphi* was named after it, and where the god was worshipped on solemn occasions with dolphins for his symbols. It is common on ancient coins and medals. A veneration for this Cetacean seems to have spread westwards from Greece, for it was borne long before the *fleurs de lis* times on the shields of some of the early French kings. It gave its name to the province of *Dauphiné*, and the eldest son of the king, as heir-apparent, was called the *Dauphin*, with the province above named for his appanage. The phrase "*In usum Delphini*" (for the use of the Dolphin or Dauphin) will readily occur to all our classical readers. The French, on whose coasts the dolphin is more frequently met with than on ours, call it *Bec d'Oie*, or "Goose-bill," a by no means inappropriate vulgar name for it, for the long, compressed snout is quite like a goose's bill, enlarged into monstrosity. The food of the dolphin is fish, Medusæ, Cephalopods, &c.; for "circumventing," as "Hawkeye" would term it, such slippery customers, the formidable array of numerous sharp laniar teeth is admirably adapted. Cut into steaks, and fried or boiled, its flesh is said to be capital eating, an assertion which we can quite believe, for the dolphin and the porpoise are at least "Highland cousins," if not more nearly related, and a gentleman assured us a few years ago that he had more than once tried a porpoise steak broiled *secundum artem*, and that it was excellent. The dolphin is by no means remarkable for gaiety of colours; it is, on the contrary, douce and sober-garmented, like all the Cetaceans. The animal of gay and brilliant colours, over which modern poets and *voyageurs* get into such raptures, and which they call a dolphin, is not a dolphin at all—not a Cetacean that breathes by means of lungs, the necessary air being inspired and again expelled through a blow-hole, but a fish proper, an animal that breathes by means of gills. The "dying dolphin," over whose ever-changing and brilliant metallic hues our poets make such a fuss, is the Coryphene (*Coryphæna*)—a true fish of the order *Scomberidæ*, or mackerel family, and is no more a dolphin than it is a whale. You have seen its first cousin, the common and beautiful mackerel of our own shores, and except in the mere matter of size, it is in its way just as brilliantly coloured and as much a "dolphin" as its congener, the Coryphene, which people who know no better will insist on calling a dolphin. The animal whose skeleton now lies before us came to our shores, doubtless, by means of the *Gulf Stream*, and probably in lusty life enough. Getting hurt somehow, it was driven ashore in a storm, and the sea-gulls, crabs, and other scavengers of the deep, soon reduced it to the mutilated skeleton form in which it was found, and forwarded to us by our always attentive correspondent. This is the first dolphin in any form that has come under our inspection, and it was with a feeling of no little pleasure, not altogether unmingled with pride, perhaps, that we stood up confident and erect beside the table on which it was laid, when at last, after some hours' hard study, we had satisfactorily completed the labours of identification.

CHAPTER XI.

Ramble among the Hills—Encounter with an aged Parishioner—Song of the Smuggling Times—A version in Herd's Collection—Which is the Original?

In the course of an ornithological ramble among the hills a few days ago—one of the few fine days of the season—we forgathered with an old man resident in a distant corner of our parish, who was returning home with a burden of fine-leaved heath (*Erica cinerea*) for making brooms with, a necessary household implement which our old men manufacture in their idle hours with a neatness and bouquet-like elegance of form and finish which we have often admired. Having saluted each other in a friendly manner, we invited the old man to sit down beside us on the mossy corner of a huge drift boulder, and give us his crack; and, as a Highlander is rarely in a hurry, and dearly loves to get hold of a good listener appreciative of his reminiscences, he readily laid aside his fragrant burden, and sat down beside us. He was a fine old man of venerable and dignified presence, and spoke the mountain tongue with a mellifluousness and round roll and rhythm that delighted us. Our *rôle* was simply to listen, only throwing in an occasional remark to keep the old gentleman straight, and make him disemburthen himself of his budget with the greatest possible ease and satisfaction to himself. In such circumstances, only manage to keep an old man, or woman—a still more difficult lot to deal with—on good terms with themselves—" playing " them, in angler's phrase, with tact and judgment—and they will pour forth all they know of any subject, with all the freedom, if also with much of the tortuousness of channel and irregularities of depths and shallows, of one of their own mountain streams; like a mountain stream, too, sometimes fairly drying up, not from lack of will to go on, but from sheer want of matter to go on with. Old age is proverbially garrulous, but it is also frequently whimsical; and it is against this latter characteristic that you have to guard in your intercourse with these old people, if you would get fair and full hold of such stores of folk-lore as they may be possessed of. A basketful of speckled trout, with a rod and cunningly hooked line beside it, on the banks of a many-pooled and eddying stream, seems to the uninitiated an easy and natural thing enough. He knows not, or forgets the fact, that the whole matter mainly lies in the act and art of angling—in putting the rod and its delicate appendages to practical and successful use. It is even so with a bundle of folk-lore. It seems easy enough to pick up these things as you wander about the country, but the actual picking up—the successful angling, so to speak—is a very different matter when you come to try it. You have, first of all, to discover the individual in whom the hidden treasure you are in search of lies hid, and then you have to extract it, and extract it as much as may be in the completest and most perfect form possible. This you will find requires all your judgment and tact, and a patience that, however Job-like, will at times be sorely tried. "*Hic labor, hoc opus est,*" as we have a thousand times found from our own experience in such matters. Our venerable *confabulator* on this occasion said a great deal that was interesting, but at present we intend only troubling our readers with the following. In telling an old story about the wife of a farmer in a neighbouring district, who seems to have been no better than she should be, he quoted a stanza of an old song which, he said, his father used to sing with great spirit when *Bacchi plenus*, in the good old smuggling days, upwards of sixty years ago. Having a pencil and slip of paper in our pocket, we took down the verse on the spot, as follows :—

"Thainig fear-an-taighe dhachaidh,
 (Cha robh fiuthair riamh ris)
'S chunnaic e géola air a chladach,
'S dh'fheoiraich de bha ghéola a' g' iarraidh !
 Géola ars ise ?
 Seadh, géola ars esan ;
Cha'n 'eil ann ach meadaran
A thug mo mhathair dhomhsa.
 'S ioma cearn a shiubhail mi,
Agus céum a dh-fhalbh mi,
Ach dà ràmh 'am meadaran,
 Cha'n' fhaca mi riamh e !

" 'S thainig fear-an-taighe dhachaidh,
 (Cha robh fiuthair riamh ris)
'S chunnaic e each aig an dorus,
'S dh-fheoiraich de bha'n t' each a g' iarraidh ?
 Each ars ise !
 Seadh, each ars esan ;
Cha'n 'eil ann ach bò laoidh,
 'Thug mo mhathair dhomhsa ;

> 'S ioma cearn a shiubhail mi
> Agus céum a thriall mi,
> Ach diallaid air bò laoidh,
> Cha'n' fhaca mi rianih e!"

These lines shall have sufficient elucidation ere we are done with them. Meanwhile, in the interests of our more inland readers, we need only observe that "géola" in the first stanza means a ship's boat. It is from the Danish and Norwegian *jolle*, a small boat. The same word, under the thinnest of disguises, is met with in the English terms *yawl* and *jolly*-boat. There were some half-dozen more verses, our colloquist assured us, but he could not remember them. Repeating over these lines by ourselves, as we took a spell at hay-making in the evening, it struck us all of a sudden that we had surely seen or heard them, or something very like them, before. It was at first like trying to piece together the disjointed fragments of a disconnected and ill-remembered dream, a difficult, and, for a time, it seemed a hopeless effort of memory to connect the lines with a nameless something of the past. Aided by our ear, however, we managed to hit upon it at last. Unconsciously, as the words were being repeated for the twentieth time, perhaps, we found ourselves humming a tune into which they fitted as easily and naturally as a well-worn glove fits the hand. Casting our hay-fork aside, we made straight for our study, and taking down Whitelaw's *Book of Scottish Song* from its shelf, we found the very thing we wanted, and which had been racing about indistinctly and will-o'-the-wisp-wise in our mind all the afternoon. On page 46 of Whitelaw's collection is the old and tolerably well-known and pawky song beginning—

> " Our gudeman cam' hame at e'en,
> And hame cam' he," &c.

prefixed to which is the following editorial note :—

"This highly humorous old ditty is preserved in the second edition of David Herd's collection, 1776. Johnson recovered the tune from the singing of an old hairdresser in Edinburgh, and published it for the first time in the 5th vol. of his 'Museum.'"

Of the song thus prefaced, the first stanza is as follows :—

> " Our gudeman cam' hame at e'en,
> And hame cam' he ;
> And there he saw a saddle-horse,
> Where nae horse should be.
> Oh, how cam this horse here ?
> How can this be ?
> How came this horse here
> Without the leave o' me ?
> A horse ! quo' she ;
> Ay, a horse, quo' he ;
> Ye auld, blind, dotard carle,
> And blinder mat ye be !
> It's but a bonnie milk-cow
> My mither sent to me.
> A milk-cow ! quo' he ;
> Ay, a milk-cow, quo' she.
> Far hae I ridden,
> And muckle hae I seen,
> But a saddle on a milk-cow
> Saw I never nane."

Almost identically the same, observe, as the second Gaelic verse given above, of which—but the English reader may judge for himself—we give a literal line-for-line translation :—

> "The gudéman came home
> (He was in nowise expected),
> And he saw a horse at the door;
> And he inquired what that horse might be doing there.
> A horse ! says she (*i.e.*, the wife);
> Yes, a horse, said he.
> It is only a calved-cow (*i.e.*, a milk-cow)
> That my mother gave to me.
> Many a place have I wandered through,
> And step have I travelled afar,
> But a saddle on a calved-cow
> Never saw I before !"

It will be observed that the humorously objurgatory eleventh and twelfth lines of the English is awanting in the Gaelic, as well as the ludicrously interrogative and impudently assertive fifteenth and sixteenth lines. These lines are either altogether awanting in the Gaelic version, or they were forgotten in the recitation of our moorland colloquist, whose exact words we have given above. Our first Gaelic verse is literally as follows :—

> "The gudeman came home
> (He was not in the least expected),
> And he saw a small boat (a yawl) on the beach,
> And he inquired what the boat might be doing there :
> A small boat ! said she;
> Ay, a small boat, said he.
> It is but a small timmer coggie
> That my mother gave to me.
> Through many scenes have I wandered,
> And steps have I travelled afar,
> But a pair of oars in a timmer coggie
> Never saw I before !"

To this there is no exact counterpart in the English, or broad Scotch version rather, but you have its equivalent probably in this stanza—

> " Our gudeman cam' hame at e'en,
>   And hame cam' he ;
> He spied a pair o' jack-boots
>   Where nae boots should be ;
> What's this now, gudewife ?
>   What's this I see ?
> How cam' these boots here
>   Without the leave o' me ?
> Ye auld, blind, dotard carle,
>   And blinder mat ye be ;
> Its but a pair o' water stoups
>   The cooper sent to me.
>   Water-stoups ! quo' he,
>   Ay, water-stoups, quo' she.
> Far hae I ridden,
>   And muckle hae I seen,
> But siller spurs on water-stoups
>   Saw I never nane !

Now, good reader, here you have an old Scotch song first published in Herd's collection a hundred years ago, and here is a Gaelic version, almost identical, asserted by our venerable hill-side colloquist to have been sung with great glee by his father, as something even then well known and popular some sixty years ago. The one is clearly a translation, or paraphrase rather, of the other. It is simply impossible that both can be original. Is the Gaelic version, then, derived from the broad Scotch ? Or, on the contrary, is the broad Scotch derived from the Gaelic ? The Gaelic version has all the signs of an original composition, and so, for that matter of it, has the English. Which is Napoleon Bonaparte, and which Pompey? For our own part, we find the question so beset with difficulty that we decline meanwhile committing ourselves either way. There is this, however, in favour of the Gaelic being the original, that the air to which the song is sung—and we have heard it admirably sung many years ago, both by Wilson and Templeton—is unquestionably Celtic, being, with some slight and unimportant variations, no other than that known along the western sea-board and in the Hebrides as "Criomadh na Cnàmh," or "The Picking of the Bones." Some of our readers may perhaps be able to throw some light on so interesting a question, at a time when Celtic literature is at length receiving some slight share of the attention it so richly merits.

CHAPTER XII.

Pets—"Merdo," a pet Billy-Goat—His Habits—Antipathy between Goats and Rats—Goat's Hoof, Horns, &c.

WE once met a man who was not in the least ashamed to confess that he never had a pet of any sort in all his lifetime. We looked at him closely, and entirely believing his assertion to be true, bade him good morning at the earliest possible moment consistent with courtesy and good breeding. Such people, we should hope, are *rari aves*—"black swans" in their way—for we think we are right in saying that in his or her day everybody has had a pet or pets of some sort or other. As for ourselves, we have had scores of pets of every kind, from the tiny wren to the golden eagle, from the fragile field-mouse to the gallant steed, that could carry us, if need were, a score of miles an hour, and was yet as intelligently tame and docile as a short-frocked girl. Of all our pets, however, the drollest and funniest is that which at this moment is scampering about our bit of lawn, and doing all the mischief he can, out of sheer love of mischief, we do believe, and because he knows that we shall very soon be out and after him; and he knows full well, too, that that is all, for as to actually catching him with a view to punishment, you might as well attempt to lay your hand upon a midnight meteor. Our present pet is a goat, a buck-goat or billy-goat, a male, a grand fellow, with horns enough and beard enough to make his fortune at a photographer's. We got him last Christmas as a present from our good neighbour and friend Mr. Buchanan of Caolasnacone; wild he was from the mountains, and as averse to anything like domestication as if he were an ibex from the Alps. With patience, however, and gentle handling, we got him to know us, and to manifest pleasure at sight of us, and then we knew the work was done. He is now the most amusing quadruped that ever played tramp with impatient feet in a gentleman's lobby. Anticipating somewhat his greatness, we gave him a great name, for we called him "Merdo," after a celebrated goat of mediæval romance—a goat so big and strong, that when all other engines had failed, he broke open, with a single dint of his head, the prison doors of a distressed damoiselle, and bore her off and away on his back with such speed and goodwill that all pursuit on the part of her gaoler—a horrible giant—was as ineffectual as if he chased the wind. We introduce our goat to the reader not so much because he really is a splendid animal worth the looking at, but because goats have for a very long time been maligned and misrepresented—vilipended, in fact, to use an old Scottish law term—and we wish to say a word or two in their favour. If you can get a chance, be sure to speak a good word of man or beast of whom much evil is spoken, were it from no higher moral motive than that thereby you exceedingly tease and annoy the evil-speakers—a class of people at whom a slap well laid on with honest, open palm is always a delight. First of all, then, we confidently assert that a goat can remember a kindness, and be very grateful therefor. Ours, soon after we got him, and before he became quite tame, had one of its hind feet seriously hurt; how it happened we could not discover. He limped painfully, and we caught him much against his will, and surgeoned him as seemed best at the moment. He soon got better, and to this present hour he acknowledges our attentions by coming to us at call, and allowing us to handle him at pleasure, a liberty which he will permit to no other human being. That he should be more friendly with us than anybody else is only, we think, to be accounted for by the fact that we chanced, as stated, to have had it in our power to do him a kindness, and that he remembers it. But apart from gratitude for favours received, a goat is, of all animals, perhaps the most attentive and attached to his quadrupedal companions of the stable and byre. Ours has had his pen so placed that the cows and pony are constantly in sight, and his affection for his companions is very remarkable. He butts at them all in turn, no doubt, and makes believe to box and buffet them, but he never really hurts them; and woe be unto the animal that any time begins a row in veritable earnest! *Merdo*, in such a case, comes forward with lightsome step, and for a moment views the combatants with sparkling, angry eyes, then backing to a considerable distance, rushes full a-tilt at one or other of the belligerents, with a force that generally suffices to end the combat. We have remarked that his conduct on these occasions exhibits less than his ordinary intelligence, for his charge is quite as often directed against the smaller and weaker of the combatants as against the larger and stronger. When a battle has thus, by his timely intermediation, been decided, his bleat is full-toned, and loud and long, as if he rejoiced at being able to proclaim that by his act it is peace and goodwill throughout the land. A goat's foothold, always and everywhere, is simply marvellous. *Merdo* will gallop at racing speed along the rough, uneven coping of a "Galloway" dyke as if it were smooth and even as a grass-carpeted lawn, never making a miss or mistake, or rather making a thousand misses and mistakes every instant, as if to show how cleverly he can recover himself at the very moment that you fancy he must come inevitably to the ground. He will ascend and descend right in the face of rocks and precipices that to an ordinary spectator seem perfectly perpendicular, and do it, too, as easily as if it were the easiest and most broad-stepped of staircases. Nothing can possibly be imagined more admirably adapted to its purpose than a goat's hoof. Take it in your hand and study its structure, and it is well worth the studying. How hard, compact, and firm are its outward edges, yet soft, cushiony, and elastic in its intermediate and inner parts, beautifully designed, in short, and meant for a goat, and for no other animal in the world.

It is a common opinion that there is a deep-rooted and natural antipathy between goats and rats, or perhaps, to put it more correctly, between rats and goats—that the rats will at once clear out of premises into which a goat is introduced, and hence it is that about mills, granaries, distilleries, &c., where rats most do congregate, a goat is very often kept, and if you ask the reason, you will be told that where a goat is kept rats dare not, for their health's sake, abide. With how much of truth this is averred we are unable to decide. It is not at all unlikely, however, that the very strong and pronounced odour about a buck-goat at certain seasons, and, indeed, at all seasons, may be so unpleasant to rats that they will, because of it, vacate localities otherwise desirable residences enough. It is a fact, at all events, worth the chronicling, that the "foot-and-mouth" murrain so common among cattle this season was later in reaching our byres, and lighter when it did reach, than was the case around us, and rightly or wrongly, we are disposed to credit *Merdo's* powerful antiseptic odours as, in part at least, the cause of the exemption. Rats, we know, cannot endure the smell of coal-tar, much less contact with it, and that the strong effluvium of a goat should also be distasteful and unpleasant to them is perfectly credible. "There is nothing unscientific," as Sir William Thomson said of his life-germ bearing meteorites from the moon, in the averment. Poets, painters, architects, and sculptors have for centuries agreed to represent, or rather misrepresent, the goat as the embodiment and sign of all moral degradation. Now, we have closely watched our *Merdo* under all possible circumstances, and we can positively assert that we can detect no more propensity to evil thoughts or evil deeds in him than might be looked for in any one of his many cousins and congeners. We should rather be disposed to assert that a buck-goat is a far more graceful and intelligent animal than, for example, a ram, quite as well behaved and moral, too, let prejudiced people shake their heads as they may. We have in our day known many quadrupeds, and some bipeds too, heterodox as it may seem, worse behaved than our very amiable and excellent *Merdo*. That a goat has faults may perhaps be conceded—every living being has; but they seem to us to be only such faults as one might reasonably look for in a denizen, naturally, of the rocks and wilds; and then, if you only say of him the simple truth, his good parts will always counterbalance all the evil in him. Our readers, therefore, will understand that our *Merdo* is a great favourite, and how annoyed we were this morning to hear a huge aldermanic-visaged tourist, who was passing our place with, we presume, his wife in a waggonette, call his lady's attention to the " pretty *nanny-goat*," when in very truth it was our big-horned hero that he talked about. We have noticed, by the way, that, comparatively common as are sea-fowl and goats, the vast majority of passing tourists, natives or foreigners, will stand to look at either when they have the opportunity. One thing more about our goat, and we have done. If you examine his horns, you will find them, for their size, of immense weight, showing the solidity of their structure. They are not round like a bull's horns, which are built for tossing and goring; nor like a ram's, which are corrugated rough and gross, intended for striking a forward solid blow that shall crush and bruise. A goat's horns, on the contrary, are much compressed in all their length, with the sharper edge in front, and we have an idea that, fairly launched at one with the full force and impetus of an irate buck, the effect would be dreadful, a gash probably as deep as could be made by a deftly-wielded sabre, and, we should say, ten times more difficult of healment. A wound from a quadruped's horns never perhaps was known to heal kindly. The insulting exclamation—

"Not for Cadwallader and all his goats,"

was the filling up of the sum of ancient Pistol's iniquities in the estimation of the much-enduring Fluellen, and earned him such a thorough trouncing at the hands of that irate and gallant Welshman; and such, say we, be the well-merited punishment always of any one graceless enough to sneer at Welshmen, Gaels, or goats!

CHAPTER XIII.

Hedgehogs—Frank Buckland—Hedgehog Pets—Hedgehogs combative—Excellent to eat—New Year Festivities—Story of Pyrrhus the Epiret—An Evening with Christopher North—Professor Blackie—" Songs of Religion and Life "—*Sancte Socrates, ora pro nobis.*

OF living naturalists, we were the first, we believe, to say a good word in favour of a much-abused animal, the common hedgehog (*Echinus erinaceus*), in connection with two of these quadrupeds which were about our place for some months as very interesting pets. They were both males, and while in our keeping they were known by the names of " Wallace " and " Garibaldi." It was at the time that Garibaldi and his doings in Sicily and Italy were being constantly talked about, and hence the name of the second and smaller-sized of our favourites. Both managed finally to escape, by tunnelling for themselves a path beneath the garden gate. They disappeared, but they seem very soon to have met each with an amiable and willing lady-love, for now the country is full of them—that is to say, you can hardly set a trap for rat or rabbit, but once a week at least, or oftener, you find a hedgehog where you expected a very different animal. We revert to the subject, which, so far as the hedgehog and ourselves were concerned, we had thought pretty well exhausted and done with, merely to notice the fact that our friend Mr. Frank Buckland entirely corroborates our verdict as to the innocuousness of the harmless and sadly abused hedgehog. This is what Mr. Buckland says in a recent article in *Land and Water*—"It always grieves me to see gamekeepers and country folks put their heavy hobnail boots on a poor hedgehog, and crush it to death. If I was an owner of shootings, I would never allow a hedgehog to be killed. The structure and number of teeth show clearly that they are insectivorous by nature. I am quite certain that they are of great service to the farmer in destroying the insect pests of the farm. I have several times given hedgehogs unbroken eggs, and although I have kept them hungry, I have never known them crack and eat them. If an egg is broken the hedgehog will lick out its contents with its little tongue. I have no doubt that if the hedgehog found a dead or wounded rabbit, he would eat it, and why should he not?" So far Mr. Frank Buckland. The reader caring about these things may recollect that we also tried our hedgehogs with eggs, broken and unbroken, and that they would not touch them; so that our appeal to gamekeepers and others, now renewed, is that the harmless hedgehog should be let alone. Mr. Buckland admits that it will eat dead rabbits; we, on the contrary, are of opinion that under no circumstances would it touch rabbit, dead or living, at least in the way of food. It will eat slugs, snails, worms, and beetles of every kind. It will also eat the common blindworm, and probably also the common snake and adder; but beyond this we are extremely sceptical as to its carnivorousness. We are certain, at all events, that it will neither eat eggs nor birds, for we have tried ours once and again with both, with no other result than that in the morning these things remained untouched as we had left them on the evening before, and for the purpose of experiment we had kept our pets on such occasions, as Mr. Buckland says, "hungry." Yet not exactly untouched either, for the hedgehog is a most curious and inquisitive little animal, and whatever you lay beside it, even if it has no thought of eating it, it will nozzle and turn over, and toss and roll about as if determined to know all about its structure and contexture at all events. Although comparatively common, of no other British mammals do our naturalists all round seem to know so little as of the little hedgehog. And the little you find about them in books, meagre as it is, is as a rule not much to be depended on. We have only further to say that the hedgehog is in its way sufficiently combative. Ours used to fight at times viciously, the *casus belli* generally being as to which of them should get first and furthest into the pillowslip full of uncarded wool in which they slept. They sometimes also, though not often, had a bit of a squealing scramble over their food, which generally consisted of a saucer full of porridge and milk, a diet to which they took from the first, and of which they seemed fonder than of anything else that we could offer them. Mr. Buckland says that they are eaten in some places, and we see no reason at all why they should not. They are most cleanly little animals, and, pig-like, are generally met with in excellent condition, round and fat. An old fox-hunter here tells us that he once had his fair share of a roasted hedgehog at a farm bothy near Perth, and that it was excellent. He did not know what he was eating till he was done with it, and then, on being told, such is the force of prejudice and habit, he avows that he felt certain stomachic qualms, indicative of a desire on the part of that organ to get quit of its *bonne-bouche*. He had been hungry, however, before eating, and after all managed to retain his hedgehog meal, and through a long ten miles after-journey he confesses he felt all the stronger and better of his tuck-in of roast hedgehog. Could we overcome the prejudices of our "womankind" as to the necessary cooking and preliminary preparations, which, we believe, are somewhat complicated and difficult, we think that, fortified by the co-operation of some healthy stomached friend to go shares with us, we ourselves could venture on our quota of a hedgehog feast any day. The best way probably would be to begin with a young and tender one, which we see no reason to doubt would, if properly prepared *secundum artem*, taste quite as well as a sucking pig, this last a dish of which the Third George was so fond, that his mouth always watered at the very sight of it.

Our New Year festivities and merry-makings are now at length happily ended, and only now, observe, for here in Lochaber we keep the Old Style, and rather pride ourselves than otherwise on our attachment to old style and old forms and traditions of every kind. Our people here seem thoroughly to enjoy themselves on such occasions, casting carking cares for the time entirely aside, and taking all the good within their reach while it is to be had, and very wise, if you think of it, they are in so doing. You remember the old story of Pyrrhus the Epiret? It is so good in every way, and so brimful of a sound philosophy, that we make no apology for calling attention to it here, even if the reader has met with it before. The story of Pyrrhus the Epiret, then, is this:—One day, upon a friend requesting to know what ulterior purposes the King might mask under his expedition to Sicily, "Why, after *that* is finished," replied the King, "I mean to administer a little correction (very much wanted) to certain parts of Italy, and particularly to that nest of rascals in Latium." "And then——," said the friend. "And then," said Pyrrhus, "next we go for Macedon, and after that job's jobbed, next, of course, for Greece." "Which done——," said his friend. "Which done," interrupted the King, "as done it shall be, then we're off to tickle the Egyptians." "Whom having tickled," pursued the friend, "then we——?" "Tickle the Persians," said the King. "But after that is done," urged the obstinate friend, "whither next?" "Why, really, man, it's hard to say; you give one no time to breathe; but we'll consider the case as soon as we come to Persia, and until we've settled it, we can crown ourselves with roses, and pass the time pleasantly enough over the best wine to be found in Ecbatana." "That's a very just idea," replied the friend, "but, with submission, it strikes me that we might do that just now, and at the beginning of all these wars, instead of waiting for the end." "Bless me," said Pyrrhus, "if ever I thought of *that* before.

Why, man, you're a conjuror; you've discovered a mine of happiness. So here, boy, bring us roses and plenty of Cretan wine!" The philosophy of our apologue is too obvious to require any explication. We recollect being once privileged to spend an evening in company of the late Professor Wilson, of Edinburgh, the world-renowned "*Christopher North*," in his son-in-law's house, Professor Ferrier, of St. Andrews. Some time during the course of our sederunt, Wilson took occasion to relate this story of Pyrrhus and his friend, and he told it so admirably and with so many happy turns of his own, that he very soon had us all in convulsions of laughter. He then made the apologue the text of a long lay sermon, bristling with apt philosophisings, such as we had never heard before, and are never likely to hear again. For this alone we reckon it one of those nights, the memory of which one treasures up as something more valuable and precious than anything else this world has to offer. A fireside sermon from such a man as John Wilson was something worth the listening to, for you might live a long lifetime and meet no other intellect of equal wit and equal shrewdness. Under the sparkling of the richest and rarest humour, and peals of the heartiest laughter, you felt all the same that, during the whole time, you were breathing an atmosphere of profoundest wisdom and world-wide philanthropy. We were then, of course, young, and more impressionable than we are to-day, but even yet we should gladly walk a rough winter day's journey to listen to wisdom so profound from lips so eloquent. An evening with Professor Blackie, too, at your own fireside, *solus cum solo*, with the curtains drawn, and no one to disturb you, is very enjoyable, for the learned Professor, although the world at large is loth to admit it, is in truth a man as thoroughly and really religious, in the best sense of that term, as he is ready-witted and warm-hearted. He has, by the way, recently published a volume of poetry, which, *ex dono auctoris*, is now on the table beside us. It is entitled "Songs of Religion and Life." That Professor Blackie should appear as a religious poet, many people will be surprised at; not we, however, for we have long known that under an air of apparent levity and *abandon*, and much *brusquerie* of manner, there is pervading the whole man a deep undercurrent of great thoughtfulness and unaffected piety. Here is a single specimen, very characteristic of the author. At first sight it sounds somewhat heterodox, but, *cum grano* and at bottom, it is orthodox enough, and conveys a censure which some people would do well to take to heart.

"SANCTE SOCRATES, ORA PRO NOBIS.

" Dear God, by wrathful routs,
   How is Thy Church divided ;
And how may he that doubts,
   In such turmoil be guided ?
When, weeping, I behold
   How Christian people quarrel,
Oft-times from Heathens old
   I fetch a saintly moral :
And while they fret with rage
   The sore-distraught community,
I look for some Greek sage
   Who preaches peace and unity,

And thus I pray :
O Sancte Socrates, ora pro nobis!
  Let faith and love and joy increase,
  And reason rule and wrangling cease,
    Good Saint, we pray thee !

"They pile a priestly fence
  Of vain scholastic babble,
To keep out common sense
  With the unlearnèd rabble.
A curious creed they weave,
  And, for the Church commands it,
All men must needs believe,
  Though no man understands it.
Thus, while they rudely ban
  All honest thought as treason,
I from the Heathen clan
  Seek solace to my reason,
    And thus I pray :
O Sancte Socrates, ora pro nobis!
  From creeds that men believe, because
  They fear a damnatory clause,
    Good Saint, deliver us !

"Some preach a God so grim,
  That, when his anger swelleth,
They crouch and cower to him,
  When sacred fear compelleth ;
God loves his few pet lambs,
  And saves his one pet nation,
The rest he largely damns
  With swinging reprobation.
Thus, banished from the fold,
  I wisely choose to follow
Some sunny preacher old,
  Who worshipped bright Apollo :
    And thus I pray :
O Sancte Socrates, ora pro nobis!
  From silly flocks of petted lambs,
  And from a faith that largely damns,
    Good Saint, deliver us !

" And some do strongly strive,
   By light of noon-day taper,
The guilty soul to shrive
   With many a jest and caper;
With candlestick and bells,
   With postures and grimaces,
With wealth of holy spells,
   And lack of lovely graces.
And when I see increase
   These feats of antic duty,
I turn me back to Greece,
   Where truth was wed to beauty,
     And thus I pray :
O Sancte Socrates, ora pro nobis !
   From quaint religion tucked in laces,
   From genuflexions and grimaces,
     Good Saint, deliver us !

" And some there be who say
   That through their veins a virtue
Doth run to charm away
   All ills that flesh is heir to ;
And from their finger-tips
   A sacred tremor passes,
To ope the braying lips
   Of Apostolic asses.
From ferment I abstain
   Of such high-churchly preachers,
And keep myself quite sane
   By sober Attic teachers !
     And thus I pray :
O Sancte Socrates, ora pro nobis !
   From men that say wide earth contains
   No truth but creeps through saintly veins,
     Good Saint, deliver us !

" Such eager fancies vain,
   Shape forth the rival churches ;
And each man's fuming brain
   God's holy light besmirches ;

And thus they all conspire
    The primal truth to smother,
And think they praise their Sire,
    By hating well their brother.
Such wrangling when I see,
    Such storms of godly rancour,
To Heathendom I flee,
    To cast a peaceful anchor,
        And thus I pray:
O Sancte Socrates, ora pro nobis!
    Let love and faith and joy increase,
    And reason rule, and wrangling cease,
        Good Saint, we pray thee!"

CHAPTER XIV.

A Wintry March—God made the Country, Man made the Town—Spanish Mackerel—An Owl making a mistake—Dog and Hedgehog—Intelligent Collies—Interchange of News.

SUCH a wintry March was never before known in the West Highlands. Yesterday we met a plucky old man, now in his eighty-sixth year, light of foot, and clear of eye, and clever of speech, as if he had not yet attained a third of that age, who solemnly assured us that in all his life long he never knew a March so inclement throughout. We ourselves can speak of the last twenty or twenty-five years, and it is very certain that in that time at least we never had such a March month as this, so persistently stormy and wild every way, as well as cold. In coming from our stable and byre a few nights ago, after seeing our pony and cows thoroughly well fed and bedded—the latter quite as necessary in its way to the well-being of your stock as the former—we stood, and while actually shivering from crown to toe in the keenness of the biting blast, that, razor-like, seemed to cut us to the very bone, we startled our servant lassie not a little, as with lantern and milk-pail she passed by us, by half-unconsciously repeating aloud a verse, the meaning of which she, fortunately for herself, knew nothing:

"The bleak wind of March
Made her tremble and shiver,
But not the dark arch,
Nor the black flowing river.

> Mad from life's history—
> Glad to death's mystery,
> Swift to be hurl'd—
> Anywhere, anywhere,
> Out of the world."

A stanza of itself sufficient to immortalise the name of Thomas Hood.

"God made the country, and man made the town," and the more we think of it, the more are we disposed to exclaim with much heartfelt fervour, "God bless the country! and God bless our own rural population! There may be sin amongst us, as, alas! sin will find its way everywhere, but of sin with all the horrors of its squalor and sad surroundings, as you meet with it in over-peopled cities, we happily know nothing." Our only son, now in business in Glasgow, fond of his work and happy in every way, yet writes, "The scenes I sometimes come across here are terrible. On a fine day, when I see the sun shining on the housetops, I often think how much I should like a run among the hills behind the manse." Cunning commentators have once and again tried to prove that Falstaff's babbling " o' green fields " is a corruption of the text, and have suggested different readings. We, for our own part, like the present reading best; it is to us very beautiful and of infinite meaning. In no other passage of Shakespeare would the general acceptance of a conjectural emendation, however felicitous, so much annoy us as in meddling with poor Sir John's babbling, bairn-like, when at the point of death, of the green fields so fresh and flowery, in which as a boy, yet innocent of "sack" in any form, he ran and scampered and shouted, as boys, boy-like, will run and shout and scamper while the world lasts.

Mr. Grant, schoolmaster of Ardgour, did something clever the other day, and something out of his ordinary "beat," too. He noticed a fish, with which evidently something was wrong, coming now and again to the surface of the sea, right opposite his windows. It was behaving as no sound and sane fish would ever think of behaving, and Mr. Grant went out at last and managed to capture it. It was shown to us next day, and we had no difficulty in recognising it as a species of mackerel, the horse or Spanish mackerel, a by no means rare fish on our shores. It was fat and in good condition, and seemed healthy every way, and we have no doubt proved good eating, though not quite so good on the table as the common mackerel. The wonder was what could have been the matter with it when it so flopped about upon the surface of the sea, and allowed itself at last to be captured. "Putting that and that together," a process in which the naturalist must often find himself engaged in, in the unravelment of such puzzles as constantly come his way, the explanation is probably to be found in the following fact :—Some time after the capture of the fish, a something was seen floating past with the ebbing tide, very much at the same distance from the shore as was the mackerel when first seen. This latter waif, on being intercepted and landed, proved to be a dead owl—a specimen of the barn owl—the *Strix flammea* of ornithologists. On being made aware of all this, we knew at once what had happened. The owl is very fond of fish, even when mice and small birds, its ordinary food, are plentiful. It often dips into a lake or stream, and seizes such small fish as, swimming for the moment near the surface, it can reach with its sharp talons. The mackerel in this case was pounced upon by the owl, but the fish was too heavy and too powerful to be taken up and sailed away with in the usual manner. The fish, however, probably struck about the head and gills, was badly hurt and stupefied, so as to be captured in the way stated, while the owl, with its claws for a time inserted in its prey so firmly as not to be immediately extracted, was dragged about and drowned. When dead, the talon tendons would become so relaxed that the fish could easily shake itself clear of its enemy. The moral of the whole is that people should beware of attempting the encompassment of a feat for which they are, upon the whole, unfit and incapable.

Backward still as is this season, and wintry, our wild-birds wisely make the most of it. Nest-building has begun in sheltered corners, although we have not as yet come across a nest with eggs in it. In anything like a calm, and with every stray gleam of fitful sunshine, the thrush, blackbird, redbreast, and chaffinch ring out their cheeriest carols. They know full well that " the time of the singing of birds has come," and only wonder how it should continue so wild and wintry at the back of the vernal equinox. The first hedgehog, probably roused from its hybernation by one fine day last week, was met with this morning by our collie dog, and there was such a row as is usual in such encounters. The dog yelped and barked, and tried to bite, but it was no use. The hedgehog curled itself up in its covering of spike armour, and being an animal of infinite patience, it just allowed the dog to bark away and fret itself into a useless passion, until it grew tired of the business, and was glad to retire, hoarse and crest-fallen, leaving its invulnerable antagonist the same bristly ball he found it. We the while sat on a dyke, and enjoyed our dog's discomfiture hugely. His looks towards us when making a dash at the hedgehog, and finding his nose hurt by the prickles—he was glad enough to leap back again, rubbing his injured organ in the moss—were so comical at times as to make us fairly laugh outright. He once or twice asked our aid as plainly and unmistakeably as if he spoke in human speech; and when, after all, we only sat still and laughed, he seemed really offended, and sulked about in a manifest pet for the remainder of the day. The same dog when in chase of a rabbit is very amusing. He is swift of foot, but not so quick-footed as a rabbit, and when, after a hot chase, the rabbit pops into its burrow and is safe, the way the dog looks at us, suggesting the immediate aid of pick and spade to dig the runaway out, is so absurd, that the herd-boy in the adjoining copse often hears us laughing aloud, and is not a little puzzled at what.

With an intelligent, well-bred collie beside you, one need never say that he is companionless or without amusement, wander where you may. Did you ever, by the way, remark how dogs seem to *speak* to each other, evidently interchanging news when they chance to meet? We were passing a shepherd's house among the hills on a recent occasion, and it was amusing to watch the meeting between our dog and some half-dozen curly tailed tykes belonging to the shepherd. Our dog, as the stranger, was instantly surrounded by his canine relations, and such a whispering, sniffing, and general *palaver* took place as made even the old shepherd smile. "Don't you think, Hugh," we observed, "that these dogs are perfectly understanding each other, and having *their* crack in their own way, just as much as you and I?" "Well, sir," responded honest Hugh, "I whiles think that dogs are in their way just as intelligent and capable of interchanging ideas as we are." "I am quite of the same opinion," we added, "and there's a bit of as good tobacco as ever was smoked. How are the sheep doing?" "Just very middling in all this bad weather. There'll be grand prices at the 'deliveries' this year, I'm thinking." "So be it, Hugh. The outgoing tenant will be pleased, and the incoming tenant will probably scratch his head as he wends him to the bank parlour to provide the wherewithal to settle for his 'stock.' Good evening,"—and so we parted. On our way home we noticed that our dog was convoyed by the two oldest and shaggiest of his canine friends till we were more than half-way down the glen, the final parting taking place after a friendly frolic round and round a green knoll that lay in our path. What news our dog gave to them, or they to our dog, we shall never know, but that an interchange of news of some kind took place we hold to be as certain as our own crack with the shepherd. It was in the course of this ramble, too, that we saw the first wild bee of the season, though what could have tempted him abroad in weather so unkindly it is difficult to say.

CHAPTER XV.

Cold Spring—An Arab Proverb—An old "Piobaireachd"—Its Origin and Date—Words attached to—Translation—A strange Charm or Talisman—Paralysis and Palsy proper.

APRIL came in pleasantly enough, and we had already begun to forget all the cold and inclemency of March, when, to the surprise of every one, the wind, that for a week had been "westlan'" and genial, went round as if at a single bound to east and north; and after a few burly blasts, snell and spiteful enough for Candlemas-tide, warning us in a measure for what was coming, brought down upon us the heaviest fall of snow of the season. The country all around now wears a sad mid-winter aspect. Agricultural labour is for the time at a standstill, and shepherds and flockmasters, who had already begun to whistle as if fairly "through the wood," are again terribly anxious, as well they may, and all the more so that this, too, is the lambing season. The snow, it is true, will not probably remain long at this date on the low-lying grounds, but on the hills and in the upland glens it must be a considerable time before the sun, even at his present altitude, and shining with what brightness he may, can dissolve the very great depth of snow that has fallen so unexpectedly as well as untimeously. It is long since matters wore so hopeless and unkindly an aspect in mid-April. Our wild-birds are fairly at their wits' end, and for that matter of it at their songs' end too, for the present. Dowie and listless, they can only cheep and chirrup their complaints in little deprecatory, expostulatory notes at the untimeous and unlooked-for turn affairs have taken. One would like to hear, in confidence, their opinion of the "clerk of the weather" in present circumstances. The Arabs have a proverb that "patience is stronger than a lion." Fine weather cannot in the nature of things be far distant. In any case, impatience and fretting on our own part, or on that of our wild-bird friends, can in present circumstances avail us nothing.

Most admirers of bagpipe music are familiar with the *port* or tune known as "Tigh Bhròinein"—*The Miserly, Miserable One's House*. To an old piper, John Macarthur of Cladaich, on Lochawe side, we are indebted for the story of the origin of this really very fine *piobaireachd*, as well as for a couple of stanzas of the original Gaelic verses attached to it, as to most Highland airs of the same class. Such scraps of information should be collected on all hands and carefully treasured up, as they never fail to lend additional interest to a tune, no matter how beautiful in itself, no less than they do to an old ballad or song. Some two or three hundred years ago, when the great Clan Campbell was at the height of its power, the estate of Barbreck was possessed by a Campbell, who was the brother or cousin—tradition is somewhat uncertain as to the exact degree of relationship—of another Campbell, the neighbouring laird of Craignish. This latter, the laird of Craignish, kept a piper, while Barbreck did not. Barbreck could afford to keep one, too, as well as his cousin, but he grudged the expense. His stinginess in this respect, or wise economy, if you so like to term it, is still commemorated in a saying common in some parts of Argyllshire—*Tha mi a's iùnais, mar 'bha 'm Barbreac gun phiobaire*—when you would admit that you want a certain thing, such, for instance, as a horse and gig, yacht, or anything else that your neighbour has, and that you might have too, and could well enough afford to have if you only liked. Barbreck was one day on a visit at Craignish, and as he was leaving, meeting the piper, he addressed him, "The New Year is approaching. On New-Year's day morning, when you have played the proper 'salute' to your master, my cousin Craignish, I wish you would come over to Barbreck and play a New-Year's 'salute' to *me*, for, as you know, I have no piper of my own to do it. Come and spend the day with us." The piper promised, and on New-Year's morning, after first playing his master into good humour, he went to Barbreck as was arranged. He played and played until the laird of Barbreck was in raptures. After a while the piper felt that he was both hungry and thirsty, and hinted as much to the laird. Food was therefore set before him, but unsatisfactory in every way as to quantity, no less than as to quality and kind. The drinkables were no better, and long ere the sun had set, the piper was anxious to return home. "Give us one more tune before you go," said Barbreck. "That I will," responded the piper, and he then and there played impromptu the tune, from that day forth so much admired and widely known as "Tigh Bhròinein"— the House of the Miserly One! The following are two of some half-dozen stanzas attached to this *port* from the very first, whether by the piper himself or by a brother bard is not known, and having a reference to its origin and history :—

"Tigh Bhroinein.

"Bha mi 'n tigh Bhròinein 'n diugh,
Bha mi 'n tigh Bhròinein ;
Fhuair mi cuireadh
'S cha d' fhuair mi mo leòr ann.
Fhuair mi deoch bhrochain ann,
A's droch aran eòrna,
Fhuair mi cas circ' ann,
'S air chiunt' gum bi 'm bròn i !
Cuireadh gu'n dreach a chràidh mi ;
Fàgaidh mi 'nochd,
Gun bhiadh, gun deoch,
Fàgaidh mi 'nochd 'm Bàr-breac,
'S cha phill mi riut tuilleadh,
A sheinn do phort failte," &c.

Only a very literal translation, such as our friend Mr J. T. Campbell of Islay delights in, can do anything like justice to these curious old lines:—

"The House of the Miserly One.

"I was in the house of the miserly one to-day,
In the house of the miserly one was I :
I went by invitation thither,
But I got no sufficiency (of meat or drink).
I got a drink of meal gruel there,
And got bad barley *scones*.
I got the leg of a hen there,
And, by my troth, she was a poor and tough one !
This is an invitation that has annoyed me ;
I will leave this to-night

> Without (I may say) food or drink;
> I will leave thee Barbreck,
> Nor will I return to thee any more,
> To play thee a piobaireachd salute!" &c.

A curious double-barrelled satire this, musical at once and verbal. It conveys an important lesson, too, which some people would do well to heed. If musician or bard visits you by invitation, and they do the best they can for your delectation and amusement, see that you treat them handsomely, for they are a *genus irritabile*, kittle cattle, a waspish race, every man of them, and, in return for any slight or improper treatment on your part, they may invest your name with an immortality of the least enviable kind. Little did the Barbreck of our *piobaireachd* think that we should have occasion to record the story of his stinginess to the honest piper of Craignish at this, a date so distant from that New-Year's day morning; nor even the piper himself that his impromptu melody on the occasion, in which, when well played, you can still recognise the screams of the tough old hen when her neck was being *thrawn*, would live and be played, and quoted and hugely admired a couple of hundred years or more after he had been gathered to his fathers.

Some little time ago we happened to meet a woman who, in speaking of a recently deceased aunt, said, "By the way, sir, in looking through my aunt's trunk the other day, the *kist*, you know, in which she kept her clothes and everything she valued most, I found a curious sort of thing which I had once or twice got a glimpse of while she lived, and by which I know she set great store, and considered very valuable. It seems to be a plant or vegetable of some kind, and I know that her idea was that while she kept it wrapped up in her dead-clothes, which you must know she had prepared many years ago, she should be free from every illness and ailment whatever, until the final illness of death itself should come." We went next day to see this wonderful herbaceous talisman or charm, and after a little examination, found it to be a stalk, and rather a large stalk, with part of the root attached, of the Great Cat's-Tail Grass or Reed-Mace, a species of bulrush, the *Typha latifolia* of botanists. It was, of course, very much dried up and withered, and had evidently been many years separated from the marshy soil which is its proper habitat. The niece either could not or would not tell us anything more about the matter, but she good-naturedly allowed us to carry the bulrush charm along with us, remarking, with an ill-suppressed smile, that she hoped it had not lost all its virtue, and that we should find it of some value, as we were at the time suffering from a sore throat. More seriously she said, at parting, that it was the truth, whether the bulrush had anything to do with it or not, that for thirty years at least, until a few days before her death, her aunt had not had a single moment's illness. A few days afterwards we rode a considerable distance to consult an old woman, with whom we chance to be a great favourite, and who is up to the time of day more than anybody else we ever knew as to the philosophy and *raison d'être* of everything in the shape of talismans, amulets, charms, and superstitious *freits* in every shape and form. She recognised the plant at once by its Gaelic name, which was new to us. She called it *Cuigeal-nam ban sith*, or the Fairy Wives' Distaff. Had she ever, we asked, known it to be treasured up as the deceased lady, its late possessor, had done, and with the same belief in its virtues? Well, not exactly, she replied, as a charm against sickness of *every* kind, but only as a very effectual charm, she had been told—for she had never tried it herself nor seen it tried—against attacks of epilepsy or *tinneas-tuiteamas*, as she called it—the exact equivalent of the vulgar Scottish name for the ailment the *falling sickness*. To have all the virtues that it ought to have, she said that it required to be pulled on midsummer midnight, or on a midnight nearest to midsummer eve possible, when the moon is at the full. It must be pulled by a person who has fasted since the preceding mid-day, who is barefooted at the time, and, if a female, whose hair is loose and ungathered, without pin, or ribbon, or comb, or cap, or covering of any kind to trammel its freely flowing in the wind as the breeze may select to deal with it. Some other particulars, she said, had also to be attended to, but she had forgotten them. Once selected and properly pulled with all the necessary ceremonies, the bulrush was to be taken home to the dwelling of the person to be benefited by its mysterious virtues. It was to be wrapped up in some one or other article of the clothes in which corpses are usually swathed for interment, the patient, as a rule, instantly feeling the benefit of the presence under the same roof of the fairy distaff charm. One remark the old lady made, which is, perhaps, worth repeating. The bulrush charm, she said, is now seldom used, just because epilepsy, at one time very common in the

Highlands, is now of rather rare occurrence. She also observed that paralysis, almost unknown in the Highlands fifty years ago, is now becoming very common, while palsy proper, or that tremulousness of the head and limbs known as true palsy, is now almost unknown, while in her younger days it was so common that there were two or three or more cases to be met with in almost every hamlet.

CHAPTER XVI.

Glen Tarbert—*Lyche-Gate* of Church at Strontian—Hedgehog—Contribution to the Natural History of.

WE wonder that it does not oftener occur to the tourist in the Highlands to act more independently for himself than he is usually in the habit of doing, by throwing his guide-book occasionally aside, and taking a route for himself, of which route, if it at all lies off the beaten track, the said guide-book maker probably never heard, and by which he very certainly never travelled. This thought struck us as lately of an early morning we were riding down Glen Tarbert on our way to Strontian. It was a lovely day, a bright sun and cloudless sky overhead, but with heavy masses of pearl-like mist here and there still lingering along the mountain tops; there was such a constant change and interchange of lights and shadows, of a glory beginning and culminating and dying away, only to begin again, and often, too, in reverse order, all in a manner so impressive and beautiful and solemn withal, that once and again we were fain to rein up our horse until he stood stock-still, while we gazed and gasped in very bewilderment of delight. The distance from Corran Ferry to Strontian is just fifteen miles, and if the tourist will take our word for it—and he can understand that in such a matter as this we can have no earthly object or end to serve in exaggerating, any more than in saying what is absolutely untrue—every furlong of these fifteen miles' length will be found worth the looking at with the most attentive, intelligent, and receptive of eyes. To describe in words, no matter how honestly done, would give but an imperfect and faint idea of the splendid reality. We do not say, observe, that Glen Tarbert is finer than many other glens along the western sea-board and elsewhere in the Highlands, far less that the already well-known and accredited tourist routes in the Highlands should be at all abandoned or superseded. On the contrary, we would have tourist routes multiplied, and the first step in this direction seems to us to be that the individual tourist and sightseer should occasionally, as opportunity offers, strike out for himself in short excursions to right or left of the usual beaten track. For our own part, we can at times enjoy the companionship of others, even a crush and a crowd, as much as most people, but, in our view of the matter, one of the main attractions of the short lateral excursions here hinted at would be their solitariness and the total absence of anything tending to distract or interrupt the sightseer in the full enjoyment of his surroundings. In all such supplementary excursions from the main route and more beaten tracks of tourists, fine weather is, of course, presupposed; and in this and other minor matters the adventurous tourist must just watch his opportunity, and endeavour to make his hay while the sun shines. In returning from Strontian that same evening, we had the pleasure of calling upon Sir Thomas M. Riddell and Lady Riddell at Horseley Hall, at this season one of the loveliest spots in all the West Highlands. Not having had an earlier opportunity, we were now taken to see the new chapel of St. Mary's, in all its parts and belongings designed and superintended to completion by Lady Riddell and Sir Thomas. It is a very pretty little church, perfect, indeed, for its size, though in the last respect, too, it is probably quite large enough for the requirements of the district. The internal fittings and decorations are in admirable taste. On approaching the main entrance we noticed that there is an arched and open cloister intended for the comfort and shelter of the worshippers on a wet or stormy day. And what immediately struck us was that, although not originally intended as such, it might quite appropriately be called a *lych-gate*, and used as such, if necessary—thus giving the pretty little building quite a mediæval character and tone perfectly in keeping with its general style of architecture. A *lich, lyche*, or *lych*-gate is a sort of cloister or piazza attached to churches and churchyards in early and mediæval times, and even up to a later period, through which a corpse was carried, and, if necessary, allowed to rest, while the officiating clergyman assumed his robes, and other necessary preparations for the burial service and interment were being carried out. *Lich* or *lych* (A.S.) signifies a dead body or corpse, so that lych-gate is just corpse-gate. We have the word still retained in our more common compound term *lyke-wake*, or nightly watching of the dead until their burial. Our Strontian trip was in all respects a most pleasant one.

We are indebted to Mr. John Bain of Stranraer for the following notes on the habits of the hedgehog, &c.,

by one who has recently given the subject much careful attention, to wit, the Rev. George Sturrock, minister of the parish of Corsock, in the Stewartry of Kirkcudbright, where hedgehogs seem to be very plentiful—more plentiful, perhaps, than anywhere else in Scotland. As a contribution to the natural history of an interesting little animal, whose true character and economy has been for some time a subject of much discussion, these notes by one who has taken the trouble to observe for himself with all the closeness and care the circumstances permitted, are of considerable value. Mr. Sturrock writes, under date 10th July, to his friend Mr. Bain as follows :—

"We had your favour of the 6th June. It looks as if I were careless, but it is not so ; the hedgehogs have required all the time. I think that, without presumption, I may now be reckoned somewhat of an authority on this subject. At least, since I saw you I have spared no pains to be so, standing often almost stone-still on drizzling evenings making my observations. The subject may not by some be thought an exalted one, but it very soon became to me quite fascinating. As to the food of the hedgehog, any difficulty, after the most careful observation, is not in saying what it will eat, but what it will *not* eat. Before beginning these observations, I thought a good deal on the subject, and as the result, that you were wrong in saying that it eat eggs and killed birds ; and that Sir William Jardine, who says that ' it is very fond of eggs, and is, consequently, mischievous in the game preserve and hen-house,' must also be wrong. Its sensitiveness to anything that menaces it, however weak or harmless, led me to think that a partridge, for example, would be more than a match for it, making it by a single peck roll up and wait for a convenient retreat, but it is evidently a subject that requires more than reflection. *My observations have led me to a different conclusion.* I have found that in captivity two hedgehogs are more than a match for a rat, and, in a state of nature, I have seen one putting a pheasant to defiance. After seeing you I made a house, a large box covered with wire-netting, and the first night I went out in search I captured two hedgehogs, one very large and another rather small. These I placed in said house or cage. At first, after all was quiet, they surveyed their quarters, and evidently looked for a way of escape. Getting tired of this, they rolled themselves up under the litter. Later in the evening, and with the aid of candle-light, we placed beside them a great variety of kinds of food, among which were some small *trout*. We then made use of the watering-can with rose, and gave them an artificial rain. They soon began to snuff about, and were attracted—likely by the smell—to a piece of pork. They soon left this, and, curiously enough, each made choice of a small trout. To this several witnesses can testify. In the morning we found everything—fish, flesh, bread, cheese, milk, &c.—had been more or less tried. On the following evening we put in a reptile which they call here a *mankeeper*, and although it could move about briskly, they soon devoured it. I am astonished at their preference for fish. This I proved by placing a variety of kinds of food as before, and hanging an *eel* by a string from the roof. This they first eat as far up as effort enabled them to get at it, and finished the rest when it was put within their reach. We afterwards starved them for a time, and then placed beside them a large rat, with no injury, so far as I know, but a leg broken in the trap. After the rat began to get quiet, our friends the hedgehogs set to work, making a sort of dart at it with the nose, and, when it resisted, rolling themselves up a little. This went on for an hour at least, and I fancied that they could make nothing of it. In the morning, however, I found it dead and completely gutted. In captivity they seem to eat anything. One in the vinery seems very fond of the thinnings of the grapes, showing that they will eat vegetables. All eggs I tried were readily eaten, *but they cannot break a hen egg with a thick shell.* The efforts they made to do this, and the way in which they persevered to do it, was extraordinary. But, both in captivity and in a state of nature, I have seen them defeated after all their efforts. Small eggs they readily devour as they come in their way, or can be reached by them. The most extraordinary thing I have to tell is, that one wet evening, when passing along the road a little below my manse, I saw a pheasant fluttering about in a very unhappy like style, and believing that its young were being disturbed by my dog, I called on him. He did not come, and I entered the field to take him away, when, to my surprise, I found a hedgehog partially rolled up, and on turning it over, found a young pheasant all eaten but the head and some bones and feathers. This I was telling a friend who is of some note in the stewartry, and he assured me that he and a friend found a partridge in a similar predicament. This I meant merely for jottings, but I have been twice interrupted, and the post is now at hand, so that with all its mistakes I will send it off. I only add this—let those who will not believe that the hedgehog is an egg-eater only go to its haunts on a damp night, and place eggs *not at its nose*, but at some distance from it, wait patiently and watch carefully, and I shall be surprised if they do not come away sufficiently convinced that the hedgehog is an egg-eater."

As the above observations were made and the notes written at Mr. Bain's request, with a view to their being sent to us, we have to thank both gentlemen for their courtesy and attention. We may remark that the term "mankeeper" for any of our reptiles is new to us. We have no doubt, however, that the blindworm (*Angius fragilis*) is the reptile meant. The Highlanders, from a mistaken belief in its venomousness and evil character, generally call it *Plaigh-Shlat*, the Plague or Distemper Switch. It is needless to say that in reality it is as harmless and blameless of life as the commonest earth-worm. It has no means or power of doing harm to beast or body, even if had the will, which it has not.

CHAPTER XVII.

Letter from the Hebrides—Curious old Song—Translated into English.

From the Outer Hebrides our friend Mr. Carmichael sends us a song which he took down on the 10th March 1869 from the dictation of a cottar woman at Howmore, South Uist, a woman who, though in a lonely position, has a keen sense of the humorous and ludicrous.

The following is the song; we retain Mr. Carmichael's orthography as being more in keeping with the Outer Hebrides pronunciation of many of the words:—

"Na Tri Eoin Chruinne-Gheala Dhonn."

Fonn—" Na tri Eoin chruinne-gheala dhonn,
  Chruinne-gheala dhonn, chruinne-gheala dhonn,
  Na tri Eoin chruinne-gheala dhonn,
  'S b' iad sid na tri Eoin !

I.

" Is dubh am fionn sin, 's dubh am fionn
  Chaidh mi butarscionn mo bhean ;
  Ma their mise 's dubh am fitheach,
  Their is' gum beil am fitheach geal !

II.

" Tha bean agam mar an deantag,
  Bean is crainnte na tom druis ;
  Bean is teogha na seachd teinteann
  Bean chruaidh chainntidh mharbh i mis !

III.

"Thogain tigh air laraich luim,
  Chairinn bonn ri maide cas,
  Thigeadh ise 's car na ceann,
  ' 'S meirig a rachadh ann a steach.'

IV.

"Dhianain treothadh, dhianain buain,
  Dhianain cruach mar fhear a chach,
  Theireadh i mar bha i beo,
  Nach robh ann ach torr air làr.

V.

"Dhianain iasgach leis an doradh,
  Mharbhain langa, mharbhain sgat;
  Chuireadh ise 'lamh na cliabh,
  'S dh-iarradh i sid 'thoirt an chat!

IV.

"Dhianain cuman air fiodh cruaidh,
  A shuidheadh gu buan air an làr;
  Chuireadh i h-anam an geall,
  Gun robh e 'call air a mhàs!

VII.

"Teinne ga fhadadh mu loch
  Gu tiormachadh cloich an cuan,
  Teagasg ga thoirt do mhuaoi bhuirb,
  Mar bhuil' uird air iarann fuar?

VIII.

"Cha truimeid an loch an lach,
  Cha truimeide an t' each a shrian,
  Cha truimeid' a chaora a h-olainn,
  'S cha truimeid' a choluinn ciall!

Fonn—"Na tri eoin chruinne-gheala dhonn,
  Chruinne-gheala dhonn, chruinne-gheala dhonn,
  Na tri eoin chruinne-gheala dhonn,
  'S b' iad sid na tri eoin!"

It is impossible, perhaps, to give the full aroma of the quiet satire and humour of these verses in an English translation, even the most literal. One must be "to the manner born," a Celt brought up amongst Celts, familiar with their domestic avocations, as well as with their speech and modes of thought, thoroughly to appreciate all that the poor wife-tormented wight suffered from the *thrawn* temper and stiff-neckedness of his uncompromising, termagant spouse. In the following jingle, however, the outsider has a tolerably fair rendering of a song that is certainly old and in many respects curious.

"THE THREE BROWN-BACKED BIRDS;" OR THE WIFE THAT NOTHING COULD PLEASE.

Chorus—" O, the three brown-backed birds,
　　　　　The brown-backed birds, the brown-backed birds;
　　　　　O, the three brown-backed birds,
　　　　　The wale of birds I trow are they!

I.

" Black is white, and white is black,
　(A quarrelsome wife is of woes the woe!)
　If I assert that the raven is black,
　She'll swear it's as white as the driven snow!

II.

" My wife she stings like a nettle top,
　Crosser in grain than bramble or thorn;
　Hotter than seven times heated fire,
　With her loud bad tongue I'm shattered and torn.

III.

" If I build her a house on a good dry stance,
　With rafters and roof all tight and trig,
　She says, with provoking gesture and sneer,
　'Was there e'er such a hovel—not fit for the pig!'

IV.

"Well can I plough, and sow, and reap,
  And build a corn-stack without bulge or hump,
  But she'll vow and declare, 'by her blameless life,'
  That ''tis never a stack, but a shapeless lump!'

V.

"Well can I fish with hook and line,
  Fish round and long, fish broad and flat,
  When, hark! from her lips, with her hands on her hips,
  'Such fish to be sure! give it all to the cat!'

VI.

"If I make a milk-cog of good hard wood,
  That will stand on its bottom all steady and stieve,
  She will swear by her soul, and by all she's worth,
  That the poor cog leaks like a very sieve!

VII.

"As well light a fire on the brown-ribbed sand,
  For to dry a rock that is washed by the sea;
  As well may you hammer a cold-iron bar,
  As to make a bad wife all she ought to be.

VIII.

"Nought to the lake is the mallard's weight;
  To the generous steed nought the weight of his rein;
  Not worse is the sheep for its coat of wool;
  Nor can *sense* give any one trouble or pain.

Chorus—"O, the three brown-backed birds,
  The brown-backed birds, the brown-backed birds;
  O, the three brown-backed birds,
  The wale of birds I trow are they!"

For very obvious reasons, no kind of poetry is so difficult to translate from one language into another as the comic or humorous and the satiric, and hence it is that literal renderings of such compositions are but rarely attempted, the loosest paraphrase being preferred even in justice to the original itself. The chorus or burden of the foregoing song seems to be only accidentally connected with the accompanying verses, probably, as is often the case, merely as the key-note to the air to which they are to be sung. It is manifestly the chorus of an older composition, probably also of the comic order, which, opportunely ringing in the ears of the hen-pecked bard, as he resolved to give vent to his grievances in song, he laid hold of and pressed for the nonce into his own service.

CHAPTER XVIII.

Sea-Fowl seeking shelter—Coming Storms—A Fieldfare in sad plight—Surgical Operation—"Sobieski" wrongously suspected—The Nightingale in Scotland.

WHATEVER may be yet in store for us before the vernal equinox has again come round, it is certain enough that, up to this date at least, we have hardly had any winter proper to speak of. Here we are within a week of the winter solstice, and the weather continues mild and open as if it were mid-April rather than mid-December. It was impossible but that to a certain extent we should feel the gales which elsewhere raged so violently at the beginning of the month; but blowing as these gales did from some point intermediate between north-east and south-east, our geographical position is such that they passed harmlessly over our heads, and off our shores rather than on them; thanks to the mountain barriers that environ us, sheltering us as they do very effectually, and in the friendliest way, from every storm, however fiercely it may blow, except such as fall upon us from the opener compass points of south-west and south-south-west. How long this mild and open weather is to continue, in a climate so inconstant as ours, and at this season of the year, it would be rash to say, but we should think not very long. A change to colder and stormier weather, the advent of true winter in short, seems to be close at hand—a bit of weather prophecy on our part solely founded on our knowledge of wild-bird life at this season. Within the last two or three days larger flocks of all sorts of sea-fowl have been crowding into our estuaries and bays, as if seeking shelter in anticipation of a coming time of trial, which their instinct, infallible within a given range, tells them is at hand; while on land, birds, now gathered into flocks, rush hither and thither restlessly and excitedly, anxiously and querulously cheeping and chirping, as if they too, almost as well as their web-foot cousins, could tell when a season of cold and storm was imminent. Sometimes, it is to be confessed, that even our wild-birds, both of the sea and land, seem to be out in their meteorological vaticinations, as well as their "featherless" fellow-bipeds of a higher order, but as a rule they are right, and may be depended upon; and at this moment we should be disposed to say, as interpreter of the sayings and doings of our feathered friends, that severe gales and a period of intense cold is about as certain as anything meteorological in our climate, with so much of the *varium et mutabile semper* about it, can ever be held to be before its actual occurrence.

Wandering along the beach a short time ago, we noticed a bird that we took to be a thrush hirpling helplessly across a field in a state of evident distress. Wondering what could be the matter with him, we managed by a little manœuvring to capture him, and found him to be not a song-thrush, but a fieldfare (*Turdis pilaris*, Linn.), in miserable condition, his breast-bone, as we ran our forefinger along its ridge, about as sharp of edge as the carving-knife that is usually set before you to operate with, so hugely to your satisfaction, at public dinners. On examining it further, we found that the cause of its hirpling and miserable condition generally was that the *tarsus* of the left leg was broken about half an inch above the toes. Wound round the latter was a long horse-tail hair, in which the bird had somehow got itself entangled, and a loop of this having, if our theory be correct, got fixed on a hawthorn twig, on the pretty dark-red berries of which these birds feed largely in the fall of the year, the fieldfare, in its struggles to free itself, got its leg broken as described, and, from pain and inability to get at its proper food in comfort, became the miserable object it was when we effected its capture. Pitying the wretched plight of the poor fieldfare, and determined to help it if we could, we took it home with us, and getting hold of a pair of scissors, at once amputated the leg at the fracture, which it was evident was not of recent date, and which no surgical skill on our part could possibly set in such a way as to give us any hope that it might eventually heal. To the stump we applied a little common tar, and wrapping a small wisp of cotton wool around it, the operation, so far as we were concerned, was complete. The next thing was to feed our patient, a delicate and difficult job in the case of a bird naturally wild and shy, and of whose proper food we had at the moment none that we could offer it. Some hawthorn berries, it is true, were still to be found here and there along the garden hedge, but in confinement at least we knew that the bird would not look at them, and to force them upon him, however carefully we went to work, we were afraid might hurt him. What he wanted was a good hearty meal—it must be forced upon him *nolens volens*, and it must obviously be such food as he could swallow readily and easily, if he swallowed at all, and such as was least likely to hurt him if he struggled, as we knew he was pretty sure to do, in its administration. Grating part of a fresh turnip into a cup full of fine flour, we made the whole, with the aid of a little milk, into a thick paste, and taking *Mr. Turdus Pilaris* in our left hand, and holding him firmly but tenderly, we forced upon him, despite his strong dislike to the operation, manifested by many a vicious nip at our fingers, pellet after pellet of the paste, until we considered that his crop was sufficiently distended, and he had had enough of it. We had now done all for him we could, and in the evening, after dark, we took him out into the garden, and placed him on a branch in the heart of a holly bush, and there we left him to the care and protection of Him without whose knowledge not even a sparrow falleth to the ground. Next morning our first after-breakfast stroll was into the garden; we looked into the heart of the holly bush, and made careful search in every direction, but nothing of our yesterday's patient, dead or alive, could we see. We met, indeed, our favourite tom-cat, a magnificent animal, striped like a tiger, and with a strong dash of wild-cat blood in his veins, prowling about; and we had an idea that if he could speak, and chose to make a clean breast of it, he knew and could tell us more about *Turdus Pilaris*, albeit *he* knew him not by that name, than anybody else; for, with many good qualities, *Sobieski*, as he is called, is but a cat after all, and, sooth to say, as ruthless among birds, when he gets the chance and thinks no one is looking on, as the Turk among the Bulgarians. In this particular case, however, *Sobieski* was innocent enough, for about mid-day a rustling in a large hawthorn tree in a corner of the garden attracted the attention of a young lady who happened to be passing at the time, and on closer inspection our fieldfare patient of the day before was discovered as comfortably perched as a single set of toes would permit on one of the topmost boughs. For a day or two afterwards the fieldfare was occasionally seen about the garden, feeding greedily on the last of the hawthorn berries, and manifestly improving in condition and strength. He then disappeared for a time, and it was odds whether he was alive or dead, until yesterday afternoon, when, with a good glass, we easily picked him up by his halting gait from among a flock of his fellows that had alighted to sun themselves in a field some five hundred yards distant from our study window. He seemed to put the stump under him fearlessly, so that it is by this time probably quite healed. What we wonder at just now is, if his "game" leg will at all interfere with his migration to the north and north-eastwards in spring; and more particularly, if it will interfere with his matrimonial prospects at the pairing season. Will a lady fieldfare (for our friend by his plumage markings is a male) be found that will accept him for a husband in virtue of his other good qualities, his game leg to the contrary notwithstanding? We shall at all events keep an eye upon him, and if he survives the winter here, it is not at all impossible, nor even improbable, that we shall see him back again some time in October of next year.

But *place aux dames!* A lady who, in the course of her reading, has met with some references to the nightingale in the works of one or more Scottish and Irish poets, writes us to ask if in the British Islands the nightingale is ever found so far north as Scotland, or so far west as Ireland? Has it any right to be called or referred to as a bird of Scotland or Ireland at all? for if not, then, she argues very sensibly, the poets aforesaid are out in their "local colouring," and, so far, are to be condemned, however *apropos* otherwise and well-worded their references to the matchless music of the plain-plumaged songster. We reply without doubt or difficulty that the nightingale proper (*Philomela luscinia*) is *not* a Scottish bird, neither is it an Irish bird. In the latter island we believe it has never been seen, nor does its appearance two or three times as a mere accidental straggler north of the Tweed give it any claim to be ranked in any sense as a Scottish bird; and the less, therefore, Scottish and Irish poets and song-writers have to do with a bird of which they can know but very little, and the people of Scotland and Ireland generally nothing at all, the better, we should say, for all parties concerned. Our fair correspondent seems to be under the impression that in England, at all events, and *everywhere* south of the Tweed, the nightingale is common. This is a mistake. Even in England it is of very circumscribed distribution, being strictly confined to certain favourite localities, forth of and beyond which it is rarely met with. A curious belief, common amongst the bird-catchers of London and its neighbourhood, is that nightingales are never seen except where cowslips are abundant. How far this is true or otherwise we have personally had no means of determining, but such a belief is at all events worth the chronicling. It is rarely met with even in England further north than about the middle of Yorkshire. Westward it is found plentiful enough, up to the very borders of Devonshire, but no further. In Devonshire itself and Cornwall it is never seen. The very partial distribution, indeed, of this bird is one of the most curious and interesting puzzles in the history of English bird-life, and deserves more attention than, so far as we are aware, it has yet received at the hands of ornithologists. As to the appearance of the nightingale in Scotland, we cannot do better than quote, for our correspondent's edification, the following note from our friend Mr. Robert Gray's excellent volume :—

"The nightingale," says Mr. Gray, "is believed to have been met with in at least two instances north of the Tweed. The first is thus alluded to in Macgillivray's *British Birds* :—' In a letter with which I am favoured by Mr. Robert D. Duncan is the following notice :—"The nightingales arrived in Calder Wood, in West Lothian, in the early part of the summer of 1826. I cannot remember so far back, but credible eye and ear witnesses, on whose testimony implicit reliance may be placed, gave me the information. Before and about midnight, while the full moon shone bright and clear, the superior warble of the male was first heard, which soon attracted a number of admiring individuals, who hastened to the spot, supposing it at first to be a scape-canary. The owner of the wood was extremely anxious to preserve them, thinking, perhaps, that they might propagate; but, with all his care and attention, some malicious and selfish individuals attempted to take them with bird-lime, but failing in their efforts, they afterwards shot the male, upon which the female left the wood."' In this case (continues Mr. Gray) it is possible that some other bird, such as the sedge-warbler, black-cap, or garden-warbler (although the two latter do not, so far as I am aware, sing at midnight), may have been mistaken for the nightingale, and that the lateness of the hour, not to speak of the 'full moon,' may have helped the deception. The second instance is given in Turnbull's *Birds of East Lothian*, wherein it is stated that the nightingale was heard near Dalmeny Park, Midlothian, in June 1839. In the belief that migratory songsters returned to their native haunts in the breeding season, an attempt was made, many years ago, by Sir John Sinclair of Ulbster, Bart., to introduce nightingales into Caithness-shire, by placing eggs, which had been transmitted from the neighbourhood of London, in the nests of robin redbreasts. The foster-parents managed satisfactorily to bring up the young nightingales, which for some time afterwards were observed flying about in the vicinity of their birthplace. In September, however, in obedience to their migratory instincts, they quitted their northern home, to which they never returned. Perhaps they were right."

Were Sir John Sinclair's very interesting experiment tried of new in one of the southern counties of Scotland—no difficult matter either, for nightingale eggs are easily procurable in spring—it might perhaps be attended with more satisfactory results. The idea of trying it in Caithness-shire was absurd *ab incepto:* as well try it in Kamschatka.

CHAPTER XIX.

Wild-Birds and Meteorological Forecasts—Stewart of Appin and the Marquis of Tweeddale—A Christening—Miss Knight and Dr. Johnson.

IT was with some confidence, as our readers may remember, that, believing in the meteorological instincts of our wild-birds, we ventured about the 18th of December upon a very decided weather forecast—to predict, in short, that a period of really cold and wintry weather, probably to be accompanied by severe gales, was at hand; and before our letter could well have been in type—before at all events it could have been in the hands of our readers—the vaticinated cold and gales were already upon us, and in such wise, too, as is not likely soon to be forgotten. Nor, if our wild-bird friends are to be further trusted, is all the elemental hurly-burly of the past twenty days by any means at end. We can hardly recollect ever before seeing such a crowding together of sea-fowl along our shores; such a congregating together of land birds along our hedgerows, in copse and sheltered glade; and in all their movements, as well as in every note of their plaintive chirpings, an evident restlessness, anxiety, and apprehension of evil days yet to come, as bad, or even worse, if worse be possible, than those already experienced from Christmas-tide to Twelfth-day. The fact that within the last few days our web-foot visitors have for the most part shifted their ground—shifted, that is, their resting-places for the night from their first selected quarters to others along the shores directly opposite—induces us to venture on another weather prediction, viz., that our next storms, probably at no distant date, will be from the south and south-west, rather than, as in the case of those already past, from the opposite direction. The western seaboard, in short, rather than the eastern, is most likely to receive the full force and fury of the next gale. Whether *propter hoc* or merely *post hoc*, whether because of our last letter or independently of it, we shall not take it upon ourselves to say, but it is the fact that letters have recently appeared in the *Times* drawing attention to the wisdom of utilising our wild-birds as weather prophets more than has ever hitherto been done. This is put forward in the columns of the "leading journal" as if the idea were entirely a new one, whereas our many readers at home and abroad will bear us witness that we have in this column advocated meteorological attention in the same direction not once and again, but repeatedly, during the last twenty years. On one occasion the late Admiral Fitzroy wrote us a long letter with reference to one of our papers on this subject, and he was arranging for a series of simultaneous bird observations during the following winter at certain selected stations along the Scottish and Irish coasts, when his sudden and sad death put an end to the scheme. One thing is certain: if the scheme which it was Admiral Fitzroy's intention to bring into active operation as an aid to what may be called instrumental meteorology, or meteorology proper, is ever to be fairly tried, the observer or observers at each station, in order to give our wild-birds fair-play and the scheme every chance of success, must be not mere fireside or closet naturalists, but practical ornithologists, conversant for years with birds and their habits in their natural haunts of unrestrained freedom. And it is well to remember at the outset that it is only when weather changes are very decided and extreme that a close study of wild-bird life can be of much service to meteorological science. As regards violent and very pronounced weather changes, such a study cannot but be of importance and value; in the course of slight and ordinary weather changes and atmospheric perturbations, our wild-birds, as a rule, are but slightly if at all affected, and from the closest study of their doings in such circumstances not much information is to be expected. We do not see, however, why the Scottish Meteorological Society should not take up Admiral Fitzroy's scheme, and give it a fair trial.

A few days ago, in the course of a friendly Gaelic "crack" with an old woman in the opposite district of Appin, we were reminded of an anecdote connected with the late Marquis of Tweeddale which we had heard many years ago, but which, until it chanced to come in our way the other day, we had entirely forgotten. About the beginning of the present century, Lord Tweeddale, then quite a young man, had his shooting quarters for a year or two together in the district of Appin. He became acquainted, as in the circumstances was unavoidable, with the last Stewart of Appin, *Duncan Mac Allain Ic-Rob,* one of those of whom Professor Aytoun has sung so spiritedly—

> "A leal old Scottish cavalier,
> All of the olden time."

Appin was at the time well advanced in years, but hale and hearty, and of a frank and jovial disposition, and the society of the district being necessarily limited, it was the most natural thing in the world that the young Marquis and the old Jacobite chief should become intimate, so intimate, indeed, that Tweeddale spent all his idle hours at Appin House, frequently remaining over nights together. Although, counting his years, decidedly an old man, Appin, as we have already hinted, was still a man of vigorous and lusty life, who bore the burden of his threescore years and ten as if they were but a featherweight, and no more a real burden to him than is half the number to men in our degenerate days. "In years he seemed, but not impaired by years;" or, to quote Scripture rather than Pope, his eye was still undimmed, nor was his natural force abated. He was married to his second wife, a stately and beautiful woman, the daughter, we believe, of Menzies of that Ilk. It so chanced that Mrs. Stewart, or the Lady of Appin, as she was usually styled by the courtesy of the people around, was confined of a son while Lord Tweeddale was in the country. Calling to offer his congratulations on the occasion, the Marquis and old Stewart made a merry night of it; and it was then and there arranged that on a given day the child was to be christened, and that, at his Lordship's special request, it was to be called after him. When the christening day arrived, and the company were assembled, the place of honour on the occasion being of course conceded to the Marquis in right of his dignity as " name-father," the officiating clergyman stopped, as is usual at a certain stage of the ceremony, and, leaning over to the old chief, asked him for the name whereby the child was to be called —henceforward known. " *Air m' osan* " (*by my hose*, a curious exclamation, unknown, so far as we are aware, in any other language)—" *Air m' osan cha'n 'eil fhios agam fhein co dhiu: cha d'fhaoinac mi.*" " By my hose," that is, " I declare," quoth the lively old gentleman, " I do not know : I forgot to ask his Lordship's first name." On the question being now put to the Marquis, he simply replied, " My name is George." " George! " exclaimed the chief, lifting up his huge grey eyebrows till they commingled with the lyart locks that still fell plentifully over his temples. " George ! why, my Lord, no son of mine shall ever be called George ; that I warrant you ! God forbid that a George should ever be known in my family. Have you no other name, my Lord ? " " Indeed, Appin," returned his Lordship, smiling, " I am plain George Hay, and nothing more." " Plain George Hay!" muttered the old man. " I promised to call him after you, my Lord, but 'George' he shall *not* be called. Minister, name him *Hay*; it is a good old name in Scottish history of which no one need be ashamed ; " and *Hay* Stewart the boy was named accordingly. Shortly afterwards the estate of Appin was sold ; the old chief died, and the family left the country. Young Hay Stewart in due time emigrated to the United States of America, where, we believe, he became a prosperous man, and died only a year or two ago, predeceasing, which was not wonderful, his long-lived nonogenarian name-father.

And, *apropos* of the Tweeddale family, let us observe that, in the course of our reading lately, we fell in with an anecdote well worth the reproduction, in which a Marchioness of Tweeddale, the wife of the fourth Marquis, is concerned. She was before her marriage the Lady Frances Carteret, daughter of Earl Granville, the "polite" of Pope's muse, and, as a young girl, was brought up by her aunt, Lady Worsley, who was a staunch Jacobite, and extremely zealous in what was always termed by its adherents the "good cause." The Marchioness of after years used to tell that on one occasion, when her aunt found grave fault with her for not regularly attending morning prayers, she replied that she did not attend because she had heard that her Ladyship (Lady Worsley) did not pray for the King. "Not pray for the King!" said Lady Worsley; "I will have you and those who sent you know that I *do* pray for the King; only I do not think it necessary to tell God Almighty *who* is King!" On the part of good Lady Worsley this is simply *naïveté*, but to the unprejudiced bystander it amounts to genuine wit, and is admirable of its kind. It reminds one of Dr. Byrom, the Manchester Jacobite's well-known epigram, one of the best in the language, of which, we believe, the following is the correct version:—

> "God bless the King; God bless the Faith's Defender;
> God bless—no harm in blessing—the Pretender;
> Who that Pretender is, and who that King—
> God bless us all—is quite another thing!"

The above anecdote is taken from a most entertaining book, *Anecdotes, Biographical Sketches, &c.*, by Letitia Matilda Hawkins, daughter of Johnson's acquaintance and biographer, Sir John Hawkins, whom Boswell so heartily detested, and whose *Life* he takes such a delight in constantly contradicting and "correcting." Miss Hawkins tells a very characteristic story of Johnson, which we do not recollect seeing before. On one occasion a Miss Knight, author of a brace of novels, *Dinarbas* and *Marcus Flaminius*, called upon Dr. Johnson to pay him a farewell visit on her quitting England, with the intention of making a prolonged stay on the Continent. Besides being exceedingly vain of her novels, it so chanced that Miss Knight was a lady of large and portly presence. When the final "good-bye" came to be said, the "Rambler" dismissed her with these words, "Go, go, my dear; for *you are too big for an island.*" This is so like Johnson as to be inimitable. One actually *sees* him rolling about like a Dutch galliot in a ground swell, and blinking that larboard eye of his—"the dog," as he said himself, "was never good for much"—as he dismissed the authoress, at once vain and obese, with the grimly equivocal paternal benediction. The reflection irresistibly occurs to one that we too not unfrequently meet with people who, at their own admeasurement and appraisement of themselves, are "far too big for an island."

CHAPTER XX.

Great Grey Shrike—Its Habits—Stormy Petrel—Terrible force of Mountain Squalls.

Our always attentive friend, Mr. Snowie of Inverness, informs us that a specimen of the Great Grey Shrike (*Lanius excubitor*, Linn.) has recently come into his possession. It is an exceedingly rare bird in the West Highlands, two or three specimens being all that have come under our notice during an ornithological career extending now—*Eheu, fugaces labuntur anni!*—over something like a quarter of a century. Mr. Snowie does not say whether his specimen is a male or female; if the former, and in full adult plumage, with the wing spots clearly marked, and the secondaries broadly and prominently margined with white, it is very valuable, and deserves a place of honour in any collection of our rarer wild-birds. As a rule, and curiously enough, it so happens that it is only females and young males in imperfect plumage that are usually captured or shot, so that you may visit a score of collections and not meet with a single specimen in the full and perfect plumage of the adult male bird. If Mr. Snowie's specimen, therefore, is a male in full feather, it well deserves preserving and setting up with the utmost care, and nowhere can this be better done than under Mr. Snowie's own superintendence. In the eastern counties of Aberdeen, Forfar, and Fife, the great grey shrike is more frequently met with than anywhere else in Scotland. The shrike, or butcher-bird, as it is sometimes called, is easily tamed, and makes an amusing cage-bird. We recollect the first living bird of the species we ever saw was during our curriculum at the University of St. Andrews. It was kept in a bell-shaped cage in the window of an apothecary's shop, and from its odd and comical gestures, and loud shrieking notes when anywise excited, it attracted no little attention from the passers-by, students and townsfolk alike, during their evening promenade along the broad pavements of South Street, the principal street in the fine old cathedral city. We had then just begun the study of natural history and comparative physiology under the justly celebrated Professor John Reid, and the reader may believe that we seldom passed the way without having more or less to say to the butcher-bird, the first living specimen we had ever seen. The shrike is much of a polyglotist, imitating the notes of other birds with surprising exactness, to deceive them, bird-catchers will tell you, though you needn't believe them unless you like, and to lure them towards it, that it may the more easily pounce upon and destroy them! Its favourite note, however, is a shrill scream or shriek two or three times rapidly repeated, and hence probably its provincial name of shrike, *q.d. shriek*. The St. Andrews bird was fed on mice and sparrows, both easily enough procured. It preferred to get hold of its prey alive, that it might have the pleasure of killing it for itself, we presume; and it was interesting to see it next suspending the mouse or sparrow that it had just killed on a small iron hook purposely placed for that use in the side of its cage, and then proceed to tear it into small pieces, which it devoured greedily and with a tremulous motion of the wings, as if to show how thoroughly it enjoyed the repast. In a wild state it usually selects a sharp thorn spine or prickle on which to suspend its victim, and hence its other common name of *butcher*-bird. Its bill is slightly notched and sharp of edge, and hard as steel, and under the command of muscles so powerful, that, on innocently presenting it on one occasion with our ungloved forefinger, it nipped us so viciously that the blood sprang —a lesson which there was little likelihood, you may take our word for it, that we should forget in our future dealings with such birds of the order as chanced to come our way. Linnæus's scientific name for the shrike is a wonderfully happy one. Too frequently in the case of birds his scientific nomenclature only serves to perpetuate vulgar errors; as a rule, however, as in this instance, nothing could be better. *Lanius* means a *butcher*, having reference to the shrike's habit of hanging up its victim, as already described, in order to tear it to pieces the more easily, its slenderness and weakness of legs and claws rendering it impossible for it to use them after the manner of hawks and falcons when devouring their prey. *Excubitor* means a *sentinel* or watchman, which admirably indicates the bird's habit in a wild state of always sitting on the exposed extremity of the branch or bough of the particular tree on which it selects to alight. *Lanius excubitor*, therefore, is the *Butcher-Sentinel*, and a more appropriate name could not possibly have been adopted.

It is rare at any season to see the stormy petrel (*Procellaria pelagica*, Linn.) along the mainland shores of the western seaboard—so rare, indeed, that although we have more than once picked up the dead bird on our shores after heavy gales, until Tuesday last we never before saw the lively little webfoot—the smallest of all the *Palmipedes*—nearer the mainland than the neighbourhood of the island of Staffa and the back of Mull. That they should be seen at this moment in our firths and estuaries is an evidence as unmistakeable and incontrovertible as could well be selected how wild, and wintry, and stormy of late has been the weather in the more open seas around the British Islands. On Tuesday morning last, which was a very stormy day, having had occasion to cross Corran Ferry, we were no less delighted than surprised to see a pair of petrels disporting themselves along the crests of the huge waves, which a conflict between an ebbing tide and a sleet shower gale from the south-south-west caused to rise and roll heavily inwards into the narrows of Corran, opposite the lighthouse. Immediately recognising the birds, we persuaded the boatmen to row in their direction, although it was somewhat dangerous to venture in an open boat into so heavy a swell, until we got quite near them, for our approach did not seem to alarm them in the least. Nothing of the kind could be prettier than to see them skimming swallow-like along the green hollows and over the curling crests of the huge waves, their little feet at times in as rapid motion as their wings, as they just touched the sloping sides of the advancing seas, pit-pattering over the great green ridges as if the little fellows were working out a sentence of a sort of wave treadmill imposed upon them by a jury, say of gannets, cormorants, and gulls, for some serious breach of the ancient laws of the Oceanic Palmipede Republic. After a while we took up a broken thowl-pin from the bottom of the boat and threw it in the direction of the petrels, whereupon they rose a little, and wheeling rapidly round, at once pounced upon the floating bit of wood, thinking, no doubt, that it might prove something good to eat; disappointed, they instantly rose again, and wheeling round with a curious *chirring* cheep, expressive of their disappointment, perhaps, they dashed off in the very teeth of the gale, and disappeared behind the crest of a huge advancing wave, to which we were obliged to turn our boat stern on, and allow ourselves to be carried on its crest onwards and inwards to the pier. The petrel, or little petrel of British zoology, is so called because it walks, or seems to walk, upon the sea, as St. Peter did, until, owing to the increasing boisterousness of wind and waves, his faith failed him, and he began to sink, when, in answer to his call for help, he was saved by the outstretched arm of Him whom alone the winds obey, and at whose bidding a great storm becomes not merely a moderate breeze, but a "great calm." The little petrel, although of all the Palmipedes the most harmless, perhaps, has as many *aliases* as any long undetected burglar that ever stood at the bar of the Old Bailey. He is called the little petrel, or stormy petrel, Mother Carey's chicken, assilay, spency, water-witch, mitty, sea-swallow, allarmoth, sea-blackbird, &c. &c. Linnæus dubs him very happily *Procellaria pelagica—*

the sea-storm bird. Colonel Montagu says that "the body of the petrel is of so oily a nature, that if a wick is drawn through from the mouth to the vent and lighted it will burn as a lamp," and that it is actually used for that purpose in the Faroes and other islands of the north. We once tried this wick experiment with a specimen that was picked up on the beach here after a storm some five or six years ago, and found that it burned neither better nor brighter than if the bird operated upon had been a sparrow or song-thrush. Our specimen, it is true, was in poor condition, and in part at least had probably died of inanition. With a freshly shot bird, full, fat, and oily, it is quite possible that our wick might have absorbed sufficient of the rank oil in which many sea-birds abound to cause it to burn with a flame of more or less brightness, though even for the rudest lamp such a bird-oiled wick must, we should think, be but a sorry substitute. We have long been wanting a good, full-plumaged example of the stormy petrel as a cabinet specimen, and for a moment had some thoughts of getting a neighbouring keeper to go with us next day in order to secure one or both of these little fellows at Corran. It was but a momentary temptation, however, which we successfully resisted and mastered: we decided to let the birds alone, a decision which we hope most people will applaud. When the weather moderates they will retire to their usual haunts to feed, and disport themselves along the hollows and over the ridges of the long, uninterrupted Atlantic swell, returning to our shores probably with a flock of their companions, in the course of some future winter that, like the present, proves exceptionally wild and stormy at all their haunts, from Ailsa Craig to Barra Head.

And while speaking of Corran Ferry, let us give an incident illustrative of the terrible and almost irresistible force with which sudden gusts of wind from adown the upland glens and corries not unfrequently strike across our lochs, firths, and ferries, making the navigation of them often more dangerous than that of mid-ocean itself, even in a storm. On a somewhat stormy day about a month ago, with the wind from east-south-east, the large ferry boat, used for crossing cattle, horses, carriages, &c. at South Corran, belonging to Mr. Thomas Maclean, and moored in what one would call a perfectly sheltered bay within a hundred yards of the pier, and not more than twenty yards from the shore, was, by a sudden squall from the mountains, which seems to have embraced it whirlwind-wise, fairly raised for a minute or two, to the height of several feet, clean and clear out of the water, and whirled round and round on its chain as rapidly and easily as if it had been a badly balanced schoolboy's kite in its efforts at incipient ascension. When the rotatory squall at length passed onward, gravitation reasserted its power, and the boat fell back into the sea again, bottom upwards. Now, such a boat as this, long in the water, and with its massive thwarts and flooring, weighs something like three tons; there was in it, as it lay afloat after a rainy night, at least a ton of bilge water, with quite another weight of chains, cables, mast, oars, &c. It will thus be understood that a boat weighing, with all its gearing, at least six tons, of whose gunwale, too, no more than twelve inches is ever exposed above water, was caught up in the embraces of a gust of wind that swirled it at the end of its heavy chain like a feather: how incredible, until one enters into the philosophy of such problems, that anything so tenuous and unsubstantial as mere wind, air in motion, could exert a force so extraordinary! A gust of similar force suddenly striking a ship under sail would inevitably cause her, in seamen's phrase, to "turn turtle," or it would knock the masts, with their rigging and tophamper, clean out of her, as if they were brittle as pipe-stems. Hence it is that, in navigating our lochs, as little sail as possible is carried, and all is ready, that everything may be let go by the run the moment one of these squalls comes rushing seawards from corrie or narrow glen, as suddenly, and almost as swiftly, as a flash of lightning.

CHAPTER XXI.

The Throstle-Cock—Substantial Breakfast—St. Valentine's Day—The Paston Letters—How to lead a Stubborn Pig the way you would have her to go.

HERE, on the West Coast, a gale of wind, with cold, raw showers, half sleet half rain, ushered in St. Valentine's morning 1877; and *maugre* the calendar and all the saints, no wonder that our woods and hedgerows continued songless and silent, and that our wild-bird friends made no sign in acknowledgment of the advent of a day wintry enough to make them think less of love-making and song than of providing, if it might be, the wherewithal to appease their hunger, and the preening and composing their feathers in the manner most conducive to comfort and warmth against a wind that had manifestly acquired its incisiveness from having been honed to a razor-like keenness of edge by long and stormy contact with the cold glittering ridges of North Atlantic icebergs. It was only three days ago that the weather cleared up a little and assumed a mildness somewhat in keeping with the season. Our birds have readily acknowledged the genial change *quantum valeat*, and at the moment of this writing the cheery notes of the bolder and hardier of them—the redbreast, chaffinch, hedge accentor, &c.—reach our ears as we sit by the open window. In the early morning, as we were dressing, the loud, clear pipe of the throstle-cock from the topmost branch of an old pear-tree in the garden so delighted us that we hurried abroad to enjoy the first unclouded sunshine of the month, and wandering far afield, returned to breakfast with an appetite such as a hero of the Homeric or Fingalian period might envy, and carrying in our hand a posy of early primroses, the very sight of which put everybody in good humour as they bent over their preliminary porridge-plates, that most excellent and indispensable substratum to a genuine country breakfast. Why, after a good substantial meal of this sort, we could ride from Nether Lochaber to the door of your own hospitable mansion at Inverness, caring little if we got nothing by the way beyond a glass of beer at Fort-Augustus to lubricate the larynx, the better to croon our favourite Gaelic ditties, a habit of ours when in the saddle, which seems, too, to please our gallant pony of the Mull breed and Spanish Armada descent, for he steps out famously, in perfect time to the air, be it slow or fast, till, when we are anxious to get on, to such lively lilts as the "Fairy Dance" or "The deil amang the tailors," he absolutely devours the way! But this is a digression. Reverting to our muttons for a moment, let us observe that we have often seen love-making among our wild-birds and nidification much further advanced on the eve of St. Valentine's Day proper than it is on this the 26th day of the month. Only last evening a large flock of chaffinches flew past us as we drove home from church, all of them males—a sure sign that amongst them, at all events, although they are very early breeders in this district, pairing has not generally taken place. And speaking of St. Valentine, we find on inquiry that, in our more rural districts at least, the number of *billets-doux* or love circulars, familiarly ycleped valentines, sold and sent through the post, is within the last half-dozen years largely on the decrease, while Christmas cards, rather an innovation in Scotland, are rapidly coming into favour. Valentine sending is now very much confined to young children, and when it is otherwise, we have reason to believe that, as a rule, they are sadly devoid of any real point or meaning, being sent and received with an indifference anything but complimentary to the memory of the match-making saint. The fact is, that in these our prosaic and utilitarian times, the good old saint has no chance; "the age of chivalry is gone," and if the weather only proves favourable on his anniversary, our wild-birds will be found more faithful to his memory than our bachelors and "maidens fair," even when most matrimonially inclined. Matrimony now-a-days is fast becoming a matter of business, a thing of contract—love and love-making, in the good old sense in which our forefathers knew the terms, being voted "spoony," "slow," "vulgar," "sentimental," "romantic," and what not. So be it, though we must take leave to doubt if the world is much the better of this particular evidence of "progress." In the famous *Paston Letters*, so interesting for the glimpses they afford us into the domestic economy and inner life of the fifteenth century, we meet with occasional delightful references to St. Valentine's Day and the love-making proper to the season something like four hundred years ago. Thus, in 1478, young John Paston, in wooing Margery, the handsome daughter of Sir Thomas Brews, very knowingly goes to work by managing matters so as to get the Lady Brews, the fair one's mother, on his side in the first instance, pretty confident, sly rogue as he was, that by the aid of such an ally the good knight, who is at the outset a little stiff in the business, may be finally outgeneralled, and forced into an honourable capitulation. " Upon Friday," writes Lady Brews to the love-sick swain, " is Saint Valentine's day, and every bird chooseth him a mate ; and if it like you to come on Thursday at night, and so purvey you that you may abide there till Monday, I trust to God that ye shall so speak to mine husband ; and I shall pray that we bring the matter to a conclusion." The young gentleman took the hint, and pressed his suit so successfully, that after that St. Valentine's eve the fair Margery was his with all her heart, the grim old knight soon afterwards yielding with tolerable grace, and coming down in the matter of dowry and " settlements" to the satisfaction of all parties. Here is a very pretty letter written by Margery to her lover after the happy engagement, largely brought about, as she doubtless believed in her heart, by the influence and friendly intervention of the good St. Valentine : " Right Reverend and Worshipful" (one would think he was Moderator of the General Assembly !), " and my right well-beloved Valentine—I recommend me unto you, full heartily desiring to hear of your welfare, which I beseech Almighty God long for to preserve unto his pleasure and your heart's desire. And if it please you to hear of my welfare, I am not in good health of body nor of heart, nor shall be till I hear from you. And my lady mother hath laboured the the matter" (the matter of dowry, on which Mr. John Paston had a wary eye) "to my father full diligently, but she can no more get than ye know of, for the which God knoweth I am full sorry. But if that ye love me, as I trust verily ye do, ye will not leave me therefore; for if that ye had not half the livelihood that ye have, for to do the greatest labour that any woman alive might, I would not forsake you." It is pleasant to know that after all their little troubles the pair were at last fairly and happily married. That ladies really honoured and obeyed their husbands in those times more than in these latter days, we shall not take upon ourselves positively to affirm, for women, and for that matter of it, men too, are, we suppose, very much the same in all ages, but judging from the style of their letters, they seem to have held their lords and masters in a degree of reverence and respect that must make our modern guidwives stare with astonishment. Writing after her marriage, the gentle Margery addresses her husband as "Right reverend and worshipful husband." But, after all, the "Dear husband," "Dear Dick," Tom, or Harry of our modern epistles may have quite as much heart in them.

When we would imply the *ne plus ultra* of stubbornness and stiffneckedness, we use the adjective *"mulish,"* and we use the familiar proverb, "as stubborn as a mule," applied to people who will neither lead nor drive, who are deaf to advice, entreaty, or persuasion, and who either stand stock-still in a posture of negative defiance, or pursue a retrograde course the very opposite and antithesis of that which we would have them follow. If we consider them attentively, however, there is a want of correct local colouring in the uncomplimentary adjective and proverb alike, as we commonly apply them. They are, in fact, foreign to our soil, having come to us from Spain, and the old Spanish dependencies, where the animal is common, and the reference has a point and meaning which it cannot possibly have in a country like ours, where a veritable mule, the semi-equine semi-asinine quadruped is about as uncommon as a giraffe or a zebra. The fact is, that the familiar proverbs of our every-day speech much require overhauling, pruning, and general revising, and to any one possessed of the requisite knowledge and leisure, the labours of such a revisal would neither be unprofitable nor unamusing. We say, for instance, "dirty as a pig," which is clearly a mistake and a libel on the poor porcine quadruped, that, in its domestic no less than in its wild state, is one of the cleanliest of animals, when the ways and means, that is, of cleanliness are fairly within its reach. If, however, we say "as stubborn, as obstinate as a pig," we are about right; the phrase, turn it about as you will, is unobjectionable. We have not the mule proper, and the familiar saying, however apt in Spain, is *quoad* us inapt and inapplicable; but we *have* the pig, and assuredly of British quadrupeds it is beyond all question the most stubborn and stiff of neck, the most deaf to advice or persuasion, to rhyme or reason; the most difficult to lead or drive, whether by wheedling, entreaty, or coaxing, or by force, *finesse*, or furtive circumvention. To be stubborn and unpliable to our wishes, particularly in the matter of locomotion, seems to be of the essence of porcine nature, ineradicable, too, by any mode of treatment to that end you may please to adopt; bone of its bone, and flesh of its flesh, and there you may safely let the matter rest, and say no more about it. The Irishman who got his pig to market by pretending strenuously to drive it for half a day in the very opposite direction, must have understood the nature of the animal thoroughly; and, born under a happier star, might have been a distinguished naturalist, the Linnæus of Carrick-on-Shannon, the Buffon of Carrick-on-Suir. And now, courteous reader, all this by way of introduction to a clever feat in pig management that chanced to come under our notice a few days ago. It was in this wise. As we were passing along the road we came upon two or three men surrounding an immense black pig, with a stiff upright mane, and one of the curliest tails we ever saw. The pig had just been taken out of the stye, which from early piglinghood had been its home, and the men were trying to get it into a larger and roomier place some score of yards distant, in order, as they informed us, that it might be killed. The pig, pig-like, would not budge, nor move an inch in the desired direction. They coaxed and fondled it by scratching its flanks and ears, and endeavoured to entice it towards the open door of the place of slaughter by holding a dish with food in it just in front of its nose, but the pig only stuck out its legs all the more rigidly, and half-grunted, half-squealed a decided negative, a *non possumus* which it was evident there was no overcoming by any such means.

A rougher style of persuasion was therefore adopted. One of the men laid hold of the large, flapping ears, one in each hand, and another man seized one of the animal's forelegs, and they began to pull with might and main, while the third man proceeded to twist and twine the pig's tail just as you have seen a seaman do with the ends of two pieces of three stranded rope before proceeding to splice them together. Stubborn and obdurate, the pig wouldn't move an inch, that is, in the right direction; it rather gained a little in a retrograde motion styewards, yelling the while loud enough to be heard by the periwinkle gatherers along the shores of Appin and Kingerloch. The man at the tail at last got mad, and, taking up a long hazel switch, belaboured the pig with all his might, but to no purpose. Move in the desired direction she would not; and the men, panting and terribly riled at the brute's obstinacy, were at their wit's end, when, fortunately, a man from a neighbouring district happening to pass the way at the time came to the rescue. "What in the world are you doing with the pig?" exclaimed the new-comer in excellent Gaelic. "With the pig?" replied one of the men, as he wiped the perspiration from his brow with his sleeve. "What are we doing with the pig, is it? Why, we are trying to get her (perverse daughter of an ugly father!) into yonder open shed, and, as you see, we are likely to be beaten in the attempt." "Leave her to me," said the stranger, a strapping young fellow, "and I undertake to put her quietly and quickly into the shed by myself, unaided!" "There's not a man in Lochaber can do it," growled another of the worsted pig-fighters. "Perhaps not," quietly replied the young man, while an incipient smile played about his eyes and the corners of his mouth. "I am not a Lochaber man, but a Lismore man, and I think I can manage the pig if you let me try." "Try away," exclaimed the man, "in the name of the legion, let us see what you can do." "Keep away then," cried the stranger, as he slipt behind the pig, and quickly and cleverly catching her by her hind legs, one in either hand, lifted her up as one would a wheel-barrow. The pig was now resting on her fore-feet, with her snout close to the ground, and, to our surprise, perfectly quiet. Giving her a slight push, just as one would with a heavily-laden barrow, he trundled her pigship, to show his command over her, once or twice backwards and forwards on the road with the greatest ease, and finally steering her in the right direction, he let her go in the furthest corner of the open shed. It was a clever feat, simple enough to be sure, like Columbus and the egg, when it was done, but all the more admirable just because of its simplicity. The philosophy of the thing seems to be this—when caught up by the hind legs wheel-barrow-wise, as described, the weight of the animal is almost entirely thrown upon the fore-feet, and on the slightest impulse, it must move forward, if it move at all; it has no *purchase* in the direction of a backward or reluctant course. Its quietness, so remarkable in the circumstances, is probably partly due to astonishment at the unwontedness of its position, and a sense of its own utter helplessness in such a case, and partly, perhaps, to the weight of the viscera thrown forward into the thorax, interfering for the time with the proper use of the vocal organs. This particular pig, while perfectly dumb in the man's hands, no sooner was let go than she yelled loud enough to take the roof of one's head off. We were glad to see that the men manifested not a particle of jealousy or resentment, as we feared they would, at the ingenuity displayed by the Lismore man in pig management compared with their own rude and ineffectual manner of dealing with porcine perverseness. On the contrary, they shook hands with him all round, and from certain masonic signs interchanged, which we pretended not to notice, we have reason to believe that on our departure they treated him to a fair share of the " refreshments " usually provided on pig-killing occasions in the Highlands.

CHAPTER XXII.

Primroses—The Primrose in Gaelic Poetry—Translation—The little Auk or Rotch—Skuas—Their habits.

THAT the sun should be bright at its present altitude at this the season of the vernal equinox is not much to be wondered at; but that with a bright, cloudless sun we should also have a May-like mildness of temperature is somewhat unusual; and you may believe that we make the most of it, rejoicing in it exceedingly after the many storms and general inclemency of the by-past winter—a winter so exceptionally stormy, that nothing like it has been known for upwards of a quarter of a century. Under a bright, genial sun, such a sudden burst, such a profusion of primroses in copse and glade, in dell and dingle, we never saw before; and of all our wild flowers, the primrose in its season is assuredly the most delightful and loveable. Our readers need hardly be told that primrose, the common name of this favourite flower (from the Latin *primus*) means *prime* rose, *first* rose or early flower, because of its early appearance in spring. The *Primulus veris* or *Primula vulgaris* of botanists is of course of like origin. While the French call it *primevère*, early spring flower, to the Highlanders, with whom it has always been an especial favourite, it is known as the *sòbhrag* or *sòbhrach*. Alastair-Mac-Mhaighstir-Alastair, the Ardnamurchan bard, makes it the subject of the following beautiful apostrophe :—

> "A shobhrach gheala-bhui' nam bruachag,
>   Gur fanna-gheal, snuaghar, do ghnùis !
> 'Chinneas badanach, cluasach,
>   Maoth-mhin, baganta, luaineach ;
> Gur tu ròs is fearr cruadal
>   A ni gluasad a h-ùir ;
> Bi'dh tu' t-eideadh a's t-earrach,
>   'S càch a falach an sùl !"

Nor does Ewen Maclachan (of Aberdeen) forget the dainty primrose in describing the early spring flowers that so delighted him, that they made, as he declares, each bank and brae, and knoll, and holm, and glade smell to him more sweetly "than all the wines of France."

> "Gur h-ionmhuinn an sealladh fonnmhor,
>   A chitear air lom gach leacainn ;
> 'S cùbhraidh leam na fion na Frainge
>   Fàile thom, a's bheann a's ghlacag ;
> Milseineach, biolaireach *sòbhrach*,
>   Eagach cuach nan neoinein maiseach,
> Siomragach, failleineach, brigh 'or,
>   Luachrach, ditheanach, gun ghaiseadh."

Burns, in "The Posie," one of his most exquisite lyrics, has a reference to the primrose, in which, unconsciously perhaps, he admirably renders the botanical *Primula* by "firstling."

> "The *primrose* I will pu', the *firstling o' the year*,
>   And I will pu' the pink, the emblem o' my dear,
> For she's the pink o' woman-kind, and blooms without a peer ;
>   And a' to be a posie to my ain dear May."

We wish, for the sake of our English readers, that we

could do anything like justice to the above Gaelic lines in a translation, but it is impossible. The following is, *longo intervallo*, something like the first quoted stanza:—

> "Primrose, loveliest, fairest flower!
> Blooming sweet on bank and brae;
> Keeking forth with gentle smile,
> And a modest mein alway;
> Hardiest flower in all the wild,
> Sweetest flower beneath the sky,
> Thou art dressed in all thy bloom,
> Ere other flowers have oped their eye."

While collecting seaware on the beach after one of the severest gales of the season, that of the 14th inst.—a sturdy, honest "equinoctial" of the old sort, however, which was so natural and so looked, that it neither annoyed nor alarmed us in the least—one of our people picked up a little webfoot bird, dead of course, which he considered a curiosity of sufficient importance to warrant his walking several miles in the evening in order to submit it to our inspection. It turned out to be a specimen of the little auk or rotch (*Alca alle*, Linn.), next to the stormy petrel, the smallest of the ocean Palmipedes. The living bird is exceedingly rare along the western seaboard, nor is it common even amongst the Outer Hebrides. The only specimens of it we ever saw anywhere on the West Coast were, as in this instance, dead birds cast up on the beach after storms. The bird is not so uncommon on the East Coast, where we have often seen it in company of puffins, razorbills, and other sea birds. Two that were shot in St. Andrews Bay, in the winter of 1847, were, after dissection by Professor

John Reid, at which we assisted, preserved as specimens, and duly deposited in the University museum, where they may doubtless still be seen. Both these were males. Although the little auk may occasionally remain to breed on some solitary outlying islets along the eastern and northern shores of Scotland, it is properly a bird of much higher latitudes, of Greenland, for instance, and Spitzbergen, of Norway and Iceland, coming south only when its own proper shores and seas are frozen over, when it must necessarily seek open water under milder skies in order to obtain its food. It is a pretty little bird; a pair of them would be a most interesting addition to an aquarium.

The same man who brought us the little auk told us that, while hand-line fishing at Corran Ferry on the previous day, he was struck with an extraordinary commotion amongst the gulls that always frequent these narrows in great numbers; such screaming, quarrelling, and fighting he assured us he had never seen before among birds usually so friendly and well-behaved amongst themselves as are all the *Laridæ*. His account of the whole affair was so graphic and interesting, for he is a most intelligent man, and in his way a very shrewd observer, that we determined on visiting the scene of riot, and finding out for ourselves, if possible, what could be the cause of quarrel. As a rule, gulls, even when they gather in large flocks over their favourite feeding-grounds, and there may be many different species wheeling about in wild confusion, are so friendly with each other, and so little given to quarrels, that although there may sometimes be a little angry scolding, what the wives of the south of Scotland call "flyting," between two or more birds that happen to select the same fish at the moment of making their pounce, and thus come into unlooked for and unintentional collision, anything like an actual fight or even a protracted quarrel is of very rare occurrence. Next day was fine, and taking our seat, with a good binocular in our hand, on the rocks opposite the lighthouse, just as the flood-tide began to make, the firth, as we expected, was filled with sea-gulls wheeling about in detached flocks and feeding on the shoals of young seth or coal-fish as they "boiled up," to use the expressive Gaelic phrase, or played here and there along the surface of the rapid, eddying stream. It was an interesting and beautiful sight, but we had seen it hundreds of times before, and it wasn't exactly what we had come to see. In a short time, however, the flock of gulls nearest us was thrown into a state of wild commotion by the arrival in their midst of what we took at first to be a pair of herring-gulls in the dark grey-marbled plumage of last year's birds; but a second and keener look, and the screams of the gulls that scattered in all directions, convinced us that what we took to be young gulls were in truth a pair of skuas,—birds which bear about the same relationship to the ordinary gull that the Bedouin Arab of the desert does to the peaceful trading caravan, or rather that the pirate schooner, with her skull and crossbones flag, bears to the honest merchantman. The skuas were not long in selecting their first victims. Two large black-backed gulls, separating themselves from the rest, flapped and flew away with loud screams of honest execration at the disturbers of their peace, and after them darted the dusky skuas, each coursing his selected victim with all the ardour and all the staunchness of a well-bred hound. The gulls were strong of wing, and in their efforts to distance their pursuers, exerted themselves to the utmost, but without avail; the skuas were not to be shaken off. They soon overtook the gulls, and wheeling rapidly above and around them, struck at them and buffeted them unmercifully. The gulls screamed in loud complaint of their treatment, and circled back towards their companions, hoping, doubtless, that their persecutors would select some fresh victims and leave them alone. But the skuas knew what they were about too well to be done in that sort of way. They stuck to their game right through the centre of the loud-screaming flock, and out and beyond began again to strike and buffet them as before, until at last, thoroughly tired out, and seeing that no better might be, the gulls almost at the same instant vomited in one large half-digested lump all the fish they had caught that morning, which was just what the skuas wanted, for they now poised themselves for a moment, falcon-wise, on quivering wings, and then, with a graceful sweep and lightning-like velocity of descent, they darted each after the falling mass which properly belonged to itself, and cleverly catching them before they touched the water, bore them away with a loud shriek of exultation, to be devoured at leisure somewhere along the solitudes of the opposite shore. It was certainly a shameful and flagrant case of open robbery and spoliation, but then, as the hymn says, " it is their nature to." Skuas are born, or hatched, if you prefer it, to act in this sort of way; and it is one of the *désagréments* of gull life to be thus treated. It is proper to say, however, that skuas do not live altogether and entirely after this fashion, for we have often seen them fishing industriously enough on their own proper behalf in the most legitimate way possible. Our own idea is that skuas, while able enough to cater for themselves when fish of any size are to be had, are unable to pick up the smaller fry, which the gulls capture and gobble up with the greatest ease, and on which they largely, mainly indeed, depend for their sustenance. When, therefore, only small fry are going, the skua is hard up, and has no other way of appeasing his hunger than by making the gulls regurgitate and disgorge in the rude manner described. With a superior power of wing, a hooked beak, and strong, sharp, black, recurved claws, it is physically superior in every way to the largest of the gull tribe, and by constant teasing and buffeting its victim, who knows full well from a sad experience that there is only one way of escape, it is made at last to vomit its undigested meal, which, precisely as we saw it the other day, is invariably caught ere it touches the water, and eagerly redeavoured as a dainty and easily-digested *bonne-bouche* by the dusky marauder. How the skua is able to distinguish between a gull that has fish in its crop from that which is still empty-stomached and hungry, we cannot tell; but that it can so distinguish is unquestionable, for it never chases a bird but one that can on compulsion disgorge the remains of a more or less hearty meal. It is probable that this questionable mode of livelihood is not peculiar to the skua among sea-birds, nor are the gulls the only birds so hardly dealt with. We suspect that, on the contrary, although we have no actual proof of the matter, it is commoner than naturalists suppose. We are led to this opinion by having observed that puffins, razorbills, guillemots, and other web-feet birds frequently disgorge the contents of their stomachs when they are wounded, and even when they chance to be captured in an unwounded state. This seems to us to be a natural and intuitive attempt on their part to appease their enemies, real or supposed, the disgorged food, in our view of it, being meant as a peace-offering by the wounded or captured bird. The skuas we saw at Corran Ferry we take to have been a pair of the species known as Richardson's skua (*Lestris Richardsonii*), a bold and rapacious bird, that does not scruple to attack man himself if he intrudes upon their favourite haunts in the breeding season. An old shepherd in the neighbourhood here tells us that he has known a pair of these birds kill a young lamb on an early spring morning on the island of Bernera, and that before night it was all eaten up, its bones being picked as clean as if one had scraped them with a knife. The people of the Hebrides, where the skua is common and its habits well known, call it *Am Fàsgaidear*, the Squeezer, because it as it were *squeezes* the undigested food from the stomachs of the gulls. When a merchant over-reaches his customers in any way, and charges exorbitant prices for his goods, or when a proprietor over-rents his lands, and deals hardly with his tenantry, where we should speak of dishonesty, tyranny, &c., the Hebrideans straightway think of the skua, and call such an one a *Fàsgaidear* or squeezer (of men), an application of the term which is not devoid of humour.

CHAPTER XXIII.

A Crooked Sixpence—A Luckpenny, or Coin of Grace—Popular Superstition—Weasel-skin Purse—Sealskin Purse—Fresh Herrings amongst the Heather.

It is commonly known, we are pretty safe in assuming, that a crooked sixpence, or some other "coin of grace," as the French peasantry term it, is frequently carried about in people's purses to ensure them good luck in money matters, the belief being not only that the owner and custodier of such a luckpenny can never be absolutely moneyless while that particular coin remains in his purse—an assertion which no one will dispute—but also that while that coin is retained safe and sound in its proper receptacle, it shall rarely if ever want one or more other coins of equal or superior value to keep it company, or, as the Highlanders say, "to keep it warm." Now, when we look into it with some attention, is even the latter part of this almost universal superstition entirely baseless? We are aware, indeed, that in dealing with popular superstitions in this wondrous age of "enlightenment" and "scientific research," the proper thing to do is, at the very least, to laugh at them; but better still, to frown at them with the sourest visage that can be assumed, and soundly to scold and threaten with ulterior pains and penalties unmentionable those who make or meddle with them in any way. And yet we are not much afraid to affirm, even if right reverend presbyteries and general assemblies frown upon us the while, that, calmly and philosophically pondered, all, or almost all, our popular superstitions are based upon a more or less substantial and reliable substratum of truth and fact, usually possessing, too, when closely examined, a vertebral column—a back-bone—of shrewd sound sense, without which they never could long find favour even with the few, much less with the many—that is, become popular in the proper sense of the term. It is, of course, only too true that man is sadly given to error, having a tendency, indeed, errorwise, even as Falstaff had an "alacrity" in sinking in ditch water, but it may nevertheless be very confidently asserted that nothing that is essentially and entirely false, nothing that is no more than a sheer, unmitigated lie, ever did or ever can become popular, so antagonistic is human nature, with all its faults and failings, to everything that is wholly and essentially false and truthless. Popular superstition may, therefore, be defined as a web of error, having always, however, some threads of truth more or less prominently interwoven with it alike in warp and woof. The truth at the bottom of the above-mentioned superstition is simply this, that a person having such a love of money, and such anxiety about it, as will induce him to treasure up a supposed lucky coin, refusing to part with it even for its full value in the direst extremity, is already what may be called a "saving" man, and is almost certain to save and hoard past an odd coin when he can, and thus the "lucky" coin has its companions, that, in a short time, become in the owner's estimation almost as sacred as the original coin itself, and the superstition is kept in countenance. What we desire more particularly, however, to direct our readers' attention to at present is the fact, not so generally known, that sometimes it is not a particular coin to which the luck is supposed to be attached, but the money receptacle or purse itself. In the former and commoner case, the coin is everything, the purse nothing. In the latter this is reversed, the coin being nothing, the purse everything. The one is a belief in a lucky penny, the other a belief in a lucky *purse*. Crossing Ballachulish Ferry a short time ago, a respectable man from a neighbouring district took out his purse in order to pay his fare. We were sitting beside and speaking to him at the moment, and the purse from which he abstracted the necessary coin at once attracted our notice, as it was impossible but it should, for to our no little surprise it was none other than a *weasel* skin, with head, feet, and tail still attached, just as if it had been a cabinet specimen of the fierce little *Mustela*, ready for "setting up." As our *vis-à-vis* placed it for a moment on his knee, with its glass-bead eyes, and the lips shrivelled and slightly drawn back so as to show the sharp teeth, ivory white at their tips and yellow towards their roots, as in all the order, as if in act to spring at you, it had a sufficiently life-like appearance to make any one unacquainted with the real state of the case slightly nervous and uncomfortable. In answer to our inquiries—cautiously entered upon, and only when quite alone with our friend—the owner of the weasel skin made no secret of the fact that he carried it, and had long carried it, as a "lucky" purse, and reminded us that there was an old Gaelic rhyme, which, however, we had not heard before, in which the virtue of a weasel-skin purse as a money-getter and a money-keeper is very pointedly referred to. The rhyme, which we took down at the moment, was as nearly as he could recollect it as follows :—

> "Neas bheag, bhuidhe nan còs,
> 'S e'n t-òr thug a dhreach da bian ;
> Gleidh sid mar sporran, air a cheangal le h-iàl,
> 'S cha bhi thu gun bhonn, geal, buidhe no donn,
> Eadar nollaig 's Féill-ròid, eadar Féill-ròid a's Féill Brian."

In English literally thus—

> "Little, yellow, hole-frequenting weasel,
> From gold is derived the colour of thy coat of fur.
> Get it for a purse, to be tied with a thong,
> And thou shalt not be without a coin, white, yellow, or brown,
> From Christmas till Rood Day, from Rood Day till the feast of St. Brian."

Féill-Ròid or *Féill-an-Ròid*, Rood Day, is the autumnal equinox ; *nollaig* is, as we have rendered it, Christmas-tide ; but what exact date is meant by the Feast of *Brian*, or St. Brian, we are unable to say, not having at the moment a proper book of reference on the subject beside us. The meaning, however, is obvious—that the man who carries a weasel-skin purse shall always have more or less money therein from Christmas to the ensuing autumnal equinox, and from that date to the Feast of Brian, that is, all the year round. The owner of the weasel-skin purse in this instance told us that he had inherited it from his father, who died many years ago, and when we remarked that it was in excellent condition still, with a close, silken pile, and that his own son might inherit it in his turn, he nodded approvingly, and added that he meant it to be so. "My father," he went on, "never wanted money in it, nor have I, and I have had my share of losses and bad times too; nor shall my son after me." "Are weasel-skin purses common?" we inquired, adding that we had never seen one before. "Well, no, not common exactly," was the reply, "but I think I know half-a-dozen, or more, among my acquaintances in Appin, Lismore, and Morven. There are other lucky purses," he continued, "besides weasel-skins, but none, I think, so good. A sealskin purse is a good and lucky one, and so is one woven of thread made from lint that, in the process of manufacture, has been 'steeped' in a loch or pool in which a human being has been drowned (!)." Did he know, we asked, *why* such purses as he had mentioned *were* accounted lucky ones, and, particularly, *why* a weasel-skin should be held in such high estimation? But he declared that he did not know any more than ourselves, and we believe that he did not, such people rarely troubling themselves about the why and the wherefore of things of that kind. All we can say from our own knowledge is this, and it is so far corroborative of our fellow-passenger's assertion, that a sealskin purse is a good and lucky one. In an old *Lusragan* MS., or Herbalist Directory, in our possession, written by a Perthshire schoolmaster upwards of sixty years ago, giving the time, place, &c. for properly gathering herbs of virtue and roots of healing, a paragraph frequently concludes with a recommendation that when gathered and dried, as directed, these are to be kept folded up and ready for use in *a strip of sealskin*. A gentleman sitting opposite to us as we write, and to whom we have just read the above, observes with a grim, cynical smile, that some time ago, under considerable persuasion, not to say coercion, *he* bought for his wife a sealskin jacket, the price of which, he avers, with a painful twist of the facial muscles, was *only* five-and-twenty guineas; that this same jacket she has ever since worn, in season and out of season, as often as she could, and that, strange as it may seem, she has not become a bit more economical on that account, but rather the reverse; and he blandly asks us to be good enough to reconcile that anomaly with our friend's sealskin purse theory. We reply that we cannot, advising him, however, meantime to purchase for his lady a sealskin purse, which she might carry about with her in her sealskin jacket pocket—a lucky purse, in short, which should always have money in it. His smile is grimmer than ever as he ungallantly, and with peculiar emphasis, exclaims, "No! any money she would carry about in a sealskin purse, or, for that matter of it, in a weasel-skin either, would be pretty certain to come out of *my* pocket, or purse, in the first instance. No, sir, I have done enough in sealskin." When a man is in that sort of mood, you know it is needless to argue with him.

When at Fort-William the other day we were told of a curious phenomenon, so rare and mysterious, indeed, as at first sight to seem inexplicable, but which, closely examined, is easily enough accounted for after all. About a week or ten days ago, some people living at Garvan, in Ardgour, part of Lord Morton's property on Lochiel-side, were astonished, as they well might be, to find among the heather, quite half a mile from the sea, as our informant assures us, several dozens of half-grown herrings and a lot of herring fry, silvery white and fresh, as if they had just been taken out of the sea. A herring in itself, large or small, is fortunately no rarity with the good people of Lochiel-side; but a lot of fresh herrings in such a place, in the proper habitat of the grouse and mountain hare, *was* a rarity and a curiosity of no ordinary kind; nor need we much wonder if, as they gazed and pondered, they scratched their heads in indication of their state of perplexity and bewilderment over a phenomenon such as the oldest among them had never seen or heard tell of before. Their perplexity, however, as to the why and wherefore of it all did not prevent them from gathering up the largest and best of the herrings, which, carried home and duly cooked, proved quite as fresh and good to eat as if they had been taken out of their native element in the meshes of their own legitimate nets. On due inquiry, we find that the day was one of the brightest and driest of the season; a smart breeze of wind blowing from the north-north-east, with now and again large, dark patches of ragged snow-showers coursing each other along the mountain ridges—a good old March day, in short. A gust of wind from out the skirts of one of those upland showers, rotating on its axis, a *whirlwind* in short, swept downwards, and striking the comparatively placid surface of Lochiel, uplifted in its convolutions a column of water in which at the moment those herrings chanced to be swimming, and carried the whole across the loch and up the opposite hill-side, until, its force expended, its rotation ceased, the whirlwind collapsed, and the herring fell amongst the heather, where they were very soon afterwards found, their silvery scales untarnished, and as fresh and fit for the frying-pan as if they had been fished for and captured in the usual way. That a column of sea-water was taken up with the fish, again to fall along with them in a shower of fine spray, is almost certain; what raised *them* must have also raised more or less of the element in which they floated; and we make no doubt at all that, had it occurred to any of the people to pluck a twig of the heather amongst which they lay, and apply it to the tongue, it would have tasted salt and briny almost as a bit of sea-wrack itself. Whoever, in a season of drought, has seen a cloud of dust raised off the highway, and carried aloft and along by a gust of whirling wind, or, better still, in the fall of the year, a heap of withered leaves caught up and whirled rapidly and multitudinously along by the same agency, need have no difficulty in understanding how fish, too, are sometimes caught up with more or less of the water near the surface of which they happen for the moment to swim, and are afterwards dropped at a longer or shorter distance from the spot at which the wildly rotating gust first found them. Although a rare occurrence, it has happened often enough to have arrested scientific attention long ago, and to have been satisfactorily explained as above.

CHAPTER XXIV.

The Crozier of St. Fillan—Its Gaelic name *Cuigreach*—Etymology and meaning of term—East Indian Hoopoe—*Upupa Longirostris*—Arrival of Cuckoo.

EVERYBODY has heard of what is called the crozier, or more properly the pastoral staff, of St. Fillan, recently recovered from its hereditary custodier, a Scotch Canadian, one of the Mac-an-Deoirs or Dewars of Glendochart, and now safely deposited in the museum of the Society of Antiquaries in Edinburgh, a relic of the olden time that no true Scotchman can behold without the liveliest interest, or contemplate, with reference to its past history, without a feeling of reverence and respect such as is felt nowhere else perhaps, unless it be in the presence of the Scottish crown and other regalia in Edinburgh Castle. Early in the seventh century Fillan first appears as an Abbot of Pittenweem, in Fifeshire, a dignity he soon afterwards resigned, in order to lead a more active and laborious life in civilising and converting to Christianity the rude Celts of the wilds of Braedalbine. Here, on the borders of Perthshire, at a place still known as St. Fillan's, he lived an austere and blameless life, and died at a good old age, and in the full odour of sanctity, in the year 649. Of all our Scottish saints, Fillan or Faolan seems to have been the most revered, as the many shrines, fountains, &c., dedicated to him testify even to our own day. For a full account of the life and labours of St. Fillan we must refer our readers to the *Acta Sanctorum*, or Lives of the Saints, a work of which even Gibbon is obliged to confess that " through the medium of fable and superstition it communicates much historical and philosophical instruction." In the Christian calendar St. Fillan's day is the 9th of January. His pastoral staff, with which we are for the moment more immediately concerned, seems to have been known over Celtic Scotland from very early times by a name or distinctive appellation, variously written *Quigrich*, *Quegrich*, *Coygarach*, *Cogerach*, &c., a word the true meaning and etymology of which has recently given rise to much learned discussion in the columns of *The Scotsman* and elsewhere. Dr. John Stuart, of the Antiquarian Society, makes it identical with our common every-day word *coigreach*, a *stranger*, and in this he is supported by the Rev. Dr. Thomas Maclauchlan, no mean authority when the etymology of a Gaelic word is the subject in dispute. And yet one is at a loss to see the force, appropriateness, or meaning of so designating a pastoral staff carried as a symbol of his authority by the servant of the Good Shepherd of the Gospel of Peace and Love. The Rev. Dr. Masson, of the Edinburgh Gaelic Church, suggests that the root may be *cagar*, a whisper, and that the word is *cagaraiche*, a whisperer, a revealer, a staff or rod of divination. Laying hold of the tradition that the relics of the saint, including this very staff, perhaps, were present at the battle of Bannockburn, and contributed in the popular belief to the victory of that memorable day, a third suggestion is, that the name may be a compound term—*cogadh*, battle; *àrach*, fosterer, urger — battle-fosterer, battle-urger, battle-victor. A fourth derives it from *cròg*, the whole hand, including palm and fingers—*cròyrach*—that which is intended to be held in the hand. Something similar is the suggestion of a fifth, that it may be *coig-mheurach*, that which is intended to be grasped by the *five fingers*. These are some of the etymological guesses—and they are no more—adventured upon in the attempt to arrive at a solution of the meaning of the appellation *coggarach* or *cogerach* applied to the pastoral staff of St. Fillan. One or two of these etymologies are worth consideration, if it were only for their ingenuity; all of them, however, as even the non-Celtic outsider must conclude, are unsatisfactory. Our own attention having been called to the subject by one of our most distinguished Scotch archæologists, we had little hesitation in coming to a conclusion satisfactory to ourselves—satisfactory, that is to say, so far as anything of the kind can be made satisfactory, and we shall not be in the least surprised if half the Gaelic scholars in the kingdom are instantly up in arms to prove us in the wrong. So be it. Meantime, we start on the supposition that the word is Celtic—of the Gaelic of the West of Scotland and Irish of the period. The word, besides, considering the object to which it was applied, *must* have had a meaning—a meaning, too, of no doubtful import — complimentary to the staff, and in no sense adverse to the bearer of the staff, or to the religion of order, concord, and peace which he, the missionary of Christianity, had to proclaim, and, if possible, make acceptable to the wild barbarians of Braedalbine; for such, and no other, were the dwellers on the skirts of the Grampians in the seventh century. Fillan taught these barbarians what they did not know before, or what they had only faintly heard of, and whisper-wise. He taught them Christianity, a religion of love, and peace, and good order, and he carried a staff as the symbol at once of his authority to preach and teach in the name of the Good Shepherd, and as a constant remembrancer to himself and to them that unity, and peace, and order were of the essentials of that religion. The name, then, by which the staff of St. Fillan was commonly known must have had a meaning, and that meaning, we believe, must be looked for in the direction indicated. The word is manifestly a compound term, and the etymology we take to be this—*comh*, or *coimh*, written in abbreviated form *co'*, or *coi"*, is a preposition syllable of frequent occurrence in Gaelic, as in Latin, English, &c., and the force and import of which are abundantly clear; *eagar* means order, discipline, system, and dropping the initial vowels of which, as they would necessarily be in common speech, we have *co'gerach* or *coi"gerach*, meaning the staff of order, or discipline, or, retaining the *co'*, the *co-orderer*, with Fillan, in his office, or co-disciplinarian. We have no desire to insist upon the correctness of our etymology, but its manifest reference to the office of the Christian missionary and *pastor* is at least *prima facie* evidence in its favour. Another name by which St. Fillan's staff was locally known in more recent times was *an Fhaireachd*, and the Dewars of Glendochart were commonly distinguished from other families of the same name as *Doirich* or *Dèoirich-na-Faireachd*, the Dewars of the Faireachd. The meaning of this word has also given rise to considerable discussion. We believe it to be from *Faire*, a watch, a vigil. There is a local tradition that, when at one time the chapel in which the relic was kept was burned to the ground, the precious staff itself was rescued from the flames by one of the Dewars, and to him, in reward for his exertions on the occasion, and to his descendants, was committed the custody of the sacred relic. The Dewars being thus highly honoured, and there being certain important privileges attached to the custodiership of the staff, they became bound to guard the relic with the greatest care, and thus came to be called *Dèoirich na Faireachd*, Dewars of the guardianship, the vigil, and watch and ward of the pastoral staff of St. Fillan, the famous *coi'gerach*. And very wonderful men, if we can but look at them with unprejudiced eyes, were these same mediæval monks and missionaries. That they have been largely misrepresented and vilified only serves to excite the sorrow as well as the surprise of the candid inquirer who has taken the trouble to look into the real state of the case for himself. They were but men, and as such, of course, had their frailties and their faults; but they were good and true men all the same, who, in the good providence of God, had a great work to do, and, upon the whole, did that work wisely and well. To the thoughtful mind, St. Fillan's staff, now happily deposited in the museum of national antiquities, is something very much more than an object of mere antiquarian interest.

A friendly correspondent who, in the far East, has

for many years been an attentive reader of the *Inverness Courier*, has been kind enough to send us all the way from Moulmein, in Burmah, two preserved specimens of the Eastern hoopoe (*Upupa longirostris*), which, however, differs so little from the *Upupa epops*, known as an accidental straggler in this country, that they seem to be the same bird. Notwithstanding the long distance these specimens have had to come, their colouring is more brilliant than was exhibited by any home specimen that has come under our examination. The prevailing colours of these beautiful birds are white, buff, and black, with intermixed shades of reddish brown, and reddish grey and orange. A distinguishing ornament is a crest, consisting of a double row of orange feathers, about two inches in length, tipped with black, which the bird can erect or depress at pleasure. From this crest the bird is said to derive its name from the French *huppe*, a tuft or crest. Others, however, say that the name is derived from certain peculiar notes uttered by the bird in the breeding season, which sound like the syllable *oop*, or *up*, two or three times repeated.

A better known bird, of plainer plumage than the hoopoe, but a thousand times dearer to us all, and about the origin and meaning of whose name, at least, there can be no manner of dispute—we mean the common grey cuckoo—was heard and seen here for the first time this spring on Thursday last, the 19th April, which is a little earlier than its usual date. We have said heard and *seen*, for unless the bird is actually seen by some one competent to recognise it, it is not always safe to believe that the cuckoo has really arrived on the faith of a mere report that it has been heard. More than a fortnight ago it was reported as having been heard in Ardgour and in the neighbourhood of Callart House, both warm and well-wooded places, likely enough spots for the cuckoo to put in an early appearance, but we could meet with no one who professed to have *seen* it so early, and as the idling herd-boy and truant schoolboy can imitate its well-known notes to perfection, and frequently do so amuse themselves when the sun shines bright and the primroses are plentiful around, we have long thought it well to wait, until it is both seen and heard, before announcing its actual arrival in the district. With the cuckoo we may now confidently look for really warm, genial weather. Up to this date the season has upon the whole been a cold and sickly one. A very severe form of influenza has been epidemic over the district for several weeks past; hardly anybody has escaped, and although we have not heard of any fatal cases, the disease, while it lasts, is exceedingly severe, and the after prostration correspondingly great. A fine, warm May month would, however, soon put us all to rights.

CHAPTER XXV.

Folk-lore from the Hebrides—An Incantation of Increase—A Confabulation in Glencoe—Periphrases as to Death and Dying—A Daughter of Allan Dall, the Bard of Glengarry.

OUR mill is a big one, and always grinding, but it is only fair to confess that hardly any one else has supplied us with so much *mealable* grist as our "Long Island" friend and correspondent, Mr. Carmichael of Uist. His knowledge of the folk-lore and *giosrogan* of the old people is certainly wonderful, so wonderful that we think that, since our good friend Mr. Macdonald of Plockton left the kingdom for the Antipodes, Mr. Carmichael stands, *facile princeps*, at the head of this particular branch of archæology. Mr. Carmichael modestly excuses himself for writing so hurriedly and incorrectly, while the fact is that he writes very well indeed; and in quoting him one can almost always use his own words, which is no small matter when, in the "dog-days," with unbuttoned waistcoat, you are panting with the heat, and wish to get up your columnful of matter with the least possible trouble—with the smallest possible amount of what the psychologists are now-a-days pleased to call "mental evolution." Let Mr. Carmichael tell the story in his own way of the "Eolas an Torranain," or "Wise-woman Wisdom," as to a plant or flower that not only ensures your cow against everything in the shape of the "evil eye," but makes her give such quantities of milk, rich and good, as soon fills your *crock* with butter, and makes every one about the house laugh, jubilant and joyous, in the midst of plenty.

"I beg to send you 'Eolas an Torranain,' a very old spell or incantation, to be said or sung in order to keep one's cows from the 'evil eye,' and increase their milk.

'Eolas an Torranain.

'Buainams' thu 'thorranain
Le'd uile bheannachd's le 'd uile bhuaidh,
Thainig na naoi sonais
Leis na naoi earranan
Le buaidh an torranain,
Lamh Bhride leam!
   Tha mi 'nis ga'd bhuain.

'Buaineams thu thorranain
Le'd 'thorradh mara 's tir,
Ri lionadh gun tra'adh
Led' lamhsa Bhride mhìn,
Colum naomh gam sheoladh
Odhran caomh 'am dhion,
A's Michail nan stéud uaibhreach
'Cuir buaidh anns an ni
   Tha mo lus lurach a nis air a bhuain.

"Thus in English—

'Let me pluck thee, Torranan!
With all thy blessedness and all thy virtue,
The nine blessings came with the nine parts,
By the virtue of the Torranan.
The hand of St. Bride with me,
   I am now to pluck thee.

'Let me pluck thee, Torranan!
With thine increase as to sea and land;
With the flowing tide that shall know no ebbing,
By the assistance of the chaste St. Bride,

> The holy St. Columba directing me,
> And St. Michael, of high-crested steeds,
> Imparting virtue to the matter the while,
> Darling plant of all virtue,
>   I am now plucking thee!'

"One of the two women," continues Mr. Carmichael, "from whom I got this '*Eolas*,' said that the *Torranan* is a flowering plant which grows among rocky places in the hills, and that the *blath* or flower is large, and resembles in shape a woman's breast, and that it is snow-white. She said the *cuach* or crop of the plant gradually fills up, '*le sugh sonais*,' with the dew of bliss, while the tide is flowing, and slowly dries up again during the ebbing of the tide. In order, therefore, to obtain the *buaidh* or virtue of the *Torranan*, the plant or flower—whether the whole plant, or simply the flower, I could not make out—must be procured during the flow of the tide, or near the time of high water. If you get at them, so my informant assured me only a few days ago, your cow or cows will give foaming quantities of milk, and your cream, butter, and cheese shall be of the richest and best. You have simply to place the *Torranan* under one of your milk-pails, and while placing it there, you repeat the '*Eolas*' three times, making at the same time a circle sun-wise, or with the sun, also three times, with the plant over the milk vessel, repeating or chanting in a loud voice, but slowly and distinctly, the spell as I have written it. The woman herself never saw the *Torranan*. It is, she says, a rare plant, and she would give *one pound* to any one who would show her the plant, and where it grows."

What plant the famous *Torranan* is, we are unable to say, although we have given the matter some consideration. The white harebell or *Hyacintha alba* is the likeliest that we can think of. We have watched it, however, and, unfortunately, it seems just as empty of "the dew of blessedness" during the influx of the tide as during the reflex. The superstition, nevertheless, is an exceedingly interesting one, and we may yet be able to throw more light upon its *raison d'être*.

While in Glencoe the other day we met a fine old man, whose lyart locks and boldly chiselled features fit him to be a sculptor's model for some aged warrior or legislator of ancient Greece or Rome, a lineal descendant, too, as he very clearly proved himself to be, of one of the Macdonalds of Inverigan, who perished in the celebrated massacre under William and Mary, "the best assorted couple, perhaps, that ever tied lots together in matrimonial bands" (a literal rendering of a line of Ian Lom's). Our venerable companion and ourselves sat for an hour together at the foot of a huge boulder, that ages ago must have tumbled into the valley from the heights above. Our talk was of many matters, and it was natural that we should speak of some people whom we both knew, though now no longer in life. What struck us as remarkable was how periphrastically beautiful was invariably this old man's reference to the dead, particularly if, when living, he had known and held them in regard. The common words for death and dying (*bàs* and *bàsaich*) were never once in such a case used. Not one of the many whom he and we knew were, in the old man's language, "dead." They had not "died;" they were merely shifted, departed, gone to another glen, as it were, where they were far better off than in this. "Chaochail iad;" "shiubhail iad;" "am fear nach maireann." They have shifted; they have departed; our friend the *non-lasting, non-enduring* one,—these, or some such delicate and kindly periphrasis, were invariably employed. And this amiable sort of circumlocution in speaking of the dead will, we believe, be found to be practised generally by the older Highlanders who still continue to speak and think in their native language. We can recollect that many years ago we were informed by the Rev. Dr. Macintyre, of Kilmonivaig, that we had grievously offended a daughter of Allan Dall, the famous Glengarry bard, with whom shortly previously we had had a long and interesting conversation about her father. She would not tell Dr. Macintyre what we had said to offend her; she would tell it only to ourselves, if we thought it worth our while to go and make our peace with her. We went, and after a while were informed that our offence lay in this: we had asked when had her father *died?—Cuin a bhàsaich 'ur n' athair?* We were then young, and couldn't exactly see how such a question should offend. "Brutes alone," she angrily exclaimed, "*die*, and when they *die*, are *dead*. Human beings—men, and women, and children—do not *die*, and are not to be spoken of as *dead*. They shift from off this scene; they depart, they go, they shift, they change, they sleep, if you like, or are gathered unto their fathers. They don't *die*, and can never with propriety be spoken of as *dead!*" We saw the thing at last, and, of course, there and then made our humblest apologies, declaring, what indeed was true enough, that in using the word objected to we did not know that we were offending, and certainly had no intention to offend. Mary Macdougall and ourselves shook hands over it, and a lasting peace ensued, but we never forgot the lesson then taught us. This periphrastic way of speaking of the dead seems to have been common in very ancient times. The Greek periphrasis we forget, but the Roman phrase for expressing that a man had died was *Abiit ad plures* (he has gone over to the majority), while we are all familiar with the beautiful Scripture expression, that when a man died "he was gathered to his people."

CHAPTER XXVI.

A "Slide" on a Frozen Stretch of River in an Upland Glen—Amazement of Black-faced Sheep at the Performance—"Lassie" also astonished—All Quadrupeds have a horror of Ice—Intelligence of "Lassie"—Finds the Cows unaided in a Midnight Storm—Age at which Dogs cease to be useful—Famous Dogs.

IF 1877 was meteorologically, and all over the kingdom from first to last, one of the most disagreeable years of the present century, this, its successor, the year of grace 1878, has, it must be confessed, so far made a good beginning, for up to this date January has been all one could desire, occasionally blustering and rude, but for the most part frosty and cold, with clear and cloudless skies. After a whole twelvemonth of slop and slush, one likes to feel the ground underfoot hard as iron, and it was with a feeling of boyish delight that, in one of the upland glens the other day, we came across a stretch of river on which the ice was so thick and invitingly smooth, that, throwing staff and plaid aside, we determined to have just one good "slide," to see if we had quite forgotten a pastime in which we once excelled. Our slide was a gentle bend in the river some fifty or sixty yards in length, and as with all the impetus of a preliminary race we shot along like a rocket, and as we arrived at the further end upright as a grenadier on parade—heels close together and full front forward—we felt rather proud of ourselves. Once, twice, thrice, half-a-dozen times, perhaps, we careered from end to end of that slide, each time with an increasing exhilaration of spirits that on that cold January morning hardly anything else could have produced. Resuming our plaid and staff, we philosophised as we crossed the hills homewards, and our philosophising went clearly in this direction, that a "slide," enjoyed as we had just enjoyed it, is a very good thing indeed, and that we had reason to be thankful that, after a quarter of a century's pretty hard work, we were still fresh and vigorous enough to do it as well, and to enjoy it almost as thoroughly as in the merry days of our youth, *consule Planco*. We came, furthermore, to this other conclusion, that the art of sliding—if you want to be very fine, you may call it *lapsiglacy*—like that of swimming, is one that, once fairly mastered, can never be forgotten. The same thing, as we happen to know, cannot be said either of skating or of curling. All ice pastimes are delightfully exhilarating, but we are not sure that there is anything to beat a good, honest slide, as we enjoyed it that morning. "Weren't you afraid somebody might see you?" was the remark of a lady to whom we were telling the story in the evening. "Afraid that somebody might see me!" we exclaimed; "no, my dear madam, I was *not* afraid. I was only sorry that half the people in the country wasn't present to see how well, how admirably indeed, I did it!" And yet we were not without spectators of our lapsiglacial pastime either, though the interest they took in our performance probably partook rather more of astonishment and alarm than of mere admiration. On either bank of the river some black-faced sheep were cropping the heather as best they could, and had we gone past them in anything like ordinary fashion, they were probably too tame and intent upon their feeding to be much disturbed by our presence. But when they saw us come down at railway speed on the " slide "—a thing they had, perhaps, never seen in their life before—they first gazed in amazement at a phenomenon so new to them, and not understanding it at all, they next crowded together and fled, until they were up the mountains on either hand many hundred yards away. But if the sheep were astonished, much more so was our excellent collie, " Lassie," the wise and intelligent companion of all our rambles. All quadrupeds have a horror of ice because of its slipperiness, but no animals, perhaps, have such a thorough dislike of it as dogs. We had once a noble Newfoundland, bold as a lion, and amphibious as a seal, that would never venture upon ice if he could help it, and if he did venture, the slightest slip and slide was enough to take all the heart out of him, until he howled with horror. " Lassie " has been our constant companion for so many years in our natural history rambles, that she has generally a pretty good idea of everything we do, and in the most extraordinary circumstances rarely evinces any stronger feeling than a pardonable anxiety and a little excitement, perhaps, when the case is critical,—the chase and capture of a rodent, or something of that sort, for example. Had the river on the present occasion, for instance, been in its usual liquid state, and had we waded along the banks looking for birds' nests or water-vole holes, " Lassie " would have quietly followed in the water or on the bank above as ordered, in case her assistance should be required, and hardly any act of ours, in the water or out of it, would have much surprised her. When in this case, however, she noticed us first throw aside our staff and plaid, and then, after a race, the meaning of which she could not comprehend, she saw us shoot along the ice like a meteor, her face was for the moment a perfect study, so visibly could we read in it a mingled expression of astonishment, perplexity, and alarm, astonishment, however, before she had time to think it all over, manifestly predominating. As we were preparing for our third slide, her astonishment had evidently given place to a feeling of anxious and honest solicitude for our welfare, manifested by her eager fawning upon us and plaintive whining when she saw that we did not give it up at once. When at last she saw us take up our staff and plaid, she leapt around us and barked for joy that we were at last done with a performance in which she at least could see nothing but danger, and her barking was proof of her sincerity, for, as a rule, she is perfectly dumb in all our rambles, full well knowing, from experience, that a barking, babbling companion, on such errands as usually take us abroad on such occasions, would be a nuisance and a hindrance rather than any assistance. Honest "Lassie" is now in the tenth year of her age, but lively and active still, and as wise as a human being—in certain circumstances wiser far than ever was any human being of equal age. Some weeks ago our cows, leaving their usual infield pasture, found, unknown to us, their way to the heather on the hills,

and when the evening came they were nowhere to be
got. They had been seen about mid-day high up
amongst the heather, and that was all that could with
certainty be said about them. The night came on wet
and wild, and dark as dark could be. What was to
be done! The cows were giving milk, and a single
night out at this season would go far to ruin them
as milkers for the remainder of the winter. No
human being could think of climbing a thickly wooded
hill in search of cattle in such a dark and stormy
night, and there was nothing for it but to give
"Lassie" a trial, though we had but little hopes that,
unaided and unattended as she must necessarily be,
she would be of much use. But, as somebody
remarked, there was no harm at all events in trying;
and first taking "Lassie" to the byre, and showing
her the empty stalls, we gave her to understand, as
best we could in good Lochaber Gaelic, that the cows
were away, and must be got, and that it was
clearly *her* duty to go and find them. With
a lantern in our hand, we accompanied her a
few yards in the proper direction, and then ordered
her, in a decided but cheery tone of voice, to be off
and get the cows. She straightway disappeared in
the storm and darkness, and we were glad to run to
the shelter of the fireside, anxious enough, you may
believe, that "Lassie" should succeed for the sake of
the cows, but not less anxious, perhaps, that she
should succeed for the sake of her own good name
and high character for intelligence in the district.
And she *did* succeed. In a little over an hour,
"Lassie's" bark, with which we are, of course,

familiar, and uttered purposely, as we know, in order to warn us that she had returned, was heard in the direction of the byre; and on proceeding, lantern in hand, to learn the result of her darkling search, we found the cows collected in the square all right, and "Lassie" standing guard over them. You may believe that we patted her kindly, and that her supper that night was as plentiful as it deserved to be.

As we have already said, "Lassie" is now in her tenth year, and in the discharge of every duty entrusted to her as lively and active as we ever knew her. And yet in a curious old book, one of the first works, indeed, that issued from the English press (1486), there occurs a couplet, according to which she ought to be now growing lazy and stiff of limb and stupid. The work in question, highly prized by the typographical antiquary, is *The Boke of Hawkyng and Huntyng*, by Dame Juliana Berners, sister of the Lord Berners who translated the Chronicles of Froissart into such delightfully quaint old English. "Hawkyng and Huntyng" seems a strange subject-matter for a treatise by a lady, and that lady, too, prioress, as she was, of Sopewell Nunnery, near St. Albans. The probability, however, is that the "boke" was written while she was still young and gay—many years, at all events, before she had anything to do with nuns or nunneries. The couplet referred to is to this effect—

> "The best dog that ever bitch had,
> At eight years is full badde."

Now, this may have been the experience of people with regard to dogs employed in hawking and hunting, about the middle, say, of the fifteenth century; nor are we prepared to say that it may not be true of dogs used in hunting, perhaps of sporting dogs generally, in our own day. We should much like to know, however, on really competent authority, if it is the fact that a hunting dog—a fox-hound, for example, or pointer, or deer-hound—is considered old, *effete*, and, in Lady Berners' words, "fulle badde," by the time it has reached or completed its eighth year. Meantime we should be disposed to doubt the truth of this couplet, even as regards sporting dogs. We are very certain, at all events, that it is not true as regards cattle and sheep dogs. A few days ago we discussed the subject with an old Highland shepherd, a man of much intelligence, and he entirely agreed with us, or rather we entirely agreed with him; for with the cattle and sheep dog—with the collie proper, that is—he has had a long and familiar practical acquaintance, such as it would be mere folly in us to pretend to. Our venerable colloquist having but little English, we had to throw Juliana Berners' couplet into Gaelic thus, that he might thoroughly understand it :—

"Aig aois ochd bliadhn', 's gle bheag is fhiach
An cù 'b'fhearr 'bh'aig gallu riamh."

He instantly and energetically denied the truth of the dictum, in the case at least of the shepherd's dog or collie, with which he was most familiar. A collie, he was prepared to say, was no more than at its prime, or very little indeed beyond it, at eight of years of age, and ought to continue a good and useful dog up to the age of twelve or even fourteen years. A dog that is "full badde" before his twelfth year must, in his opinion, have been a "fulle badde" one all along. As nearly as he could remember, he had in his day owned quite a score and a half of different sheep dogs of his own, and the very pick of these were at their best when they were between five and ten years old. Another shepherd, a much younger man, and from the south, assured us more recently that few shepherd's dogs know all they ought to know till they are between five and six years old, and that their first noticeable ailment is generally a diminution of activity and speed in gathering and "wearing" sheep, which most shepherds thought was owing to their getting stiff in the joints, but which he maintained was more frequently due to laziness, a laziness resulting from the cunning that teaches a dog as he advances in years that it is foolish to over-exert himself when it can at all be avoided. In proof of this last statement, he averred that a ten-year-old dog that may be generally called lazy, and stiff, and slow, can, "when he likes himsel'," and indeed often does, perform his hill-side duties with all the vivacity and all the speed of his five-year-old "form." But even granting that a dog is a little slower in performing his work at and after his eighth year, this shepherd was of opinion that he is all the surer, that he is still more valuable than at any earlier period of his life, because of his riper intelligence and general common sense. Our own experience of such dogs leads us to a similar conclusion, that an eight-year-old collie may be a very good and useful dog indeed, and is not necessarily "full badde" by reason of either mental or bodily decrepitude till he is several years older. Talking of dogs the other evening, we were asked this rather curious question, "Which would you say were the most celebrated dogs connected with poetry? Suppose you had the chance, which of them would you like best to know?" It was a somewhat puzzling question; but after a little reflection, we replied that we thought that of the dogs connected with poets and poetry we should be most glad to have had an opportunity of knowing and kindly patting Ulysses' *Argus*, the brave old dog who, recognising his master after an absence of so many weary years, crawls to his side, licks his feet, and then

> "Takes a last look, and having seen him, dies;
> So closed for ever faithful Argus' eyes:"

Fingal's *Bran*, so celebrated in the old Gaelic heroic ballads; Byron's *Boatswain*, and Scott's *Maida*.

CHAPTER XXVII.

Cold January—Pet Days—Rainfall—Highlander's standard in gauging a Fall of Snow—Anecdote of Alasdair Macdonald, the Ardnamurchan Bard—Shoemaking—Shoes sent home unblackened.

IN the philosophy of the old people here, the best winter weather that we can have is storm and cold—cold in the honest, tangible form, so to speak, of frost and snow, so intense that, after a few minutes' exposure to it, you are unable for the moment to make a *crubhan-cait* (a cat's claw), that is, to bring together the points of your fingers and thumb, by reason of the benumbment of the muscles that are necessary to the act; and storm so violent that the hardiest sea-birds are fain to scud before the gale, and, like so many disabled ships, to seek the shelter of the best protected creeks and bays along the seaboard. In the folk-lore of the Highlanders, it is a maxim, founded on a long experience, that the severer the winter, the more likely are the succeeding seasons to be all they ought to be. So much storm and cold, they argue, is due in every twelve months, and when should the storm and cold come most opportunely but in winter, the season expressly set apart for it? Better and more natural, they say, to have all the inclemency of the year collected within the compass of three or four consecutive months, than scattered irregularly, untimeously, and at random over the area of the twelve. So impressed are they with the truth of this philosophy, that it is rare, even in the severest winters, to hear a Highlander complain of storm or cold, no matter how violent and intense. He will put on one or more extra articles of clothing, and give his cattle an extra sheaf at feeding time; he will come into his cottage so benumbed that he can hardly take firm enough hold of the horn spoon with which he is to sup his "kail" or porridge, but not a word of complaint shall you hear from him as to the over-inclemency of the weather. If you make a remark in that direction, he replies that the weather is seasonable and natural, and that there is reason to be thankful that it is so rather than otherwise. Meet an aged Highlander on one of these pet days that sometimes occur in mid-winter, when it is clear, and calm, and mild, as if it were a day in early summer. You remark in a cheery, congratulatory tone of voice that it is a fine, warm day, beautiful, summer-like, or something to that effect, and you naturally expect that he will be as much pleased with the bright, warm, sun above, and the peaceful calm around, as you are yourself. Far from it, however. He doesn't like, he will tell you, "fine" days out of their proper season. It is the middle of December or January, and he will remind you that the proper weather for those months is intense frost, drifting snow, or wild, impassioned storms; and, if you understand his language, he will quote you old meteorological proverbs and weather "wisdom-words" by the score, in corroboration of the soundness of his views of the matter, and the utter fallacy and untenableness of yours, if you venture to differ from him. The reader, therefore, will understand the meteorological character of the month of January just past, when we say that the people were upon the whole highly pleased with it. It was cold enough, and stormy enough, to be characterised by them as the most seasonable and "natural" January month for several years past. If the present month of February, or even the first half of it, only proves cold and wintry enough, our weather-wise people promise us a bright and pleasant spring.

Within a comparatively recent period, when meteorological science was still in its infancy, and the honest rain-gauge yet a rarity, people always exaggerated, though for the most part unwittingly perhaps, the amount of rainfall for any given period. Now-a-days, however, it is pretty widely known that a single "inch" of rain in four-and-twenty hours is really a large quantity, and held in check by the unbiassed testimony of a very simple and useful instrument, one or more of which is to be found in every district; people have learned that it is wise to speak of rain generally, and even of "heavy falls" of rain when they occur, with circumspection and caution. In speaking of a fall of snow, however, people still talk loosely; for, unchecked by anything like a *snow*-gauge, they almost invariably exaggerate the quantity on the ground. With regard to last week's fall of snow, for example, you read in the newspapers that in this or that particular locality it was "six inches," "between six inches and a foot," "two feet," and on the hills and uplands "several feet" in depth, the truth being, nevertheless, that a fair, undrifted fall of six inches in depth is of extremely rare occurrence—so rare that it does not occur once in twice as many years. Drifted snow, of course, may accumulate to almost any depth, but a snowfall that clothes the country *generally* with a covering of three or four inches in depth may safely be called a "heavy" one, and such a fall is rarely exceeded in this country. With such a fall, it is of course to be understood that there may be wreaths and drifts of many feet in depth, according to the conformation of any particular area of country, and the force and direction of the wind. You are always pretty safe in taking a Highlander's estimate of a snowfall, for unless he wilfully exaggerates, his standard of measurement is always at hand, and always in use wherever he wanders, on the lower lying lands or on the mountains. That standard is none other than his own *leg*, and by the constant use of that gauge, his estimate of the depth of snow at any time and anywhere may be accepted as fairly accurate and approximately correct. Thus, if you ask a man about the depth of snow on the ground after a fall, he will tell you that in the particular direction in which he has had occasion to travel it reached to the opening of his shoe (*gu beul na bròig*), or to the ankle (*gu ruig an t'aobran*), or to the small of the leg (*gu caol na coise*), or to the calf of the leg (*gu ruig an calpa*), or to the knee (*gu ruig an glùn*), or to the thigh (*gu ruig an t'sliasaid*), or to the waist or girdle (*gu ruig an crios*). Beyond that he does not go, rarely, indeed, so far, and for two good reasons—first, because a greater depth of snow than reaches to one's girdle is rarely encountered, and, secondly, when it does occur, it is not difficult to understand that a wise man is not particularly anxious to gauge it. We asked a shepherd the day after the last snowfall what might be the depth on his beat, and he answered at once, and we believe honestly, that it reached to between the ankle and the small of the leg (*cader an t'aobran's caol na coise*, were his own words), some three or four inches, that is, which in the West Highlands is a large fall.

Everybody having any acquaintance at all with Celtic literature must have heard of Alexander Macdonald, commonly called Alasdair MacMhaighstir Alasdair, the Ardnamurchan bard, the Tyrtæus of the '45. He stands in the very front rank of modern Gaelic poets, almost without an equal, indeed, whether the subject be the impassioned war-song or the peaceful pastoral, the varied scenery of mountain, glen, and peopled valley, or the wild tumult of ocean waves in a storm. To Highlanders, at least, anything connected with such a man must be of interest, and we make therefore no apology for introducing the following anecdote. Bailie John Cameron, of West End House, Fort-William, happening to call upon us, took occasion, in the course of conversation, to quote some Gaelic lines, a sort of epigram, which we could not recollect to have ever heard before. On our expressing a desire to know all he could tell us about the origin and occasion of the lines in question, Mr. Cameron gave the history of the curious jingle as follows. The epigram, he said, was by the celebrated Alasdair Macdonald, when he was quite a young man. The bard's father was, as is well known, an Episcopalian clergyman, and happening once on a time to have occasion to go to the district of Rannoch, in Perthshire, his son, not yet known as a bard, accompanied him. Alexander, while in Rannoch, found it necessary to order a pair of new shoes from the shoemaker of the hamlet in which his father and himself were temporarily resident. The shoes came home in due time and were paid for; and though the price charged was considered high, it was not grudged, the shoemaker assuring the young man that they were in the height of fashion, and sole and welting and uppers of the best material and most substantial workmanship. The shoes had not, however, been worn many days when they became leaky and generally out of sorts, and a close examination of the materials and workmanship convinced the embryo bard that the shoemaker was neither more nor less than a rascally cheat. The young man was of course indignant, and determined to have his revenge, and as publicly too as possible, when an opportunity should offer. On the following Sunday the bard's father called the people of the hamlet together to worship, and as they were at a considerable distance from their own stated place of worship, all the people of the place collected to hear him. Amongst the rest was the shoemaker, who, it should be observed, was an exceedingly tall man, long, lank, and lean. The young bard acted on the occasion as reader and precentor to his father, and at a certain stage of the service, to the consternation of the worthy minister, and the amusement of the rest of the congregation, with whom the shoemaker was no favourite, he chanted the following lines, which, like so many barbed arrows, went so straight to the mark that the luckless shoemaker was covered with shame and confusion of face :—

> " Ailein, 'Ic Ailein, 'Ic Uilleim,
> Fhir-dhubhaidh nam bròg ;
> Fhir a dh-fhuaigheas le snòd na gearr bhuinn ;
> Ailein, 'Ic Ailein, 'Ic Uilleim,
> Fhir-dhubhadh nam bròg,
> 'Stu 'n rògaire 's mò a tha 'n'a Albuinn.
> Ailein, 'Ic Ailein, 'Ic Uilleim ;
> Gur a fad' eadar t'uileann 's do shealbhan ;
> 'Snam bithinn a'm ghurrach air mullach do chinn,
> Gum faicinn Cillfhinn a's Braidalbainn !"

We give a translation, though the point and pith is almost entirely lost in an English rendering.

> " Allan, son of Allan, son of William,
> Thou that art the blackener of shoes ;
> Thou that sewest the inner shoe-soles with unrosined thread.
> Allan, son of Allan, son of William,
> Thou blackener of shoes,
> Thou art the biggest rogue in all broad Scotland.
> Allan, son of Allan, son of William,
> Far is the distance from thy elbow-joint to thy wind-pipe ;
> If I were but perched on the top of thy head,
> I could see hence all the way to Killin and over Breadalbane."

That the general reader may have some idea at least of the pith and point of these lines, some little elucidation is absolutely necessary. It will be observed that the shoemaker is addressed not by his name and surname—the latter, we believe, was Campbell—but patronymically, after the manner of the Highlands. He is reproached with being a "blackener" of shoes, because in old times it was the custom of the craft to send new boots and shoes home to their owners unblackened on the welt, and altogether unpolished and unvarnished, that the sewing of the seam, and workmanship generally, might be seen and examined in its naked reality, and approved or disapproved of, as the case might be. There is no doubt that it was an honest, well-meant custom, calculated to check badly finished or "scamped" work, as it is called; and Mr. Ruskin, we daresay, would be glad to devote, if the thing were suggested to him, a whole number of his *Fors Clavigera* to the advocacy of a return to so healthy and honest a custom in other crafts as well as in shoemaking. It would seem, however, that even in Macdonald's time the custom was getting into disuse, for his shoes were sent home in such a polished, and "blackened," and non-naked condition, that they could not be minutely examined, and the maker's word had to be taken that they were all they ought to be, which a few days' wearing proved they were *not*. How improper it was to sew, welt, and sole together with "unrosined thread" will be readily understood. The reference to the distance between Crispin's elbow and throat is meant to lead, by a ludicrous step, up to the concluding hit at the lank longitude of the entire man, from the top of whose head, if only he could manage to get perched upon it, the young bard declares he could have a most extensive view—all the way to the village of Killin, and over the heights of Breadalbane. The unlucky shoemaker soon found that he had made a bad job of it in more ways than one. The rhyme was in everybody's mouth, and as often as he heard it, it ceased not to vex him till his dying day.

CHAPTER XXVIII.

Safe from East and North-East Storms under the Lee of Ben Nevis—Story of a Ballad of the Maritime Highlands—A Fragment—Translation.

WE may now look, and with some confidence, to a continuance of bright, dry weather, and any one having land to deal with deserves to be called a sluggard, and nothing less, if he doesn't get everything into the ground with all possible speed. The old Highlanders of the West Coast and Hebrides, wiser in their day than their School Board-patronised descendants, had this saying—

"Biodh e fuar no biodh e blà,
Bi glic a's cuir do shiol 'sa Mhàrt,"

which, being interpreted, may run something like this—

"Weather cold or weather warm,
March-sown seed ne'er met with harm."

And although, according to the Gregorian calendar, the present writing is correctly dated in April, it is to be remembered that it is still the *Mhàrt* or March of the old people who computed the months and seasons according to the Julian calendar. Another agricultural saying of the old people, founded on practical experience, and well deserving the attention of their descendants, is this—

"'S fhearr aon là le surd Earraich,
Na tri latha le surd Samhna,"

which may be rendered thus—

> "Better in spring, the work of one good day,
> Than three at Hallowmas, work as you may."

Reverting to the recent storm, it is proper to say that it was but comparatively little felt here. Nestled as we are under the broad lee of Ben Nevis and his brother mountains, such storms as come from the north and north-east pass high over our heads. In the case of such a storm, we "hear the sound thereof," and see the mad scud of its clouds as they tumble along in wild and ragged confusion Atlantic-wards; it never harms, and rarely even incommodes us, except in the way of a little delay, perhaps, and occasionally a wet jacket, if one has to cross a ferry.

It is many years since we became acquainted with an old and exceedingly interesting Gaelic song, for a complete and correct copy of which we had inquired and searched everywhere with but indifferent success. In the Hebrides, and all over the Maritime Highlands, no production of the Celtic race is better known than the composition in question, though, so far as we are aware, it has never yet appeared in print, nor, although almost everybody knows the beautiful air and the argument or story in its minutest details, is it easy to meet with any one who can repeat more than two, or at most three, verses of the song itself. The song in which we have so long been interested has no distinctive title or name by which it can be referred to; like many similar compositions in other languages, it is best known by a single line, which indicates the keynote of the tragedy—

> "Nach truagh leat bean òg 's i ga bàthadh?"

The story is briefly this :—A young woman happily married, and already the mother of two children—one, as the song itself relates, two years old, and the other three months—invites her younger unmarried sister to visit them. In a short time a criminal connection is formed between the husband and this young woman, his sister-in-law, a state of matters of which the poor wife, devoted to her children, and believing herself happy in her husband's love, has no suspicion; how could she possibly suspect, asks the story, her own born sister of such wickedness? The guilty husband and his guiltier paramour resolve to rid themselves of the deeply wronged and unsuspecting wife on the first favourable opportunity. This opportunity soon presents itself. One day in the spring of the year, during the low tides of the vernal equinox, the wife, leaving her children in charge of her sister, descended to the big ebb-shore in order to gather dulse and the rarer shell-fish only to be got at such seasons. Venturing seawards as far as possible, she fills her creel with shell-fish, and then directs her steps to a *sgeir-mhara*, or rock of the sea, that at low ebbs is exposed and dry, but is usually covered by the tide, in order to gather dulse, the largest and best that could be got. The dulse gathered, the woman sits down to rest, for the day is bright and warm, and she is tired with her exertions; her head droops; she turns on her side, and falls asleep. Her husband and her sister calling her, and getting no answer, go to the *sgeir-mhara*, and finding her sound asleep, they weave and plait her long and abundant locks with the tough grass-wrack and tangle that grew luxuriantly and as conveniently for their purpose as possible, around the shapely arm on which rested the sleeper's cheek. Their evil work done, the man fled from the scene, but his accomplice only removed to the opposite shore, there to wait and watch, in order to be able to convey to her companion in guilt certain and sure tidings of their victim's death. The woman on the rock awakes from her sleep to find herself already encompassed by the fast rising tide, while her hair is so firmly interwoven with the wrack and tangle that she can only raise her head a very little; but that little suffices to show her her sister seated above high-water mark on the opposite shore. She calls aloud and supplicates for aid in her terrible distress, only to be jeered and laughed at by her cruel sister, who avows that she has no pity for her, and will give her no help. It is at this point that the song, as we have been able to recover it, begins.

"Oran Cianail.

"'A phiuthar ud thall, no hùg ò,
'An cois na tràghad, hùg ò,
Thig a nall, no hù, hoirinn ò,
'Sin do làmh dhomh, hùg ò.

"'Nach truagh leat bean òg, no hùg ò,
'S i ga bathadh, hùg ò;'
'Cha truagh, cha truagh, no hù hoirinn ò,
Is beag mo chàs dhiot hùg ò.'

"'Nach truagh leat féin, no hùg ò
Cor mo phàisdean, hùg ò?
'Bhios a nise, no hù hoirinn ò
'Caoidh am màthar, hùg ò?

"'Fear dà bhliadhna, hùg, ò,
Fear 'na ràithe, hùg, ò;

Cha'n fhaigh e 'nochd, no hù hoirinn ò,
Cìoch a mhàthar, hùg, ò.

" ' Iarraidh esan, no hùg ò,
Cioch a mhàthar, hùg ò,
Ach cha'n 'fhaigh e, no hù hoirinn ò,
Ach an sàile, hùg ò.

" ' Cuir fios uamsa, no hùg ò,
Gu 'm thriuir bhràithrean, hùg ò,
Ach dean a cheileadh, no hoirinn ò,
Air mo mhàthair, hùg, ò.

" ' Mo thruaighe mise, no hùg ò,
'S fuar-fhliuch sleamhuinn, hùg ò,
'Tha mo leabaidh, no hù hoirinn ò,
Air bad feamainn, hùg ò.

" ' 'S fliuch mo chluasag, no hùg ò,
'S fliuch, 's cha nàir dhi, hùg ò,
Fliuch le 'm dheoir, no hù hoirinn ò,
Fliuch le sàile, hùg ò.

. . . . . .

" ' An easgann fhuar no hùg ò,
'Na glas-làimh dhomh, hùg ò ;
'S am partan donn, no hù hoirinn ò,
'A streap ri'm bhràghad, hùg, ò,' " &c.

. . . . . .

The following, though not a literal translation, is a sufficiently faithful rendering to give the general reader a good idea of the manner and matter of the original :—

"A VERY TRAGICAL BALLAD : FROM THE GAELIC.

(A FRAGMENT.)

" ' Sister that sittest safe on land
  (Alas, and woe is me !)
Come hither, and reach me a friendly hand
  (Cruel and cold is the sea).

"'For a drowning wretch some pity have
  (Alas, and woe is me!')
'No pity have I, nor help to save,
  Tho' cruel and cold is the sea.'

"'For my children's sake, have pity, I pray
  (Alas, and woe is me!)
They'll break their hearts that their mother's away
  (Cruel and cold is the sea).

"'Two years and a day is the age of one
  (Alas, and woe is me!)
Of my babe's life not three months have run
  (Cruel and cold is the sea).

"'For his mother's breast he'll weep and pine
  (Alas, and woe is me!)
'Twill yield him to-night but the salt sea brine
  (Cruel and cold is the sea).

"'O tell my sad and woful case
  To my darling brothers three;
But hide it from my mother dear,
  Who nursed me on her knee!

"'Sad my heart and low my head
  (Alas, and woe is me!)
Wet and slimy my grass-wrack bed,
  In the cold and cruel sea.

"'Wet, indeed, my sea-wrack pillow
  (Alas, and woe is me!)
Wet with my tears and wet with the billows
  (Cruel and cold is the sea).

. . . .

"'Manacled fast are my hands in the tightening folds
  Of the slimy eel;
The great brown crab as it crawls and crawls
  On my breasts I feel!'"

. . . .

The remainder of the ballad, which we have been unable to recover, but which we can well remember hearing sung in our boyhood, tells how the tide slowly rose until it reached and covered the lips of the poor victim, who continued to the last, until her accents became but a sound of bubbling indistinctness, to plead and pray for mercy in language so touching and beautiful, that it rarely failed to move the listeners to tears. We forget whether the ballad tells that retribution, speedy and terrible, overtook the guilty accomplices; the elucidatory prose narrative, which was always told in connection with the subject, certainly does. On a midsummer night lightning from heaven struck the cottage as they slept. In the morning the neighbours found the end of it in which slept the guilty pair shattered and burnt, their bodies reduced to a foul and fetid mass of cinder. In the other end, which was untouched by the fire, the children were found clasped in each other's arms, and sound asleep—"unharmed," says the narrative, "because of their innocence, by the wrath-fire of God."

For the best and completest version in our possession of the above fragment we are indebted to our neighbour, the Rev. Dr. Clerk of Kilmallie. How old this ballad may be we cannot positively say. Very old men recently in life knew it in their childhood from old people, whose story was that they too knew it in *their* childhood. We should therefore say that it is as old at least as the middle or even the beginning of last century—perhaps much older—and from internal evidence it seems to belong to one of the Hebrides or to the sea coast of Argyllshire. It is proper to say, however, that the people of Uist and Skye, as well as those of Mull and Morven, and some other places, claim it each for their own, generally pointing out in corroboration of their claims the very rock on which the woman perished, and the spot on which sat the sister whose hard and cruel heart could not be moved to pity. From the prose narrative, and from a still unrecovered verse of the ballad itself, the day was warm and bright, and it was *in the heat of the day* that the shell-fish gatherer, *at low ebb*, found her way to the rock on which she fell asleep. It must have been low water then about mid-day at the scene of the ballad tragedy, and this fact so far localises the story, for such a state of tide at that hour in the West Highlands only occurs in some of the inner Hebrides, and along the Argyllshire coast, say from the Sound of Jura to the Point of Ardnamurchan.

CHAPTER XXIX.

Demons of the Dust-Cloud and Spindrift—Gaelic Rhyme—Demons sometimes visible in form of Lambent Flame—Wit-Word Combats—Meaning of a Gaelic Phrase.

EASTERLY winds, cold and keen, frequently intensifying into such squalls as sent the *Eurydice* to her fate; squalls that sent the spindrift careering adown Loch Linnhe in huge columns of comminuted spray, half-a-dozen or more together, very pretty to look at from a distance as they swirl and gyrate in their mad waltz Mull and Morven-wards—such, with a bright sun overhead by day, and a slight touch of frost by night, has been the sort of weather prevalent here for the last twenty days; capital working weather, as you may understand, with dust enough, too, taking the familiar proverb in its literal sense, to counterpoise in value the ransom of all sovereigns of Europe, as sovereigns are appraised now-a-days, ten times over. A neighbour of ours, an old man, who has for many years been a dabbler in occult philosophy and thaumaturgy, will have you believe that at this season in each and every dust whirlwind on land and spindrift column at sea there is present an invisible spirit of evil animating and, when a special disaster has to be brought about, intensifying all their gyrations. These evil spirits, he says, are let loose for seventeen days and nights together at the season of the vernal equinox, with the power to do much mischief, though not nearly so much as they have a mind to. Their busiest time is in Annunciation week. At sea they take the form of sudden squalls, waterspouts, and spindrift columns, which cause wrecks and drowning, driving, besides, the fish from the shallows into deep water, so that the fisherman baits his lines in vain. On land their object is to check and crush back vegetation into its state of mid-winter torpidity; but failing in this, they swirl about in clouds of dust, which, being inhaled, causes grievous sickness in man and beast. Against the demon of the dust-cloud, as it swirls along the highway, a wise man will take this precaution: as it approaches, you are instantly to close your eyes and mouth as tightly as possible, at the same time turning your back upon it until it has swept by, mentally repeating —for you are not to open your mouth, nor as much as breathe, as long as you can help it—this rhyme :—

> "Gach cuman a's mias a's meadar,
> Gu Pòl, gu Peadair 'sgu Bride;
> Dion, a's seun a's gleidh mi 'o olc 'so chunnart,
> Air a bheallach, 's air a mhullach
> 'Sair an tullaich ud thall;
> Pòl a's Peadair a's Bride caomh!"

These old rhymes and incantations, abrupt and inconsecutive as they frequently are, and with such recondite allusions, are extremely difficult to translate, though to the competent Gaelic scholar and antiquary the general drift and meaning may be plain and patent enough. The above lines are something like this :—

> "Be the care of milk-pail, and bowl, and cog
> Given to Peter and Paul and Saint Bride :
> Wherever I wander protect me, ye Saints!
> Let not evil or harm me betide;
> Hear me, Peter and Paul, and gentle Saint Bride!"

We have spoken of the demons of the dust-cloud and spindrift as invisible, and invisible they will always remain to the incredulous and uninitiated; but our informant says that under certain conditions, which he declined to explain to us, the spirits may be seen as they swirl past in their vehicles of dust or spray, generally in the form of a blue lambent flame, that, to prove its spiritual and unearthly character, is always inclined backwards—in a direction, that is, directly opposite to the wind, however fiercely it may blow at the moment. These flame demons he has often seen himself. There is also a rhyme to be said by mariners in spindrift season at sea. He had forgotten it except a few words, and could not therefore repeat it, but he promised to procure it for us from a brother thaumaturgist in a neighbouring district when next they chance to foregather. This man, we beg our readers to understand, is a person of more than average intelligence and shrewdness in the ordinary conduct of life, and yet he spoke as to this matter with a gravity, and an evident reluctance to speak at all, that satisfied us that he was perfectly and seriously in earnest, and really believed his own averments. Can it be possible that under certain electrical conditions of the atmosphere a visible flame is sometimes generated in the dust whirlwinds of March? If so, one can readily understand how such a superstition should in time gather round a nucleus of fact so remarkable and rare. We may depend upon it, that, interwoven with most superstitions, and more especially with those that are connected, as in this case, with natural phenomena, there is always more or less of fact and truth to be detected, if we could only lay our hands upon it.

Last week we spent two or three days very pleasantly in Badenoch amongst a highly intelligent and hospitable people. The only drawback was the intense cold, which, borne on the edge of keen, easterly winds, seemed to pierce one through and through, and that, too, although there was a bright sun overhead, and the lark on quivering wings, at a height that made it seem no larger than a bee, trilled forth his best and blithest lay. There is a great deal in Badenoch that one would like to see, but our time on this particular occasion was fully occupied with matters of too much importance to be neglected in favour of antiquarian or folk-lore research, however interesting and enticing. All that we picked up worth the chronicling in this column was the following:—The reader must understand that in the old time it was a custom in the Highlands—a custom in the remoter midland districts not yet entirely extinct—for the shrewder and more intelligent inhabitants of neighbouring districts, and sometimes of neighbouring glens and hamlets, to engage, when they chanced to meet at kirk or market, fair or funeral, in "wit-word" combats, a sort of epigrammatical *duello*, in which the people at large took a lively interest, the charge and counter-charge, the attack and repartee, being repeated from district to district, and remembered, if they contained anything particularly good, long after the wit-word combatants themselves were gathered to their fathers. It seems that some generations ago a wit-word war of this kind had long existed between the people of

Bohuntin, in Brae-Lochaber, and those of Killiechonate and Insh, on the south of the Spean, and so evenly were the wit-wordmongers matched, that it was impossible to say positively that either party had had the best of it. The victory was finally decided for Bohuntin in this wise. One day there was a meeting of some sort at High Bridge, where all the Brae-Lochaber people were assembled. In the course of the day the good man of Killiechonate (*Fear Chillechonaite*) came up to Donald Bane of Bohuntin (*Domhnull Bàn Bhohuntuin*) and launched this wit-word shaft:—"*A Dhomhnull Bhàin Bhohuntin tha buille agam ort*" ("Donald Bane of Bohuntin, I have to launch a wit-word shaft at thee!"). "*Cuir i mata*" ("Launch it, then"), quoth Donald Bane. "'*Sleamsa na h-nile ni a'thair an t'saoghal*" ("Everything that is on the world is mine"), said the good man of Killiechonate. "'*Sleamsa,*" retorted Donald Bane, "'*sleamsa 'a saoghal fein: Tog thusa do chuid 's bi 'falbh!*" ("Mine is the world itself. Take up, therefore, your property, and be off with you, bag and baggage!") And, by the unanimous vote of the assembly, it was allowed that Donald Bane had the best of it, that the superiority of wit and ready repartee was with Bohuntin; and there, continued our colloquist, himself a Bohuntin man, it remains to this day. We picked up this on the top of the Fort-William and Kingussie royal mail coach,—a most useful institution, by the way, and a great boon to the districts of Lochaber and Badenoch, admirably conducted by the proprietor, Mr. Hugh Macdonald, and driven in excellent style by John Warren, an exceedingly attentive man, and our whilom-neighbour, honest Donald "Frenchman."

CHAPTER XXX.

Splendid Wild-Bird Season—Sea-fowl at Work—Following in the wake of Steamers—Sharpness of Eye.

Such a splendid wild-bird season this has been! Hardly a single instance of a deserted nest, of abortive incubation or addled eggs, has come under our notice this year. Throughout it has been all our feathered friends could wish, and they, to their credit be it recorded, made the most of it. At this moment the wealth of bird-life everywhere is something wonderful—mavis and merle, chaffinch and greenfinch, and yellow-hammer, linnet, goldfinch, blackcap, and whitethroat, pipit and lark, and tit and bunting, in hundreds upon hundreds, whithersoever, evening or morning, you select to direct your ornithological ramble. Sea-fowl, too, are exceedingly numerous this year; and nothing can be more graceful and beautiful than the evolutions of a flock of black-backed gulls, greater and lesser, black-heads, kittiwakes, terns, and skuas, at this season, as they gather over a shoal of herring fry that has been hunted to the surface by their invaluable allies, the web-foot divers. The graceful buoyancy of flight and perfect mastery of wing exhibited by gulls, terns, and skuas in such circumstances, is something wonderful. They poise and shiver, and dip and dart; they wheel and glide hither and thither, upwards and downwards, zig-zag and aslant, in the most beautiful and graceful curves, and all so easily that their most complicated evolutions seem to be the merest matter of course, and to be no more a matter of effort or exertion than it is for them to float, lighter than the foam itself, when with folded wings they settle on the waveless surface of the summer sea. The stridulous clang and scream of a single gull, or of two or more gulls when they fall out and quarrel over a stranded fish, or other *ejectamentum* of the deep, is decidedly harsh and unpleasant to the ear—about as discordant, perhaps, as any notes that bird or beast can utter. It is otherwise, however, when hundreds are collected, keen and excited, and upon the whole it is to be understood *pleased*, over the murmur and ripple of a fish shoal "*aboil*." Then the notes of the different species, as they poise and dart and wheel, become blended into a wild harmony, admirably in keeping with all the surroundings, and musical enough, after a fashion, to be heard not merely with interest, but with pleasure. Before parting with these graceful and beautiful birds, let us draw attention to the marvellous quickness of sight possessed by the sea-gull, a quickness of sight, too, no less remarkable for the immense distances over which it is constantly exercised to good purpose, than for its unerring accuracy and keenness when brought to bear on objects of almost microscopical minuteness. Let the surface of the summer sea—of the Linnhe Loch, suppose—be calm and placid as the deep blue sky that overarches it; if on a sudden you notice the mirror-like sheet gently darkening with the gurgling ebullition of a fish fry shoal "aboil" (the Highlanders of the West Coast and Hebrides say *goil éisg*; *bruchd èisg air ghoil*, a shoal of fish *aboil*, or *aboiling*—that is, breaking to the surface as if in play ; in English we use *ebullition*, a word borrowed from the Latin, and of precisely similar meaning, in the same sense), then, in less than two minutes by the watch in your hand, half a dozen or more gulls have already arrived, and are screaming excitedly, and dipping, and darting, and diving over the shoal, while others with strong and powerful beats are to be seen winging their flight from all directions towards the centre of attraction. And yet, before that shoal broke to the surface aboil, you could safely have sworn that there was not a wing of gull or tern in sight within miles and miles of you. Coming from Fort-William the other evening we had an opportunity of putting the quickness of sight in sea-gulls to a very practical test, for the edification of a companion who was somewhat sceptical as to all we had just been saying on the subject. The steamer was going very fast, in the rapid " race " of a spring-tide ebb, something like twenty miles an hour, and yet a baker's dozen of gulls were following in her wake— following easily and lazily, so to speak, without apparent effort, and with but little beat of wing, circling and wheeling in graceful curves over the boiling waters just escaped from the torture of paddles and keel, as they spread in a broad belt of hissing, gurgling foam astern of us. The gulls, we saw, were keenly on the watch for anything worth picking up that might be thrown overboard. Running down into the cabin, we got hold of a small water-biscuit, with which we returned to the quarter-deck, prepared to overwhelm our sceptical friend with proof positive and practical, immediate and direct, that there is perhaps no other bird of land or sea so exact, sharp, and keen of sight as the common gull of our own shores. Breaking the biscuit into four parts, the largest of which was less than an inch square, for it was a very small biscuit, we handed one of the fragments to our companion, directing him to drop it quietly into the surging, seething waters just abaft the starboard paddle-wheel. The bit of biscuit, be it understood, was of the same colour as the hissing foam into which it was dropped, and by which, slightly submerged, it was of course rapidly carried astern. Once dropped, it is needless to say that it was utterly invisible to our eyes; we could only at the best guess its whereabouts, and yet, before it had dropped thirty yards astern, a large black-backed gull, though it must have been somewhat incommoded at the moment by the steamer's smoke, in the centre of which it was sailing, detected the *flotsam* at once, and dipping with headlong dart into the foam, secured it! It detected and picked up the other bits of biscuit, one by one, as they were dropped into the sea, with equal dexterity, venturing up at last so close to the stern of the steamer, that with its large bright eye it seemed to be keenly watching all our movements. The biscuit disposed of, we put our hand into our pocket and taking out some old letters, we tore off the "Queen's head" corner of an envelope, and slipped it overboard, in order to see what Mr. Gull would say to it. The beautiful bird detected the waif at once, and made a dart at it as if to pick it up: but, no! when within a yard or so of it he became aware that, whatever it might be, it was nothing in his way, and he glided upwards again in graceful curves to his favourite station on a line with the topmast truck. As a final experiment, we dropped a small chip of wood right over the steamer's bows, over which, the instant it appeared astern, the gull, making a slight stoop, hovered for a moment, but straightway shot upwards and away, clearly showing that it took in at a glance the not unimportant fact to it, that whatever the flotsam might be, it was certainly nothing of which even a hungry gull could make any use, although the race is almost omnivorous, and with the digestion of ostriches.

CHAPTER XXXI.

Puss-Moth Caterpillar—The Astronomy of Buddhist Priests—Galileo—Chinese Encylopædia in 5020 Volumes!

A FEW days ago there came to us from Alness a small box which contained what there was no difficulty in recognising as the caterpillar of the puss-moth, one of the largest and handsomest of the order, and remarkable for the soft downy fur with which its body is covered, feeling to the touch like the fur of the cat, and hence its common name of *puss-moth*. It is sometimes also called the sphinx or sphinx-moth, because of its caterpillar or larva. When it has ceased feeding, it has a habit of reposing in the attitude of the Egyptian sphinx—erect, and solemn, and grave—an attitude which it manages to assume by firmly grasping the twig on which it may happen to find itself for the moment, with the claspers with which the posterior segments of its body are furnished, thus enabling it to raise the fore part of its body into an almost upright attitude, which is maintained until, under the calls of hunger, it again desires to feed, when it lets itself down again on the twig, and crawls along in usual caterpillar fashion. The puss-moth caterpillar is usually found on the willow and poplar, though we have also met with it on the cherry and privet. It is by no means an uncommon larva in localities where natural woods abound, and this year has been quite plentiful in our immediate neighbourhood. Though sometimes prettily coloured, the sphinx larva is of rather formidable and even repulsive aspect. The head is heavy and bulldog-like, looking as if it could bite hard, if it only could get hold of one. But to the uninitiated its chief terrors would seem to lie in the tail, which is armed, earwig-wise, with a couple of suspicious-looking tentacles or darts, long and pointed, as if they were meant to sting. The creature, however, is perfectly harmless, and can neither bite nor sting; and wanting the power to do harm, it almost certainly wants the will. The use of the bifurcated caudal appendage seems to be to brush away the ichneumon fly, that is, the deadly enemy of all caterpillars, piercing their bodies with its needle-like ovipositor, and laying an egg which in due time produces a larva after its kind that slowly feeds on the viscera and other internals of its living home, until it shrivels up and dies. The caudal tentacles of the sphinx are, in short, defensive weapons against the attacks of parasites, and are used in brushing these away when they attempt to settle on its body, just as a horse uses *its* tail to whisk away the flies that tickle and torment it.

The etymology, by the way, of *caterpillar*—a word used more than once in the foregoing paragraph—is curious. According to Bailey, and he seems to be right, it is a compound term from the old French *Chate peluse*—the *cat-furred* worm—applied to all hairy caterpillars, though the reference with us is only found in connection with one species, and that not in its larva, but in its perfect state—*puss*-moth. We speak of hairy caterpillars, to be sure, but without a thought of the *cat* in the connection; and we are assuredly right, for the hair of most of our hairy caterpillars is rather in the form of tooth-brush tufts than like the soft, sleek, silken fur of, for example, our favourite tabby "Bella," as she sits on our shoulder crooning low and soft in our ear even as we write these lines.

An anonymous correspondent, with whose handwriting we are familiar, and to whom we have often been indebted for friendly aid in the course of our folk-lore and antiquarian gleanings, sends us a newspaper cutting containing the following bit of news from Japan:—

"The Buddhist priests in Yokohama recently declared that the sun moves and the earth stands still. Some students ridiculed the assertion, and were attacked by a mob and mortally wounded. Japanese only were concerned in the affair."

What our correspondent meant us to say about this, for the slip bears his usual *nota bene* mark for close attention, we are at a loss even to guess. We can only meantime observe that it very naturally reminded us of what occurred at Rome, in the Convent of Minerva, on the 22d June 1633, two hundred and forty-five years ago, when, before the "Most Eminent and Most Reverend Lords Cardinals, General Inquisitors of the Universal Christian Republic against Heretical Depravity," Galileo Galilei, "son of the late Vincenzo Galilei, of Florence," only escaped a worse fate even than that of the Japanese Copernicans, by publicly re-embracing the errors, knowing that they were errors, which they had ridiculed, and solemnly abjuring the truths for which they suffered. The two propositions of the stability of the sun and the motion of the earth were thus condemned by the "*Theological Qualifiers*" of the Inquisition—

"1. The proposition that the sun is the centre of the world, and immoveable from its place, is absurd, philosophically false, and formally heretical, because it is expressly contrary to the Holy Scriptures.

"2. The proposition that the earth is not the centre of the world, nor immoveable, but that it moves, and also with a diurnal motion, is also absurd, philosophically false, and, theologically considered, equally erroneous in faith."

To these propositions Galileo, on his knees before the Holy Inquisition, solemnly assented, abjuring and cursing as damnable heresy and error anything and everything that disturbed, or had a tendency to disturb, the Ptolemaic system of astronomy as then accepted by the Church and the world at large. It is a sad and sombre picture enough; humiliating, too, and painful to contemplate, the shadows of it all the darker, intensified rather than relieved, by the solitary beam of light that flashes across the gloom when the old man, rising from his knees, stood erect, and, with a stamp of his heel on the ground, was heard to mutter, "*E pur se muove!*" ("For all this it *does* move!"); as if he had said, "Notwithstanding my abjuration, the earth *has* a diurnal motion on its own axis, and an annual motion round the sun. Copernicus is right; Ptolemy and the Inquisition are wrong!" Our early friend Sir David Brewster, under whose guidance we first voyaged to the stellar spheres, in his Life of Newton, thus refers to the scene :—

"At the age of seventy, on his bended knees, and with his right hand resting on the holy evangelists, did this patriarch of science avow his present and past belief in the dogmas of the Romish Church, abandon as false and heretical the doctrine of the earth's motion and of the sun's immobility, and pledge himself to denounce to the Inquisition any other person who was ever suspected of heresy. He abjured, cursed, and detested those eternal and immutable truths which the Almighty had permitted him to be the first to establish. Had Galileo but added the courage of the martyr to the wisdom of the sage, had he carried the glance of his indignant eye round the circle of his judges, had he lifted his hands to heaven and called the living God to witness the truth and immutability of his opinions, the bigotry of his enemies would have been disarmed, and science would have enjoyed a memorable triumph."

No fear, let our correspondent rest assured, but that matters will come right—slowly, perhaps, but surely—in Japan, as in the fullness of time they came right in the western world. The truth is great, and must prevail in the end.

From Japan to China is but a leap; and as a sort of counterpoise to the Ptolemaic-Copernican tragedy at Yokohama, here is a bit of very extraordinary and curious news about China and the Chinese. Lately there reached London for the British Museum a copy of what may be called the encylopædia of Chinese literature, from 1100 B.C. down to 1700 A.D., in 5020 volumes!—certainly and far and away the most voluminous work the world has ever seen, or is likely ever to see. It is supposed to contain, as well it may, everything of any consequence in Chinese literature for 2800 years, and an extraordinary *omnium gatherum* of celestial wit and wisdom it must be. Even if one knew the language thoroughly, what a task it were to wade and flounder through this prodigious dead sea of Eastern literature, for all the pearls and coral it can possibly contain! The work, it seems, is one of only a hundred copies printed, and was obtained and in a manner smuggled out of the Celestial empire only at great trouble and not a little danger by Mr. Mayer, Secretary of Legation at Pekin. It reaches the British Museum at a cost of some £1500, by no means a large sum for a work of such unparalleled magnitude and vast importance. A literary friend in London, who mentions the subject in a recent communication, asks, "How, my dear fellow, would you like, supposing you knew the language, to read—honestly and studiously, mind—these 5020 volumes?" We reply we shouldn't like it at all! "*Naviget Anticyram*," would soon be the cry of our best friends. We should probably be mad as a March hare, and fit only to be consigned to the care of our friend Dr. Arthur Mitchell, long ere we had voyaged half-way across so difficult and dark a sea!

CHAPTER XXXII.

The Pearl Mussel in Highland Rivers and Streams—Story of a Pearl belonging to Stewart of Appin—*Byssus* of *Mya Margaritifera* a Specific in Affections of the Eye—Pearls in the Common Mussel—Mussel sometimes poisonous.

WHILE at Banavie the other day we were shown some very pretty, pea-size, pinkish pearls, the nacreous secretions of the fresh-water pearl-bearing mussel of our Scottish streams, the *Mytilus aquarius* or *Mya margaritifera* of conchologists. The mussels in which these pearls were found were taken out of some of the semi-stagnant pools in the upper waters of the Tay and its tributaries, which, owing to the dryness of the season, yielded to the mussel fisher a readier and richer harvest during the summer of 1878 than for many years past. The two finest pearls in the collection were of a slightly oval form, and of a delicate, slightly striated, pink hue. A third, equally large, would have been quite as valuable but for a slight depression in the bulge of one side, which somewhat marred its symmetry. The fresh-water *Margaritifera* is a much more common bivalve than is generally supposed, for by diligent search it is to be found in many of our Highland rivers and streams, in which its existence has perhaps never been suspected. We were once shown here at our own door a small collection of very pretty pearls found in mussels picked up in one or more of the Moor of Rannoch streams. The late Mr. Maclean of Ardgour once sent us three large mussels that were taken out of the Sanda on his property, which, however, on being opened and carefully examined, contained no pearls. Nor, though slightly disappointing, was this surprising, for it is not to be supposed that a pearl is to be found in every mussel, one in three or four being considered a fair average even for the best localities. The largest and finest Scottish pearl we ever saw was worn as a pendant by an attachment of golden wire to a very fine old silver *fibula* or brooch of exquisite workmanship, at one time an heirloom in the family of Stewart of Appin. There was a curious tradition connected with this pearl,—that it was found in the stomach of a huge salmon, killed with the leister on the River Awe, in the reign of one of the Scottish Jameses, and that the king himself was present when the fish was struck and landed. There is, of course, nothing really impossible in such a story, though the probability is that the pearl was in truth taken out of a margaritiferous mussel found in a pool of the Awe, or in one or other of the many streams that fall into the loch of that name. The *byssus* or silken *beard* of the *Margaritifera*, by which it anchored itself to rock, gravel, or stone in its native stream, was at one time in great request in the Highlands as a specific in affections of the eye. Properly dried, it became a soft and silken tuft, which, if gently rubbed over the eyelids, cured them of inflammation and *sty*. Toasted before the fire until brittle, and ground into a fine powder, a small pinch of it blown by the operator's breath into the eyes was a certain cure in all forms of ophthalmia. The burnt and pounded shell of the *Mya* itself was, according to one of our authorities, given in milk as a cure for colic; according to another authority, it was rather given as a cure for heart-burn and *glas-shile*, a sort of painful gastric salivation, an ailment fortunately less common now-a-days than formerly. It is perhaps not generally known that pearls are frequently to be found in the common mussel of our shores—the *Mytilus edulis*— more rarely, however, in the larger kinds sometimes eaten—hence the specific *edulis* in its scientific name —than in the smaller variety generally found on stony beaches where a streamlet falls into the sea. These small pearl-bearing mussels are not uncommon along our Nether Lochaber shores. We have often collected dozens of these pearls in a single season; but, unfortunately, they are so small as to be of little, if of any value—mere "seedlings," bearing about the same proportion as to size to the larger and really valuable *Mya* pearl that "*sparrow-hail*" shot, in the language of sportsmen, bears to "buck" or "swan" shot. The common mussel, though styled *edulis* or the *eatable*, is at certain seasons more or less poisonous, whether owing to certain circumstances of locality, or to a certain peculiarity of constitution in the eater, is not easily determined. The smaller variety, the pearl-bearing musselet just mentioned, which, in default of a distinctive scientific name, we may venture to style the *Mytilus margaritifera minor*, may be eaten by everybody with perfect safety, perhaps because it is chiefly found on stony beaches constantly washed by the limped waters of mountain streams.

CHAPTER XXXIII.

Weather Prognosticators sometimes "out in their reckoning"—Magnificent Double Rainbow over Glencoe—Cats—A One-Eared Cat a Treasure—How it came about—Rival Rhymes—Cat's Whiskers.

It will readily be admitted that navigation is an exacter science than meteorology, and yet we all know that even the best of seamen may at times be "out in his reckoning;" otherwise that very expressive phrase of such constant and happy application in the conduct of every-day life had never been received into the currency of our familiar phraseology. And if a navigator may sometimes be out in his reckoning, much more, *a fortiore*, may the meteorologist, whose science, as a science, is but yet in its infancy, and who, still enveloped in the Newfoundland fogs of uncertainty and haphazard conjecture, can meantime only grope his way as best he can in the direction of opener waters and clearer skies. Therefore it is that, for our own part, when at any time we make a weather forecast that is not duly verified by the event, we have no difficulty at all in frankly admitting that we were in error—that, by any number of degrees you please, we were "out in *our* reckoning." In our last paper we ventured, very guardedly it is true, but still we *did* venture, to predict fine weather for the greater part of October and up to the middle of November, and it is only honest now to confess that, instead of fine weather, we have had it, up to this date at least, very much the reverse—wet and slush, and the fretful sputterings of veering winds, never long enough in any one quarter to enable them to blow an honest, downright gale. And yet, had the weather turned out all we ventured to predict, we could not have seen what we saw the other evening—a sight, the magnificence and splendour of which must haunt us till our dying day. It was a double rainbow, both perfect arches of glory, of the vividest and most brilliant colouring, spanning the dark gorge of Glencoe! It was about five o'clock in the afternoon, and the sun being then on the horizon, the rainbow arches were as nearly as possible perfect semicircles, spanning the entrance to the glen, with their northern limbs resting (from our particular standpoint) on a field near Invercoe House, and their southern limbs in the garden plots of the hamlet of Carnach. We happened to be crossing the ferry of Ballachulish at the time, and even the ferrymen rested on their oars for a moment to admire a spectacle such as neither they nor we had ever before seen anything of the kind to equal in brilliancy and beauty. Under the bright and glorious arches the gorge of Glencoe itself was one ink-black sea of surging cloud and rain, while from the rapid shiftings of the cloud masses higher up it was evident that a mighty storm was at the moment raging along the summits. A third, or "supernumerary" bow, as they are termed, was for a short time visible in the interior of or within the "primary" arch, a phenomenon of extremely rare occurrence, and never seen except when, as in this case, the primary and secondary bows are of exceeding vividness and brilliancy of colouring. Coleridge, or somebody else, has said, and very finely said, that "the savage is a poet when he paints his idol with blood; the countryman returning from the labours of the field, when he stands to gaze on the rainbow;" and if this be true, all the people about the ferry of Ballachulish during a particular quarter of an hour that evening were poets for the nonce, even if they knew it not. Neither in poetry nor in prose that we know of is there any reference to the rainbow equal to the beautiful words of the author of *Ecclesiasticus*, or the *Book of Wisdom*, the sage and eloquent *Son of Sirach:*—" Look upon the rainbow, and praise Him that made it; very beautiful it is in the brightness thereof. It compasseth the heaven about with a glorious circle, *and the hands of the* MOST HIGH *have bended it.*"

In our last paper we had something to say about rats, and here is something which may not be uninteresting to our readers about cats, the antipodes and born antagonists of the marauding rodent. The other day, while Bailie John Cameron of Fort-William was sitting with us in our study, our favourite cat "Bella" leapt with a friendly purr upon his knee, and meeting with the desired recognition in the shape of a word of kindness and some soft stroking, not against the grain —remembering the homely adage and the motto of the great Clan Chattan, there might be some danger in *that*, even with "Bella"—but *with* the fur; and "Bella" was soon stretched at length on the Bailie's knee, with half-shut eyes, contentedly crooning her siestal song. Pleased with the friendliness of the cat, and admiring the glossy sleekness of her fur, Mr. Cameron observed that he supposed she was not much of a thief; that she did not at least meddle much with the milk and cream, seeing that her ears were evidently of the normal length, intact and uncurtailed. Like a long-forgotten dream it instantly dawned upon us that there was some connection between cats' ears and cream, though what that connection was we could not at the moment remember, and we begged the Bailie—to whom we acknowledge our indebtedness for much curious folk-lore—to explain. All cats, Mr. Cameron observed, are fond of milk, but, like their betters, fonder still of cream, when they can get it, and a cat that has fairly gone in for cream will manage to get at it, do what you will to prevent him. In utter neglect of mice and rats, and such "small deer," its legitimate and proper game, a real cream-loving cat will sit and watch and wait about the milk-house door and window for a whole day and night, if necessary, until sooner or later his chance comes, and he slips in like a shadow to regale himself with "a deep, deep draught" of something more delicious to his taste than the best Rhine wine; and how heartily he has fared may be detected by the observant eye in his protuberance of bulge and somnolent tendencies in "rest and be thankful" attitudes for hours thereafter. When cats take to these disreputable courses, two evils are inevitable—mice and rats superabound, and butter becomes a scarcer commodity than it need otherwise be, and of inferior quality what there is of it. The easiest and most effectual way to put a stop to such feline depredations would, of course, be to kill the cats, and have done with them; but the old saw holds good in the case of a cat as of a dog, that the very worst use you can put him to is "to hang him." Long, long ago, then, in the Highlands, the problem to be solved was how a cream-stealing cat was to be turned from its evil ways without actually killing him, or so maiming him as to render him worthless in his legitimate feline pursuits. From sad experience they were aware that hardly anything short of this would do, and yet they were loath on many considerations to proceed to extremities if in anywise it could be avoided. They had a proverb in which was neatly rolled up, as within a cigarette, much sound philosophy, a proverb by which they were largely guided in their dealings with criminals of all sorts, and equally applicable to quadrupeds as to bipeds, and the proverb was this—*'S feàirde bràth a breacadh gun a brisdeadh.* Literally, a quern (hand meal-mill) stone is the better of being pitted and indented (with many blows of a hammer), *so that you do not break it.* The proverb is an old one, of a date long before the age of water-driven grinding mills, and when hand querns were in common every-day use over all the Highlands. The meaning is that a criminal or evil-doer of any sort was to be punished with all necessary severity where the case required it; the end always in view, however, was to be the *reformation* of the culprit, not his utter ruin from over-severity of bodily punishment, and least of all his death. The question, then, was how a cat, in this case a convicted cream-stealer, was to be deterred from evil, and if possible reformed, without putting him to death, and with as little interference as possible with his acknowledged usefulness as a rat and mouse hunter? After, we may be sure, much thoughtful study and experimenting, the plan finally hit upon as at once the most efficacious, deterrent, and least harmful to the culprit himself, was to cut off his left ear as close to the roots as it could be cropped. A cat once so treated never had the courage to look a dish of cream in the face again, while as a mouse-killer he was, wonderful to relate, vastly sharpened and improved by the operation. Thenceforward a one-eared cat about a house was indeed a treasure. He never under any circumstances would touch cream; in the language of the East, "his heart was hardened" against it; nor dare a rat or mouse peep out of its hole where a cat that had undergone the aural operation was on the premises. But how was the discovery made? Who first tried or suggested the lopping off of a cat's left ear as likely to cure him of cream-stealing? Know, then, good reader, that, like many other great and wonderful discoveries and inventions, this also was due to the merest accident. The tradition is, that on a Sunday morning in the long ago ante-Reformation times, a stalwart Highlander was left in charge of a shieling, with all its treasure of milk and cream, and butter and cheese, while the females of the establishment went to confession at the chapel several miles adown the glen. The Highlander, whose name, according to the tradition, was *Beathean*, anciently a Christian name, but now a surname under the form of Bethune, Beaton, Mac-*Vean*, &c., was strictly enjoined by the women folks to keep a sharp eye on everything, and more particularly on the cats and cream dishes, the churning of the week promising to be excellent, if only these two could be kept separate until the churning day came round. For some time after the departure of the females Beathean was a most wary sentinel, keeping watch and ward, and going his rounds with the most praiseworthy vigilance. For a moment only did he sit down to rest him on the turf seat close by the shieling door; but in that moment one of the cats, the biggest and blackest of the lot, and an inveterate thief, slipped past him unseen, while Beathean, with his eyes directed to the heavens, was mentally forecasting the likely weather for the morrow. On his next round he thought it well to peep through the milk-closet window, and there, to his horror and shame, was the black cat sitting by the best of all the cream dishes, and up to the whiskers in the delicious fluid! Beathen was wroth, as was no wonder. He then and there drew his dirk, in a rage, and through the open window hurled it at the whiskered delinquent, intending, in the words of Burns, to "spit him like a pliver." The aim, however, was too hurried to be exactly true. The keen-edged weapon shore off the cat's left ear, but the animal was otherwise uninjured. With a spit and a hiss, that appalled even Beathean, the cat flew past him through the open window, as if on wings, but Beathean could show that cat's left ear as a trophy of his valour and a proof of his vigilance, and was content. When his wounds got healed, the cat went about the place as usual, but it was noticed that he never on any account would go near the milk-closet, never meddled with cream even when he could get at it easily, and even refused to taste it when it was offered him *ex gratia*. It came thus to be known that cats could be cured of cream-stealing by simply depriving them of their left ears; and it was long the custom so to treat cream-stealing cats all over the Highlands, a custom not quite unknown even at the present day. Mr. Cameron remembers seeing one-eared cats in Ardnamurchan in his younger days, and these were unquestionably mutilated in the interests of the cream dish. In Lochaber, too, we find on inquiry that, within the recollection of many people who are as yet but on the borderland of their grand climacteric, two, or three, or more one-eared cats might be found in every hamlet. Mr. Cameron quoted a rhyme, with which many of our readers must be familiar, in which the custom is very pointedly referred to. In the olden days the bards of different clans and different districts frequently exercised their wit in chaffing and satirising each other, and many of the "wit-word" rhymes of such contests are still repeated as Parthian shafts with which to wound an antagonist in argument when more legitimate weapons fail. A Lochaber bard, who had some real or fancied grievance against the people of Uist, once attacked them in a pungent satire, of which the following stanza survives:—

> "Ged 'bhithinn cho sean ris a charraig,
> 'S m'aodan air preasadh le aois,
> Cha phòsainn bean òg a Uist,
> Cha toir mo chridhe dhi gaol."

To which the Uist bard replied as follows:—

> "A mhic a bhodaichain chabaich,
> O bhun Lochabar nan craobh.
> *Cleas a chuit a dh-òl an t'uachdar;*
> *Bheirinn dhiot a chluas on mhaoil.*"

The point and sting of these epigrammatic rhymes are apt to be lost in a translation, but the following is about as good an English version as we can supply:—

The Lochaber bard *loq.* :—

"Though I were old and grey as is the lichened rock,
  With many years my face all furrow'd o'er,
An Uist maid for wife I'd shun and mock—
  I *could* not love a maid from that dull shore."

Uist bard *responds* :—

"Of worthless, toothless father, worthless son!
  Spawn of Lochaber's dismal woods and meres.
Silence! or, *as to lewd, cream-stealing cats is done,
  Close by the roots I'll crop off thy long ears!*"

The Lochaber bard having been the aggressor, and his attack on the females of Uist being deemed as ungallant as it was gratuitous, we have noticed that when at any time the above rhymes are repeated, it is on the understanding that the Uist bard has by much the best of it, the threat to cut off one's ears being considered the most galling insult that can be offered to an opponent.

The other day an old woman, whom we were questioning on the subject of cats, gave us another curious bit of popular lore regarding them. It has long been known, she assured us, that if you cut off the whiskers of a cat, he will, *ipso facto*, be utterly spoiled as a mouse-hunter until they grow to their proper length again; and even then, a cat with a second growth of whiskers is never so good a mouser as he was with his original moustache. She recollected that long ago, when two persons quarrelled in a hamlet, it was not an uncommon thing for one of the parties to cut off his neighbour's cat's whiskers, with the view of ruining him as a mouse-hunter. A spiteful and shabby thing to do, she confessed, but it was occasionally done, and she promised to try and remember an old song in which the thing was referred to.

CHAPTER XXXIV.

Meteorological Observatory to be erected on Ben Nevis—Electric Discharges on top—Curious Story.

WHAT Mont Blanc is to the Continent of Europe, Ben Nevis is to Great Britain—its loftiest and lordliest mountain. It is true that Ben Macdhui for a time, erecting itself as it were a-tiptoe in the eagerness of its rivalry, disputed pre-eminence of altitude with our own grand old Ben, but the last Ordnance Survey knocked the Aberdeenshire mountain's pretensions finally and for ever on the head, and, on the strictest scientific calculations, declared Ben Nevis to be, *facile princeps*, the lord and king of British mountains; not merely *primus inter pares*, observe, like a moderator of a synod or assembly of the kirk, but *primus altissimus* literally and absolutely; fully, besides, and curiously enough corroborating the correctness of the local traditions that, by a sort of infallible instinct, not uncommon in such matters, had without question or doubt so regarded it for many ages. We may now, then, adopt as applicable to our own burly Ben the chant of the Spirit in *Manfred* :—

> " Ben Nevis is monarch of mountains :
> They crown'd him long ago
> On a throne of rocks, in a robe of clouds,
> With a diadem of snow."

Now, on the top of this the highest of British mountains, we are to have a meteorological observatory, and that a set of meteorological instruments at such an altitude from year's end to year's end will, after a while, tell us many an interesting and curious story of weather shiftings and changings is unquestionable; but who is to be resident keeper of the instruments? *quis custodiet ipsos custodes?* He must, in a very literal sense indeed, be *up* to his work. He must be sound in lungs and limbs, and all the rest of it, and even when, after careful selection, you have got him up there, it is not of every one, mind you, that it can with confidence be said that he is the right man in the right place. Let us suppose, however, that after some little seeking the right man is got, with the *mens sana (et meteorologica) in corpore sano*, we have still one little hint to offer to the patrons of the exalted undertaking before they send their man to do battle at such an altitude with the demons of fog, and frost, and cloud, and rain, and snow, and storm, and solitude. And the hint that we would venture to offer is this—they shall insist upon it that the observer, for his own personal comfort, and in view of certain not improbable eventualities, shall, before his ascent, have his hair cropped, as closely cropped, please, as scissors can crop it, and be clean shaved, without a vestige of moustache or beard on lip, or cheek, or chin —all hirsute and capillary appendages, in short, however ornamental at the sea level, are to be eschewed as highly inconvenient and *de trop* on a mountain summit of such altitude as Ben Nevis.

What do you mean? the reader will very naturally ask, and in order to make ourselves fully understood in the matter, we must beg to be allowed to briefly summarise a story which will be found told at length, and very admirably told, in a letter to Sir David Brewster, published in the third volume of the *Edinburgh Journal of Science*. Know, then, good readers, that some forty-five or fifty years ago the late Rev. Dr. Macvicar of Moffat, a gentleman of many and varied accomplishments, as well as a sound and popular preacher, while yet a young man, and accompanied by Sir Walter Trevelyan, who still survives, and some other friends, made an ascent of Ben Nevis. It was on a hot and somewhat hazy day in June, about the worst month in the year, let us observe *par parenthèse*, for the ascent of any Scottish mountain. About mid-day, and only a little while after they had got to the top, a snow-shower from the south-west swept angrily over the mountain. While this shower lasted a singular noise was heard on all sides, a sort of hissing and crackling such as proceeds from a point on an excited prime conductor or a strongly charged Leyden jar. This hissing and crackling in all directions continued for upwards of an hour and a half, and clearly indicated the emission of pencils of electric light, which very probably would have been visible to the eye had the day been only a little cloudier and darker than it was. The electric discharge was noticed on an umbrella belonging to one of the party, as well as on almost all the sharp-pointed rocks around. Sir Walter Trevelyan, who seems to have lagged behind in the ascent, happened to reach the summit just as the electric phenomena were most pronounced. He was carrying his hat in his hand at the moment, and his companions were not a little astonished to see his hair and beard standing stiff and erect on end—an additional evidence, if additional evidence were needed, of the activity of the electric emission. Standing round the cairn, the other gentlemen of the party also uncovered, and the beautiful phenomena of electric attraction and repulsion were at once perceived on their hair and beards as well as on Trevelyan's. The hissing noise indicated that the electric fluid was positive, and was streaming from the mountain in pencil-jets characteristic of that state.

Now let the reader imagine, as best he can, the unenviable condition of a poor man subjected for weeks and months to the active electric currents that in some form or other are probably in everlasting play about the summit of our monarch Ben. If a longhaired and full-bearded man, just fancy what his appearance must be when the electric jets are at their liveliest. He is a married man, let us suppose, and on some fine day his wife ascends to pay him a visit at his giddy observatory. Hearing her voice outside his hut of solid and Cyclopean architecture—and solid and Cyclopean it must needs be if it is to stand at all —he rushes forth to meet her, and as in his ardour he advances to embrace her, she stares in horror and aghast at the aspect of a man more like a raving maniac just escaped from the tortures of some cruel asylum than the sane and sedate husband of their sea-level home.

Of his whilom petted and well-kempt locks that were wont to carry their "shed" so evenly and to lie so smoothly, lo! each particular hair now stands stiff on end, "like quills upon the fretful porcupine," while of his moustache and beard, once so glossy and flowing, and of which, in happier if less *exalted* days, both were wont to be so proud, each separate hair stands out stiff and strong, and sharp of point, as was the bristle on the back of the Caledonian boar that, as he measured its length from tail to snout with naked foot, wounded the great Fingalian *Diarmaid* to the death. As he still advances, and bends his head in order to salute her, she screams in terror, as well she may, for there is about his head and face a crackling and hissing as of thorns aburning, with now and again a shower of sparks and miniature jets of vivid fire, such as leap from the glowing bar that the smith, with brawny arm and heavy hammer, beats upon his anvil! He would, nevertheless, probably still endeavour to clasp the wife of his bosom in his arms, despite her terror and screams; but suddenly he halts, stammering and staggering in utter amazement, for the electric currents have by this time found their way into *her* as well as into him, and there she stands before him a living Leyden jar, surcharged with the subtle fluid, until at all points she is neither more nor less than a hissing, crackling, spark-emitting electric machine! *Her* hair, too, erst so sleek and silken, now stands up stiff and erect as a tuft of heather, while her jaunty little hat, with its ostrich-plume adornment, trembles atop a full yard above the head it was meant—partially at least—to cover! The distracted husband——but no! let us drop the curtain, a curtain of Lochaber mist, on a scene which may be imagined without much mental effort, but which no pen can adequately describe. Of this, one thing, however, you may be sure enough—before that loving pair can embrace in anything like comfort, they must descend half-way down the mountain, so as to be somewhat out of the way of the direct action of the electric currents.

But expunging so heart-rending a picture (there is at present a protest against what is called "dismal" art—a protest in which we heartily join) from the mental retina, let us suppose that the Ben Nevis top meteorological observer is not a married man at all, but a full-bearded bachelor, ambitious of scientific honours and *ennuyé* with the humdrum conventionalities of sea-level life. Your observer then is, we shall suppose, a bachelor, and, if a bachelor, the chances are any number of hundreds to one that he has left behind him, for the present, on a lower level, some one whom he delights to think of, even on that sterile mountain top, as his "little bunch of roses," and who, in her turn, ceases not day nor night to think with fond and affectionate regard of her lover up there in his cloudy altitudes, chained, so to speak, to the rocky summit of Britain's highest mountain by his devotion to science, like Prometheus on Caucasus, with, however, not a love-sent vulture gnawing at his liver, but rather a Venus-commissioned dove, emblem of love! gently pecking at—tickling rather than really hurting—a far more interesting organ, his heart. Can anything be more certain than that in such a case his ladye-love, or some complaisant matron in her behalf, gets up a picnic party of half-a-dozen of their mutually most intimate and particular friends to visit the interesting hermit in his lonely solitude? Some fine morning shouts of merry laughter, sweet and musical as the chime of silver bells, startle the hermit as, resting on his left knee, he is in the act of blowing the fire in order to get his morning pannikin of coffee aboil. His heart responds to the silveriest chord in that laughter peal with a bound; he throws the Laodicean pannikin into the dark shadow of one of the foundation boulders of his hut; he rushes forth to receive his visitors, and as these gather in an admiring circle round him, the echoes of that mountain altitude, that never before responded to anything cheerier than the scream of the eagle, are now startled into glad reverberation of the clapping of a dozen lily hands, and the silvery laughter of half-a-dozen of the prettiest girls in Lochaber, now prettier than ever with their cheeks aglow with their morning climb, and their own Ben Nevis for a pedestal! After a while some of the party scatter among the boulders to collect rare lichens, or such other curiosities as may fall in their way; others make bold enough to enter the hut to have a look at the display of Negretti and Zambra's instruments, ranged along the walls; while in a few minutes, and by the merest accident, of course, the observer finds himself close by the side of *one* young lady of the party, "themselves, by themselves two," as the Spaniards phrase it, and separated from the rest by the whole height and breadth of the *cairn*. Meantime, however, unknown to them all and unthought of, *mons parturiit*, the mountain is in labour, and the birth is neither a "ridiculous mouse" on the one hand, nor a volcanic eruption on the other, but an active discharge of streams and pencil jets of positive electricity, and as the faces of the pair behind the cairn approach each other by an attraction *not* electrical, there is, ere their lips have met, a crack as of an exploded percussion cap, and from the tip of the observer's nose right into the tip of the same organ (of delicate and Grecian outline) on the face of his companion, there darts with a hiss and a crackling a vivid spark of fire that makes the young lady draw back her head with a little scream and a shudder as if she had been shot. With a terrified glance at her lover, whose hair and beard——But *halte là!* and again no! we cannot finish this picture any more than the other. The imaginative reader, giving free play to his fancy, must finish it for himself.

CHAPTER XXXV.

Comfortable condition of the People at Term-time—The old Quern Hand-mill or *Bràth*—The *Cnotag* or *Eòrnachan*, the Knockin'-Stane or Pot-Barley Preparer—Knockin'-Stane Stick and Sword Combat.

ALTHOUGH November, up to this date, has been abundantly cold and stormy, with frequent snow showers on the mountains and over the moorland wilds, it has been fairly bright and dry along the seaboard; the winds having been mainly from the east, a quarter whence at this season of the year we may safely enough look for storm and cold and snow, but which as a rule does not give us that wintry rain which, in the form of sleet and slush, makes everything so disagreeable, and which rarely fails to bring influenza, " colds " in every form, and *catarrh*—that last, by the way, good reader, being to our thinking the very ugliest word to look at that can be printed, as what it means is one of the most trying ailments, short of mortal disease, that a human being can suffer under. Under meteorological conditions, which must be set down as exceedingly favourable, when compared with the state of matters elsewhere over the kingdom, people have been able to wind up their harvest operations satisfactorily enough; and for the winter, come as it may, it is pleasant to know that everybody is fairly well prepared; for, adverse, and even hopeless at times, as was the state of matters during the season of growth, things turned out latterly so much better than was expected, that the land in due time largely yielded her increase, and now, thank God, instead of anything like dearth, there is abundance. Matters assumed a still brighter aspect when it was found that at Fort-William market on Wednesday last the price of all kinds of cattle, instead of being largely "down," as was expected, was on the contrary high and well sustained throughout. With abundant and well secured crops, therefore, followed by good local markets, our people are about as well off this year as ever we knew them. They will pay their rents not only without complaint or murmur, but with the greatest good humour and cheerfulness, having wherewithal besides to pay their honest debts otherwise, and to pass the winter in comparative comfort and ease, grateful to a beneficent Providence the while, like the sensible and pious people they unquestionably are.

We are old enough to remember having seen the old and venerable *quern* or hand-mill—the Gaelic *Bràth*—in actual use on more than one occasion in our early boyhood. This was in Morven upwards of forty long years ago. Very many of our readers connected with the Hebrides, and with those districts of the mainland remotest from direct communication with the south, must perfectly recollect seeing the same little machine in daily use for the supply of that famous *graddaned* meal, which was so sweet to the taste, and on a plentiful allowance of which, in various forms, was reared a peasantry remarkable for their symmetry and strength, and not less remarkable for a state of robust health that seldom knew any serious ailment even into the decrepitude of extreme old age. It was only when meal-mills driven by water-power became sufficiently numerous over the country, with their " thirlage," their " multures," and their " sequels," firmly secured to them under order of the lairds and others in authority, that the *quern* fell first into disrepute, and quickly into total disuse, partly because, under the mill and thirlage " customs," its use became in a manner illegal, but mainly because the *graddan* quern meal, although abundantly palatable and sweet to the taste, was nevertheless both darker in colour and coarser in grain than was the produce from the self-same corn as turned out by the water-mill, with its greater power and more complicated machinery. Quern stones only survive in our days as objects of some antiquarian interest, and just rare enough to be worth a few shillings in the archæological market. We have recently had brought under our notice a very handsome specimen of an implement of allied use with the quern in the shape of a knockin'-stane, as it was called in the south and east of Scotland—the Gaelic cnotag of the mainland—the *eórnachan* of the Hebrides. This particular specimen of the knockin'-stane is an almost square block of the Syenite of the district, some sixteen inches in length, fifteen inches in breadth, and about the same in thickness. The centre is hollowed out to a depth of some twelve inches, in the shape of an inverted truncated cone, about ten inches in diameter at the mouth, and very gradually lessening downwards, until its bottom diameter is something like six or seven inches. This

Syenite mortar must weigh considerally over a hundredweight. It was used in the old times for husking barley in, so as to make it fit for pleasant comminglement with other materials in the preparation of broth, a dish for which the people of Scotland have always had a huge liking, and which they delight to have presented to them "thick and slab." The Gaelic verb signifying to husk or shell pulse or corn is *cnot*, so that the appellation cnotag, by which the "knockin'-stane" was known to the Gaels of the mainland, signifies the husker or husking machine. The *eórnachan* of the Hebrides is of course from *eórna*, barley, and, more pointedly than cnotag, indicates the proper use of the implement, the (pot) barley preparer. In preparing their pot-barley, a handful or two of the thrashed out grain was first hand-dried and browned on a thin sheet of iron over the fire, or, more simply, before the red embers of a brisk fire on the hearthstone. When sufficiently hard and brown, it was thrown into the cavity of the cnotag, and smartly poked at, and rapidly swirled about with a short, stout cnotag-stick—*maide cnotaig*—until in a few minutes the grain was separated from its husks, which, having been fannered or winnowed in small quantities by the breath of the operator, until the husks were all blown aside, and nothing but the grain remained, it was ready for use as one of the most important ingredients in the preparation of a broth that must be of considerable substantiality and "body," as the wine merchants say, or it is worthless. The weak, watery soups of the modern dinner-table, "white" or "brown," your genuine Highlander of the past (and, *entre nous*, perhaps of the present) would turn up his nose as at a thing of nought, because of its too much fluidity, and deficiency in honest weight and substantiality. The cnotag or husking mortar was sometimes of wood, necessarily a large block, round or square, which, when not in use, was usually turned upside down, and made a capital winter night's seat in some cozy corner by the ingle. A specimen of a genuine wooden block cnotag would be very interesting, and, archæologically, extremely valuable, as they were much less common than the stone mortars, stone being preferred not only as the more lasting material, and that did not require to be of such bulk as the wooden implement, but because the husking operation was quicker, and easier, and more perfect in every way when the work was done, not as between wood and wood, but as between wood and stone. It may easily be understood how the working of a wooden pestle in a wooden mortar must be less satisfactory in the husking of any kind of grain, than the same work as done by a wooden pestle in a mortar of stone. Hence it is that wooden block cnotags were less common than those of stone, and are now so extremely rare, that we have ourselves never seen even a single specimen, although we have had a description of them from old people who had seen them in proper use, and had sat upon them when, bottom upwards, they were used as stools by the winter fire. The place for the cnotag of stone, on the contrary—also turned upside down when not in use—was close by the door outside, a convenient support for the gudewife's washing-boyne, or in the summer a ready seat for " granny," when, in the words of Pliny, "taking the benefit of the sun," her grandchildren meanwhile romping about her knees. Quern stones are comparatively common, because, be it remembered, there were necessarily *two* stones to each quern, and because every family having corn to grind required its own especial quern. Wooden cnotags are, for the reasons above stated, extremely rare, if, indeed, there is at this moment any known specimen in existence. Nor are even stone cnotags at all common, for the reason mainly that they never were common in any broad sense of that term. Instead of each family having a cnotag of its own, as was the case with a bit of rude machinery in almost constant use like the quern, the cnotag was usually the property in common of a whole hamlet, one amply sufficing for the pot-barley wants of a score, or twice a score, of neighbouring families. Why, nevertheless, it may be asked, do we not meet with them more frequently than we do? for even if we allow only a single cnotag to each hamlet, they ought to turn up oftener than they do. The secret of their almost total disappearance lies in the fact that, being usually squared blocks of granite or whinstone, necessarily of considerable size and weight, they were used for building purposes, when shops having multiplied throughout the land, and the pot-barley of commerce could be had—a month's supply of it—for a few pence, or in exchange for a couple of dozen of eggs, then, indeed, was Othello's occupation gone, the cnotag was no longer required for its original purpose, and it was readily utilised, *quantum valeat*, for building purposes, for which, from its size and shape, it was admirably adapted. We have no doubt at all that in the corners or lower tiers of the front or gable of at least one cottage in most hamlets there is hidden away a granite or whinstone cnotag, if we only knew where to look for them. The cnotag-stick, or pestle, seems to have been peculiarly shaped, and must have been a formidable weapon; for in one of the old sgeulachds or fireside tales of the West Highlands, the hero of the story is represented as on one occasion bravely encountering a giant who had invaded his dwelling, the giant, after a fierce fight, getting the worst of it at the hands of the Gille Maol Ciar, as the hero was called, although his only weapon, so suddenly was he attacked, was the maide-cnotaig, or husking-mortar pestle, which fortunately at the moment lay ready to his hand. A somewhat more modern story describes a celebrated witch "of the period" as riding from Knoidart to Harris on an "Eórnachan-stick" (eadar Cnoidart, 's na h-Erradh a marcachd air maid' Eórnachain),—and why not? There is no good reason that we know of why a husking-mortar pestle with a witch astride should not be quite as swift and willing a steed for the nonce as the conventional broomstick itself. In an MS. collection of old Gaelic poems in our possession there is a very ludicrous song all about a laird who, in the days when lairds still wore their native garb, with the indispensable sword and dagger, had occasion to confess that a "cnotag-stick," wielded by a brawny arm, was no contemptible weapon, whether of offence or defence.

The song tells how the laird, having had to find fault with one of his smaller tenants, resolved to visit him at his house, and give such a blowing-up for some misdemeanour of which he was supposed to be guilty as might deter him from ever doing the like again. The man was at home, occupied at the moment in weaving a peat creel. He bluntly disavowed all knowledge of or participation in the alleged misdemeanour, and gesticulated wildly in confirmation of his innocence. The laird got very angry at what he believed to be sheer contumacy and defiance, and in his wrath drew his sword. The man laid hold in self-defence of the weapon readiest to hand, which chanced to be the " maid' córnachan " or cnotag-stick. A furious combat ensued, most ludicrously described, the result being that the laird had to turn his back ingloriously, and take to his heels; the cnotag-stick warrior shouting after him in derision :—

> " Theich thu, 's cha b' fhiach thu,
>   A shiochaire ghingaich !
>   Faire, faire ort a ghaisgich !
>   Gus am paisg mi thu a'm spliucan ! "

("Thou hast had to run ingloriously, thou worthless one ;
  Thou splay-footed starveling !
Better stop, O thou most doughty one !
  That I may wrap thee up, tobacco-wise, in my spleuchan !")

The idea of calling upon his frightened laird to stop in order that he might twist him up like an ounce of tobacco, and lay him so twisted in the odoriferous recesses of his sealskin spleuchan, is admirable for its grim humour and utter contempt for everything like lairdic dignity and authority. This very amusing composition seems, from internal evidence, to be connected with the island of Mull.

The particular cnotag which has thus formed the text for a longer dissertation than we had intended was discovered here during the early summer of the present year. Its history has been easily traced as the cnotag or husking-mortar of the Mackenzies of North Ballachulish for many generations. Its age cannot well be less than two hundred years, and it may very possibly be much older. It has recently found its way, through our distinguished friend Sir Robert Christison, Bart., to the National Antiquarian Museum.

CHAPTER XXXVI.

November Meteor Showers—Occultation of Stars—Superstition—Old-Wife Herbalist—How a Cow was rescued from the effects of the Evil Eye—Virtue of an Oatmeal Bannock—Fox caught sleeping—Badgers.

THERE is no longer any doubt about it: winter is down upon us in snell and surly earnest. The hills are covered with snow down to the water line, while sleet and snow showers, fierce and furious, descend upon us from the north-west with all the intensity of cold derivable from recent contact with the glacier mountains of Greenland and the thick-ribbed ice-fields of the palæocrystic sea. We were duly at our post on the night of the 13th or 14th, and a bitterly cold night it was, but the drift of clouds was too widespread and too continuous to permit us to see anything of the meteor showers due on that date, if, indeed, meteor showers there were to be seen. About midnight it cleared up a little in the south-east, and two or three "falling stars" of average brilliancy were recorded, but they were only such falling stars as may be seen on any winter night that the stars are visible at all, and the probability is that there was no meteoric display of any consequence to be seen, even if the weather had been as favourable for observation as it was very much the contrary. On the night of the 10th there was an occultation by the moon of the Pleiades, or, to speak more correctly, of some of the more notable stars in that beautiful group. The sky was fortunately clear from about nine o'clock till midnight, so that, by the aid of a fairly good telescope, a very satisfactory observation was made of the immersion and emersion of the occulted stars. Almost as interesting as the occultations themselves was the near approach of several other stars to the edge of the moon. as full-orbed and round she hung like a shield of burnished silver in the midnight sky. There will be no other occultation of any consequence during the present year.

A friendly correspondent—a Lochaber man born and bred—sends us an interesting letter about the *Cailleach Lusraigean*, or old-wife herbalist, of whom, as our readers will recollect, we had occasion to make " honourable mention," as they say at the agricultural shows, in a " Nether Lochaber " of recent date. Our correspondent is old enough to remember her as a personage of wide and somewhat uncanny reputation throughout Lochaber and the neighbouring districts, though it is but justice to her memory to state that if at times she encouraged and promoted what seemed to her to be suitable and likely enough love-matches by ways and means that, closely examined, were of but questionable propriety, she also frequently used her influence and skill in preventing such alliances as she was persuaded were undesirable, if not improper, and likely only to lead the parties concerned into an aftertime of misery and want. According to our correspondent's recollection of her reputation throughout the country in his boyhood, he is inclined to believe that she was an exceedingly shrewd and clever old dame, who had many good points about her, and was more useful than people will now-a-days readily believe, in the happy adjustment of many little matters in which nobody else, perhaps, could interfere to any good purpose. Our correspondent tells us the following bit of curious superstition, of which he himself was an eye-witness, and of which the *cailleach* herbalist was the hierophant. It happened on a certain occasion that a cow belonging to his uncle yielded but little milk, and that little so *wersh* and watery as to be of little or no value. It was clear enough that something was wrong, though what that something was it was difficult for the uninitiated to discover, for the cow was abundantly fed, and apparently in lusty enough health. It was at last suggested by a " wise " neighbour that the animal was probably under the spell of an " evil eye," and it was resolved to apply to *Mairi 'n Eirinnich* (the Irishman's Mary—so called because she had been married to an Irishman; she was herself a native of the island of Barra) for advice and aid as to the best way of counteracting and neutralising the evil influence at work in the case of a cow that up to that occasion had borne the character of being one of the best milkers in the country. Mary, like our learned sheriffs when the cause before them is of more than ordinary gravity and importance, took the case to *avizandum*, and it was only after full and careful consideration of the matter in all its bearings that she decided what was best to be done. She sent for our correspondent's aunt, who usually attended upon and milked the cow, and to her she gave the following directions. She was to knead a large circular *bannock* of oatmeal bread, and in the centre of this bannock, when duly baked and fired, she was to knock a circular hole of a given diameter. Holding the bannock thus centrally perforated in her left hand at milking time, she was to direct the stream of milk from the teats in succession into the pail *through the central hole*, and this she was instructed to do for nine days consecutively; and our correspondent has a perfect recollection of seeing his aunt milking the cow, bannock in hand, in the curious manner stated. He is unfortunately unable to say positively whether *Mairi 'n Eirinnich's* cure was successful or otherwise in neutralising the evil spell, or how the matter ended; but he thinks it probable that the cow gradually recovered her character as a bountiful milker, and that the herb-wife got the credit of it all. From inquiries made in various likely places since the receipt of the above communication, we find that, in the popular superstition of the Highlands, an oatmeal bannock was deemed of sovereign efficacy in the prevention of many such evils as people were supposed to be liable to from across the dim and shadowy borderlands of the mysterious and supernatural. Thus, a bannock suspended above the door of the apartment in which a recently born babe and mother lay was accounted a safeguard against such pranks as the *Men of Peace*, or fairies, might be disposed to play with both or either. The pungent odour of a bit of oatcake toasted close to the fire, until it smoked and burned, was supposed to be so disagreeable to evil spirits of every kind, that they cleared out of a dwelling *en masse* under the force of this very simple and very easy rite of purification. An unbroken oatcake bannock laid on the pillow beside a sleeper was a sure and certain prevention of nightmare and evil dreams, while a ship at sea was considered tolerably safe from lightning-stroke and fire-bolt if only, when the thunder-storm came on, an oaten cake was suspended somewhere in the rigging. Up to the present day it is accounted unwise to leave any kneaded dough in the lump unbaked. Whatever is once kneaded must be made into bannocks, and, if possible, fired before the family retire for the night, otherwise evil spirits, with more or less power for mischief, will make themselves busy about the dwelling till sunrise. A highly intelligent old lady in a neighbouring district tells us that when she was a girl—some seventy years ago—her grandmother was in the habit of sewing a small bit of oat-cake into the breasts of the bodices of herself and sisters four times in the year, namely, on Beltane Eve, Midsummer Eve, Hallowe'en, and on Candlemas Eve. The cake, our informant said, was in this case specially baked for the occasion, and always with some "carvy" (caraway) seeds intermixed with the oatmeal. It was meant as a safeguard and charm against "evil," but what particular form of evil she doesn't know. She thinks it was probably meant as a safeguard against evil in every shape—*gach seors' uile.* These bits of oatcakes were left sewed up in each girl's bodice till their return from church on the Sunday following, when they were taken out and burned in the fire. These superstitions as to the sanctity and virtue of bread and fire are very curious, and deserving more particular consideration than we can at present bestow upon them. To the thoughtful student they speak of very remote times, and of other and far distant lands, for they point very unmistakeably, as we think, to the ancient worship of Ceres and the fire-worshippers of the East.

To catch a weasel asleep is proverbially an impossibility, and one would think that to catch a cunning hill fox napping might be set down as something equally unlikely. No instance of the capture of a somnolent weasel is, we suppose, on record, but that a fox may be caught fairly off his guard, however rarely, is abundantly testified by the following story, recently communicated to us by a gentleman in Badenoch. We had better let our friend tell the story in his own way :—" While a shepherd of the name of Alexander Campbell, from Dalwhinnie, was on his rounds on the 20th October (Sunday, which was a very windy day), he came on a full-grown fox *asleep*, and, after a hand-to-hand struggle, managed to secure him. He was a very fine specimen of the male fox, in exceedingly fine coat, and very fat, which perhaps accounts for his drowsiness. It may perhaps be urged that he was wounded, but no such thing ; his four pads were as whole as possible, and his being in good condition shows that he was otherwise all right. He was lying in a bed of dry moss, in the shelter of a little tuft of heather. This, as nearly as possible, takes the pith out of our old Scotch proverb, ' Catch a weasel asleep.' I am sorry to say that the man gave him such a beating with his stick before he captured him that he died soon afterwards. How do you acccount for his sleeping so soundly, and being so taken off his guard ?"

Our correspondent himself has about hit the right nail on the head. The fox was in comfortable condition, fat, and of course all the more tired with his early morning wanderings, in which he had doubtless fared sumptuously; a case of *furtum grave*, depend upon it, though it probably lay light enough on his conscience. The spot in which he was caught napping is, we may be sure, though our correspondent does not say so, rarely trodden by human foot—never before, perhaps, by that shepherd himself. The day was stormy, and the wind over heather and bent made wild music. The shepherd probably advanced not *with* but *against* the wind, and his trusty stick was in lively contact with the sleeper's head while poor Reynard was still revelling in all the joys of an imaginary chase and stalk through the fair fields of happy dreamland. A curious proof, by the way, how common badgers were at one time in the Highlands, and how comparatively rare were foxes, is to be found in the fact that we have no proper specific word for foxhunter in Gaelic, for the man, that is, whose profession and business it is to trap, and kill, and keep down foxes on our sheep farms as best he may. Such a man is to this day called a *Brocair*, literally the *badger*-man or *badger*-killer, though now-a-days and for long his business is to kill foxes, which are common, not badgers, which are rare.

CHAPTER XXXVII.

Intense cold—Bird-Pensioners in frost and snow—Their tameness—Fond of Scraps of Flesh and picking Bones—Stupidity of Cochin-China Cock—Cochin-Chinas and Bantams—Ninth Ode of First Book of Horace done into English.

Not for upwards of a quarter of a century has there been a winter of equal severity in the West Highlands. So intense has been the frost, and so continuous, that not only has "the owl, for all his feathers," been acold, but all our wild-birds, even the hardiest and most active, such as the thrushes and finches, have suffered terribly, hundreds having already died miserably from sheer cold and hunger, while the survivors can only limp about in sad and sorry plight, mere skin and bone, so perfectly stupid, too, as to be utterly heedless of danger from prowling cat or circling hawk. And when a bird is brought to *that* state, that cat or hawk, or stoat or weasel may have him if they like, and he will make little or no effort to escape, there is no more to be said; then may you believe, beyond all question or doubt, that his case is desperate indeed. We certainly never did see our feathered friends and favourites in such a plight before. We have on several successive mornings picked them up off the ground in our own high-walled and well-sheltered garden, as well as in a neighbouring copse, in which, some time during the night, they had dropped down dead off their perch; and we have, in quite a score of instances, found them dead on the branch, to which their feet were frozen hard and fast, in which case, however, death was to them a real mercy, for it probably reached them as they slept the profound and dreamless sleep of those whose blood is curdled in their veins by intensity of cold. Had they awakened to the cold grey light of the morning, with their feet frozen to the bough, they must have died a still more miserable, because a more painfully conscious and lingering death. We notice that in hundreds of cases the survivors are limping about lame from frost-bitten feet and toes; many of these, too, must die, while those that see the spring and early summer will see it crippled and deformed, and have but little chance in the battles of love and life with those that have the good fortune to survive the winter without hurt or loss of limb.

If we bring our meteorological tables under minute inspection, we shall no doubt find that once or twice, or even thrice, during the past five-and-twenty years the cold, thermometrically appraised, has been quite as intense as during the present winter; but the severest winter, be it understood, is beyond all question that which is most detrimental to animal and vegetable life—that which bears hardest on the well-being of living organisms; and, looking at it from this stand-point, it is questionable, from all the inquiries we have been able to make on the subject, if we have had a winter of equal severity—in the West Highlands at least—for upwards of fifty years. A winter is severe when the fall of snow is universal over a district or kingdom—not necessarily of great depth, but to be found everywhere from the highest mountain summits down to the sea level, and to the last tide-mark of the sea itself. When this snow is instantly caught and fixed and bound down by intense and long-continued frost down to or below zero, then the earth becomes hard and cruel of heart, as if it had been turned into one mass of solid iron; and it matters little—less at all events than might be supposed—whether the average reading of the thermometer is 5° or 35° below the freezing-point, for with a frost-bound earth and temperature long-continued at and below freezing-point, animal life must instantly begin to suffer, and where the vitality is weakest, death, *cæteris paribus*, will first ensue. Usually, in ordinary winters in the West Highlands, the feeling of cold is rather to be characterised as the negative of heat than anything else. It is as if you had been sitting in a room in which the fire had almost or altogether gone out, and you felt it uncomfortable in consequence. It is a feeling of a something that was pleasant being now amissing, rather than the actual presence of a something else of a totally different character and essence. The cold of this winter has been of a very different sort, not a mere negative of heat, but a positive, palpable, tangible cold, keen and cutting as a sword-blade; or, as a man had on Handsel Monday morning observed to us, it was sharp-pointed, and seemed, on the swirl of a north-east wind, as determined to penetrate as a gimlet (*Air chuairtaig na gaoith tuaithe, tha'm fuachd an diu', le'r ceud, cho biorach ris a ghimleid!*) It is with cold of this kind that animal vitality finds it so difficult to combat successfully. We notice that on a calm, or comparatively calm day, no matter how really cold it is, some scores of feathered pensioners whom we feed twice a day with bread crumbs and table scraps, although they pick up our *largesse* eagerly enough, are yet a little shy of us, scattering on the slightest alarm, and taking refuge in the neighbouring trees and hedges until they begin to think that the danger is past, and that they may return in safety. When, however, it is a day of intense and *piercing* cold, that is, a cold day with high winds, razor-edged and keen, our feathered friends act very differently. The cold then seems so to penetrate and interpenetrate their very being, heart and brain and marrow, that they lose all sense of fear; they will pick the crumbs from between our feet and off our open palm, and if we walk outside, and for a moment cease feeding them, they will follow us in all directions, the boldest—that is, the coldest and hungriest—alighting on our head and shoulders, as if to expostulate with us on the impropriety and cruelty of keeping our dole in our pockets, instead of scattering it around with a liberal hand as usual. These pensioners consist of blackbirds, thrushes, chaffinches, grey wagtails, wrens, ox-eye tits, and hedge and house sparrows, and occasional stragglers of other and rarer species. That all of these should greedily pick up bread crumbs and other table scraps in these hard times is not wonderful, but we were not a little surprised the other day to see them all, without exception, pounce upon a shoulder of mutton bone which we had just thrown out upon the frozen snow, believing that it would be esteemed a *bonne bouche* only by the blackbirds and thrushes. The bone had still a good deal of flesh adhering to it, which, however, we were careful to cut and carve into as rough and ragged a state as possible, that the birds might the more easily manage the picking of it. All of them, finches and buntings as well as the more carnivorous insect-eaters, instantly fastened upon it like a pack of famished hounds, wrestling and tumbling over each other in their eagerness to share in what must have been to them a really delicious feast, for in less than an hour the bone was picked clean—as devoid of every shred and particle of flesh and cartilage as the parlour poker. In feeding these birds from day to day, one curious thing we observed was how stupid in some respects are domesticated animals as compared with their wild congeners. A huge feather-legged Cochin-China cock sometimes found its way to the parlour window as we were in the act of feeding our wild-bird pensioners. When we threw out a plateful of crumbs and scraps, all the other birds gobbled up their food very fast by going shrewdly and sensibly to work, each selecting bit after bit of a suitable size, to be instantly swallowed with little or no trouble, wrens, finches, and thrushes only taking up such bits as they very plainly judged were suitable to their individual powers of deglutition. It was amusing, however, to see the stupidity of the big Cochin-China. He greedily pounced upon a big bit, so big that he could not swallow it, and rather than let it drop in order to pick up a more suitable and sizeable bit, he invariably stuck to it, like a fool as he was, and is, and will be to the end of the chapter; straining and striving to swallow it until you feared he would inevitably choke himself in the attempt, all the time walking about on the snow with uncertain steps, and his eyes as if they would start out of his head, like a bagpiper who would fain strike up a merry lilt, but who finds his drones and chanter at sixes and sevens in defiance of all the wind with which he can supply their ear-splitting discordance. The idea never seemed once to enter the head of the stupid Cochin, that by taking up smaller and more manageable bits he would be much the gainer in the long run; for when, after terrible straining and striving, the bit in his throat had become at length compressed and lubricated enough to be swallowed outright, and he looked round for more, there was no more for him; the wiser wild-birds had, by a very different process to his, finished it all up even to the smallest crumb, so that there was none remaining, and the Cochin-China had to stalk about in the snow, looking very disconsolate and foolish, and yet manifestly unable to see wherein his foolishness lay, for the next time he got the chance he acted in a precisely similar and equally stupid way. The fact seems to be that, while many animals gain in *nous* and intelligence by domestication, others, notably of birds the gallinaceous tribe, become stupider and less sagacious every way than in their wild state; and of all feathered creatures the male Cochin China, and his first cousin, the Brahmapootra, are, we take it, far and away the most absurdly stupid and least intelligent, the most cowardly, too, and the most ungallant, their most prominent characteristic being a stupid, awkward selfishness, that frequently receives its just reward, when the very hens of their own particular species, provoked by their loutishness and general incapacity, turn round upon them and give them a sound thrashing. It is not a little curious that the *Bantam*, also from the East Indies, and a compatriot and countryman, so to speak, of these same "feckless loons," should be, on the contrary, a remarkably intelligent bird, and as gallant and plucky as it is intelligent. We had one of these little fellows some years ago, weighing but a pound and a half, and if Cochin or Pootra, of five times his weight, dare even to look at him otherwise than submissively and respectfully, he was at the offender like a flash of lightning, drubbing him round and round the yard, until the cowardly lout crouched down exhausted by his splay-footed gallopade, with only strength and sense enough left in him to thrust his head into a wall crevice, under the bottom of a shut door, or into a bunch of nettles, so as to save it from further punishment, while the plucky little Bantam marched back to the ladies of the harem with a lofty step and air of self-importance and pride such as Napoleon may have worn on the eve of Austerlitz. The reader will, perhaps, laugh at us for making the confession, but it is the truth all the same, that even on the table the flesh of these big louts is less palatable to us than that of other fowls, mainly, we do believe, because we have so often been annoyed at the cowardice, ungallantry, and other demerits of the living bird.

None of the Odes of Horace has, perhaps, been so frequently quoted as the famous Ninth Ode of the First Book, beginning—

"Vides, ut alta stet nive candidum
Soracte, nec jam sustineant onus
Sylvae laborantes," &c.

In severe winters, when the snow lies deep and the frost is keen, it is almost impossible to avoid quoting more or less of this charming lyric, a polished gem, with a *raison d'être* and a philosophy that concerns all, and that all can understand; so exquisitely perfect as a lyric that no amount of quoting, the severest of all tests, perhaps, in the case of such compositions, can render it commonplace or vulgar. The Ninth Ode has been rendered into English verse by some of our best poets and most successful translators; but in all such renderings with which we have any acquaintance, much of the subtle humour and charming *naiveté* of the original is lost. It is one of those lyrical gems so absolutely perfect that it cannot be adequately translated into another language—certainly not into English. The nearest approach that we have seen to the exquisite Horatian touches so characteristic of the original, is curiously enough in the letter of a sporting correspondent of the *Field*, in a recent number of that popular journal. It is, however, rather a paraphrase than a translation, but the following lines are Horatian all over:—

> "Behold with rime Soracte's top is crown'd,
> The woods are bending with their weight of snow:
> The rivers in an icy trance are bound
>   And cease to flow.
> Come, thaw the cold: pile logs of wood on high
> Upon the blazing hearth—with liberal hand,
> Old wine, my friend, from cobwebb'd bins supply—
>   The choicest brand!"

CHAPTER XXXVIII.

Old Gaelic Rhyme, Meaning of—Golden Eagle at Kelvingrove Museum, Glasgow—Golden Eagle on the wing—Circling *Sguir-na-Ciche* of Glencoe—The Epithet *Chrysaëtos* first applied to it by Aristotle—Its predominant Colour—Professor Geddes of Aberdeen—His *Problem of the Homeric Poems.*

ALTHOUGH not quite so hyperborean as it was, the weather is still cold enough and stormy enough for the last week in January, usually a mild period with us here on the shores of the Linnhe Loch. The pleasant thaw of the middle of the month came not a moment too soon, for things were beginning to look serious even in our part of the West Highlands, where, as a rule, we are more familiar with winter as, in the words of the old sea-song, a "blustering railer," than as the implacable and ruthless tyrant of intense frost and marrow-piercing north-east winds. Our lochs are still swarming with Arctic sea-fowl, and a return to a longer or shorter period of very decided cold and storm is not improbable. But, come as it may, the worst at least is past; a cold and stormy day when the sun, on his return journey northwards, is back again half-way through *Aquarius*, must always be more endurable and better every way than a cold and stormy day while the sun is still in the heart of Capricorn. On this subject the old Highlanders had a curious rhyme worth quoting, for they were a remarkably shrewd people in their reading and interpretation of meteorological, and indeed of all natural phenomena :—

> "Ri fuachd Calluinn
> Math clò olainn;
> Ri fuachd Feile-Bride
> Fogh'naidh cisfheart."

Cisfheart, or *closart*, was a particular kind of woollen cloth, what we should call now-a-days a *light* tweed. The meaning of the rhyme we take to be that, whereas the thickest and heaviest woollen cloth is necessary to protect one from the cold of New-Year time (12th January, or Old Style), a lighter sort will suffice in the case of any possible cold at Candlemastide, 12th February. So marked and decided, the old Highlanders desired by means of this rhyme to intimate, was the increase of temperature, and under a higher sun and rapidly lengthening day, so easily combated was any degree of cold that could possibly befall at Candlemastide, or the Feast of Saint Bride, as they termed it, as compared with the intenser and more persistent cold of the short and sunless days of New-Year time.

Last year a distinguished French naturalist wrote us asking if it was true that the golden eagle was extinct in the Highlands of Scotland. He was induced to make the inquiry, he said, by having recently seen a statement to that effect in a German zoological journal. It was a startling, and for the moment even a puzzling question; but on due consideration we replied to the effect that we thought it was *not* true; that we hoped and believed the noble bird was *not* extinct; that, on the authority of shepherds, foresters, gamekeepers, and others, we had good reason to believe the golden eagle still exists, and is occasionally to be met with in the more inaccessible mountain solitudes of some of the Outer Hebrides, as well as on the mainland. We were obliged to write less confidently on the subject than we could have wished, for the truth is, that since the spring of 1869 we have not recognised a single specimen of this magnificent *Raptor* in the unfettered freedom of his mountain home. For nine years, in short, the only living eagle of this species (*Aquila chrysaëtos*) we had seen was that at the entrance to the Glasgow Kelvingrove Museum, a chained captive! still, indeed, with some remains of "pride in his port," and not a little of "defiance in his eye," but, *quoad ultra*, no more to be compared with the same bird in the unfettered freedom of his native wilds than the Napoleon of St. Helena could be said to be the Napoleon of the Pyramids, Austerlitz, and Jena. Had it been possible by an effort of mere volition on our part then and there to snap the chain that tied that captive to his perch, and instantly transport him to the freedom and protection of the upland solitudes of Glenevis or Lochtreig, take our word for it, it had certainly been done. As it was, we could only contemplate the captive—sullen and savage, as was no wonder—for a moment with a feeling of sympathy so intense that it amounted to actual pain, and we hurried on, the proud and indignant glance, however, of an eye fiery and fearless, that reflected a spirit not to be subdued by imprisonment while life lasted, haunting us for days afterwards. You may believe, then, good reader, that we were not a little delighted on Thursday last—proud, if you can understand it, as well as pleased—when by the merest accident we had the good fortune to see not one, but a pair of these noble birds hunting over the corries and along the mountain slopes of Caolas-na-Cone and Glencoe. Thursday was one of the finest days of the season, cold, but calm and clear, without a wisp of cloud in all the blue. About three P.M. we were walking along the beach under Callart Cottage, where Lochleven begins rapidly to contract, until, a couple of miles beyond, at Caolas-na-Cone, it becomes so narrow that a Fingalian hero of the "swift-footed Achilles" order, once in the ardour of the chase is fabled to have leapt across at a bound, and thought little of the exploit. As we strolled along the shore we had all our eyes about us, less, indeed, from any expectation of seeing anything new or wonderful than from a habit from which an ornithologist finds it difficult to divest himself, when the surroundings are at all such that something in the way of his favourite science may turn up in any direction and at any moment. Glancing along the mountain sky-line to the right, the eye was arrested by a black speck over the great corrie of Caolas-na-Cone, a speck almost immediately joined by a second speck, the two slowly circling and zig-zagging in the direction of *Sguir-na-Ciche*, the Pap of Glencoe, directly opposite the spot on which we stood. That they were birds, and big birds, was certain; and finding a convenient hiding-place at hand, we stretched ourselves on a bed of silvery sand, between two large granite boulders, and waited patiently in the hope that the birds might come near enough to be identified. While lying thus, we bethought ourselves of an old *ruse* of ours, which has already stood us in good stead in many an ornithological ramble. We filled our pocket-handkerchief with dry drift-weed, abundance of which lay within our reach, and tying the four corners together, we threw it up on the grass above high-water mark, some twenty yards from where we were lying. We took care, however, not to tie our handkerchief so tightly but that some of the dark-brown sea-weed could be seen protruding through the openings, in order that it should appear in as strong and startling a contrast as possible with the whiteness of the handkerchief in which it was bundled. All birds are amazingly inquisitive, and a hungry *Raptor* is inquisitive and bold beyond all others; and hence it is that we have found that placing somewhere along their beat anything odd-looking in size and shape out of the ordinary, and that *may* have life in it, though for the moment it seems lifeless and immoveable, will "fetch" a bird, to use an expressive Americanism—that is, attract his attention—and, if you are concealed in the neighbourhood of the object of attraction, bring him nearer to you than you could possibly manage by any amount of stalking and circumvention otherwise. In a few minutes the birds, moving in graceful circles, and occasionally crossing each other's paths like yachts in a trial to windward, were right over the Pap, along the shoulders and skirts of which they hunted in the most beautiful manner, quartering their ground, in sportsman's phrase, like a couple of well-bred pointers. That they were golden eagles we were already certain; their immense spread of wing, their easy and graceful flight and manner of hunting, placed their identity beyond all question. As we hoped, however, and expected, we had soon a nearer look at them. Gliding adown the northern shoulder of the Pap, with a single beat of their huge wings they had crossed the loch, and were circling right above us at an altitude of five hundred feet, perhaps, looking black as ravens against the blue background of the heavens. It was only for a minute or two. Too keen of sight not to discern that the stuffed handkerchief was a sham, and suspicious that it might also be a snare, very likely aware of our presence also, well hidden as we thought ourselves, and quiet as we lay, by a simple and scarcely perceptible dip of the point of one wing, and a corresponding elevation of the other, the magnificent birds were in an instant half a mile away, hunting over the green slopes of Mam Challairt and Camusnahehroe, where, however, they found nothing worth the picking up, for, as we were leaving the shore, they were disappearing over the mountains to the north, looking for a ptarmigan along the summits, failing which, they were pretty sure of a hare in Laroch Mòr beyond. We question if Dr. Schliemann was better pleased on the eve of his most successful day at the archæological "diggings" of Ilium or Mycenæ than we were as we drove home that evening, in the knowledge that not only was the golden eagle not extinct in the Highlands, but that a pair of the lordly birds had their home and hunting-ground among our own magnificent mountains of Lochaber and Glencoe.

Aristotle was the first to apply the epithet *chrysaëtos* —golden—to distinguish this species of eagle, a species of very wide geographical distribution—

"The bird of Jove, of every bird the king!"

from its immediate congeners. That he meant the epithet to be interpreted in its natural sense is evident from his description of the bird, in other words, as being "yellow in colour." Exception, however, has been taken to the appropriateness of the epithet *chrysaëtos*, because, according to the observations of some very distinguished ornithologists, the prevailing colour is not golden or yellow, but a very dark brown; and it is certainly the fact—a very significant fact, too, in this discussion—that the bird is known in the Highlands of Scotland as *An Iolair Dhubh*, or the *Black Eagle*. Others, again, affirm that Aristotle is perfectly right, for that the bird has quite enough of yellow about him to make the epithet fairly fit and appropriate. The truth, we should say, is that both parties are right. The plumage of the bird while comparatively young—up to its tenth year, say—has quite enough of russet yellow about it to justify Aristotle's epithet in the opinion of most people who are not "particular to a shade," while, as the bird advances in life, the plumage grows darker and darker, until it attains a tawny rust-colour, which quite as much justifies the Gaelic epithet *dhubh* or black as the more juvenile plumage justifies the *chrysaëtos* of Aristotle. We have seen specimens of both colours. The *Iolair Dhubh*, however, is known in the Highlands by another and much more poetical name, *Iolair Suil na Gréine*, namely, the eagle, that is, with an eye bright and fiery as that of the sun itself, or with an eye that can stare the sun out of countenance, so to speak; that can look into the burning heart of the solar orb without winking—a feat impossible to any other creature of air, or earth, or sea.

By the kind attention of Professor Geddes of Aberdeen we have for some time had beside us his recently published, very learned, and very remarkable work, *The Problem of the Homeric Poems*, a book written by a scholar for scholars, a work not to be merely read, but to be thoughtfully studied by the light which is in itself, augmented or modified from time to time, as occasion may arise, by the many side-lights bearing upon the problem, the most interesting of all literary questions, from the labours of other workers, ancient and modern, in the same field. It is a work, indeed, that the general reader of average culture may read with no little interest, and pleasure, and profit; but the reader who would thoroughly appreciate the prodigious learning and wide research of this remarkable volume, and, in the quaint language of an old author, "eat with delight of its very marrow," must be of academical training, and conversant with the language and literature of ancient Greece in such wise as is very much the exception rather than the rule even among people of superior education and culture otherwise. The *raison d'être* of Professor Geddes' work is briefly this. The traditional and orthodox view of the two great Homeric poems, the *Iliad* and *Odyssey*, is that they are both the work of one man, an ancient Greek bard, whose name was Homer; but as to when he lived, where he was born, and how he composed these wonderful epics, there is no certain knowledge, only vague and valueless conjecture. This is the view regarding these poems and their authorship that obtained among the Greeks themselves, and the view that, up to a comparatively recent date, was adopted by the most distinguished Homeric scholars in all lands, with hardly a whispered doubt or murmur of dissent. It is proper to observe, however, that even in Greece some two thousand years ago there was a small party of scholars, the "Chorizontes," or *Separatists*, as they were called, who held that the two great Greek epics were of different ages, and of course by different authors—the earlier or older poem, the *Iliad*, by Homer; the later or more recent poem, the *Odyssey*, by some nameless minstrel, of great poetic power indeed, but upon the whole only an imitator of, and second and subsiduary to, the great original Homer after all. For some twenty centuries, then, Homeric scholars and critics were divided into two camps, the one containing a numerous and well-disciplined army of orthodox *Traditionalists*; the other, a mere handful, the heterodox *Separatists*, whose influence was so small, for they spoke with bated breath, that they may be said to have existed only as the heretical exception that went to prove the orthodox rule. Towards the close of the last century, however, arose the *Wolfian* school of heretics, so called after their distinguished leader, Frederick Augustus Wolf, Professor of Classical Literature in the University of Halle. Wolf, a profound scholar, and a man of marvellous critical acumen, found, or thought he found, so many discrepancies in the Homeric epics, such "mighty gaps and commissures," so much to be accounted for and adjusted in various directions, for which the Traditional and Separatist theories were utterly insufficient, that he had no hesitation in turning his back on both camps, and boldly propounding a theory of his own—a theory on which alone, he was of opinion, all the difficulties of the great Homeric question could be satisfactorily explained. The *one* Homer of the Traditionalists was not enough, nor even the *two* Homers (or Homer and later minstrel) of the Separatists. He held that the Homeric epics were built up of many ballads and martial songs, the composition of *many* Homers, so to speak—of many different bards, that is—belonging to the great epic cycle of Grecian song. This startling theory Wolf proceeded to substantiate with so much critical ingenuity and learning, that it straightway found favour with many of the most distinguished scholars, not only in Germany, but generally over the Continent, and even in England. The Wolfian camp, in short, was soon filled with many willing and able recruits, and on the Hellenic field, on which there were formerly but two camps, there were now three—the Traditionalists, the Separatists or Chorizontes, and the Wolfians.

What Professor Geddes tries to do in the volume before us, and does so well that he will assuredly have many followers, some of whom have even already intimated their allegiance, is to point out a *via media*, a middle way, towards a full and final settlement, if possible, of the great Homeric problem. In the great epic known as the *Iliad*, he finds a certain number of books so closely associated with Achilles and his exploits, so clearly the outcome of the "wrath" of the godlike hero, that he calls the group so distinguished the *Achilleid*. These Achilleid cantos, too, he finds pervaded by an archaic tone, an air of *eld*, not so noticeable, if it exists at all, in the cantos outside the Achilleid group. This *Achilleid* Professor Geddes believes to be the oldest part, the kernel, so to speak, of the *Iliad* so called, and to be the production of an old Thessalian bard, who lived a thousand years, perhaps, or more, before the Christian era, and whose name has perished, though his work survives. The remaining cantos of the *Iliad* not included in the Achilleid group are the composition, along with the *Odyssey*, of a later minstrel, and this later minstrel is none other than Homer, *the* Homer with whose name is associated so much of all that the world has for thirty centuries agreed to hold in highest honour as the pride and glory of epic song. It is impossible, within the space at our disposal here, to do anything like justice to the ingenuity and learning with which Professor Geddes works his way, step by step, through the many difficulties that beset him in laying out and *macadamising* his *via media* solution of the Homeric problem. He has not, indeed, convinced us that he is right. After as honest and careful a study of his work as the long and stormy nights of the last fortnight of the old year and the first fortnight of the new enabled us to bestow upon it, we still cling to the unity of the *Iliad*, believing that *one* minstrel, even Homer, "father of verse," was the author of it all from first to last, from the opening invocation to the Muse in the first canto to the closing line of the twenty-fourth :

> "Such honours Ilion to her hero paid,
> And peaceful slept the mighty Hector's shade."

And all this, discrepancies, "gaps and commissures" admitted, and to the contrary notwithstanding. As to the *Odyssey*, we believe that it, too, is the work of the same bard that sung "the tale of Troy divine." We cannot believe in two Homers, far less in many Homers: Nature is not so lavish of her great poets. All the difficulties and discrepancies in both poems, all the gaps and commissures visible under the microscopic lens of Wolf, are to be accounted for, we think, partly by the admission that Homer sometimes nods; that he is at times, nay, very often, *impar sibi*, winging a lower and more devious flight than when, filled with all the divine *afflatus*, he soars aloft in the full plenitude of his poetic powers, and partly by ascribing all the more glaring faults and flaws, of whatever nature, to the interpolations and omissions of the raphsodists while the poems were still in an unwritten state, and to the carelessness or dishonesty of collectors and transcribers after they began to appear in a written form. Be this, however, as it may, what there can be no doubt at all about is that the Professor of Greek in the University of Aberdeen has written one of the most scholarly and learned books of the century in any language; and henceforward no one who has not read and thoughtfully studied *The Problem of the Homeric Poems*, as discussed and sifted by Professor Geddes, can pretend to a knowledge of the question in all its bearings. It is such a book, as to its subject-matter, as only a scholar of the very first order could have written, while among scholars of the highest order it is rare to find a literary style so perfectly lucid and logical throughout, so entirely free from the obscurity and paradox that too often make the books of very learned men a hard task to read, and a harder still to comprehend. The publishers are Macmillan & Co.

CHAPTER XXXIX.

Meteors—Professor Blackie—Homer—The Descent as a Meteor of Pallas Minerva—A sparkling swift-descending Fireball Meteor ought to be called a *Minervalite*—The "*Dreag*" of the Gaels—An exploding *Dreag* in 1746—The great Meteor Shower of 1866.

FEBRUARY has come in, even as January went out, cold and calm and clear, with enough of brilliant sunshine to counterpoise all the frost and chill of the hours of twilight and darkness. Of late, indeed, we have had no such thing as darkness properly so called, for even when the last moon was but a faint and pallid fragment of an ill-defined and sickly orb in rapid wane, and while the present moon was still but a thin and sharp-horned crescent in the west, the nights were brilliantly starlit and clear, the practised eye, otherwise unaided, being able to detect and identify small magnitude stars—in Taurus, for example, and Orion and Leo as they culminated—with a readiness and ease that indicated a remarkable transparency of atmosphere, rare in this country at any time, and rarest of all, perhaps, at this particular season of the year.

One night last week, as we were observing an occultation by the moon of a star in Taurus, a fiery meteor of large size and exceeding brilliancy lit up the south-western heavens with a surging wave of pale green light of such dazzling intensity, that for a few seconds the moon and stars were but the shivering ghosts of themselves, so tremblingly pallid and deathly was their hue in the presence of the fierce and fiery stranger. The meteor, as we saw it, seemed to issue from the left shoulder of Orion, then on the meridian, and thence to drop, or rather to dart, obliquely westwards, until, somewhere over Duart Castle in Mull, it burst into a thousand brilliant fragments, a reddish green luminous train that marked its track remaining visible for several seconds after the disruption and extinction of the meteor proper itself. Similar meteors of the fireball exploding order we have frequently seen, but never, perhaps, an example so splendid in all its belongings as this one; for it was not only of intense and almost blinding brilliancy in itself, but at the moment of explosion it was splendid in the number and exceeding brilliancy of its disrupted fragments, as well as in the broad train of light, like a strip of confused and ill-defined rainbow, that marked out its path adown the heavens from Orion to within the horizon line over the ancient stronghold of the chief of the Macleans. We wished exceedingly that, of all living men, our excellent friend Professor Blackie had been beside us at the moment, that he might see this meteor for himself even as we saw it. Why, it may be asked, of all men Professor Blackie? why in the particular circumstances should *his* presence, rather than that of any one else, be so desirable? Well, courteous reader, if you grant us your patient attention for a few minutes, you shall be made to understand the connection between the learned Professor and this same fiery meteor of ours. In the Fourth Book of the

Iliad Homer tells how Jove, at the urgent request and incessant " nagging " of ox-eyed Juno, sent Pallas Minerva to incite the Trojans to a breach of the peace—to a breach, that is, of the league, truce, armistice, or whatever it may be called, into which the contending hosts had entered shortly before, in order that the quarrel might be settled by single combat, after a fashion with which we are so familiar in the history of chivalric ages. The blue-eyed goddess, nothing loth, darts from the heights of Olympus on an errand, about the morality of which the less said the better. Literally translated, Homer's description of the descent of Pallas is as follows :—" Thus having spoken, he (Jove) urged on Minerva already inclined ; she, hastening, descended the heights of Olympus ; such as the star which the son of wily Saturn sends as a sign either to mariners or to a wide host of nations, and from it many sparks are emitted. Like unto this Pallas Minerva hastened to the earth, and leaped into the midst (of the neutral space between the armies) ; and astonishment seized upon the horse-breaking Trojans and the well-greaved Greeks, looking on." Now, it is clear that although Homer here employs the usual word for star (*astēr*), he cannot of course mean a star in the ordinary sense of the term in his own language any more than in ours—he cannot, that is, mean a fixed star or a planet. He must mean a celestial something, not exactly a star, but at the same time of so much of the nature of a star as to make the term upon the whole apt and proper enough, and sufficiently intelligible to those primitive peoples for whose delight and edification he sung his matchless *epos*. Commentators have been a good deal puzzled as to what is really meant. Pope thinks that a *comet* is the thing, and translates accordingly :—

> "Fir'd with the charge, she headlong urg'd her flight,
> And shot like lightning from Olympus' height,
> *As the red comet*, from Saturnius sent
> To fright the nations with a dire portent
> (A fatal sign to armies on the plain,
> Or trembling sailors on the wintry main),
> With sweeping glories glides along in air,
> *And shakes the sparkles from its shining hair;*
> Between both armies thus, in open sight,
> Shot the bright goddess in a trail of light;
> With eyes erect the gazing hosts admire
> The power descending, and the heavens on fire!"

But it is very certain that Homer in this passage cannot mean a comet, for it is only to the astronomer of comparatively modern times that a comet is known as a fact to move swiftly; to the ordinary eye it moves slowly, and is besides visible, when visible at all, for weeks and months together; whereas what Homer means is something that moves with exceeding swiftness, something that darts with extraordinary velocity, even for a heavenly body, and which, in some part or other of its course, emits sparks. Professor Blackie in his translation avoids the danger of being too particular, for he is confessedly in doubt, and translates "a *meteor-star*," which, although not sufficiently precise, is yet by any number of millions of miles nearer the mark than Pope's "comet." Blackie's lines have much of the true Homeric ring in them, and are worth quoting :—

> "Thus he; and spurred with needless words Athenè's eager bent,
> Down from Olympus' lofty brow with rapid swoop she went:

> As when the 'Thunderer' *from the sky hath shot a meteor-star*
> To sailors toiling through the seas, and soldiers camped in war,
> A flaring sign; and thick the trailing sparks are scattered far;
> So in a trail of light to earth down shoots the maid divine,
> And leaps between the hosts; while strange amazement held
>   the eyne
> Of horse-subduing Trojans, and the stout well-greavèd Greeks."

The compound "meteor-star" of this passage is so good, so sufficiently suggestive, that we should never have dreamt that the learned Professor had the slightest doubt or difficulty in the matter, were it not for a note in which he confesses to be much puzzled by the "sparks" which his "meteor-star" is described by Homer as emitting. The Professor sees clearly enough that Pope's "comet," even if supplied with a tail the broadest and brightest you can imagine, will never do; it is too slow, its course is not sufficiently earthwards, and it does not emit sparks. He thinks a "shooting star" is meant, though he frankly confesses that he never saw shooting stars casting out sparks in the way described. But a shooting star of the ordinary type, with which we are all so familiar, will not do any more than Pope's comet. The course of shooting stars is not necessarily earthwards; they move in all directions, up (speaking for the moment unscientifically) as well as down, and are far too common to be a wonder or a terror either to soldiers or sailors. Let us see what is really wanted. Pallas darts from the top of Thessalian Olympus, the serene abode of the Immortals, a mountain 9000 feet high, nearly double the height of our own Ben Nevis, and her course must from such a height be a swiftly descending one, a downward "swoop," to use the Professor's own word,

T

for she has only to cross the Ægean in order to alight on the Trojan plains at the foot of Ida,—a few seconds, in the case of a goddess urged to do Jove's errand quickly, clearly sufficing. Such a "star," then, as will serve Homer's purpose in the connection must be a brightly luminous body, that seeks the earth swiftly, and by an almost perpendicular descent; it must be visible but for a brief moment, just long enough to impress the spectator with a due sense of the magnificence of its fiery splendour; it must emit sparks, a sign of rapid extinction and dissolution (in the case of a goddess, simply of invisibility under that particular form); and, finally, it must be of comparatively rare occurrence, so rare as to be always more or less an object of wonder and terror, and a "portent dire" to the beholders. Now, it is evident enough that neither comet nor shooting star, properly so called, will serve our purpose under all the conditions stated. But as the Fingalian proverb has it, *mur e Bran, 'se 'bhrathair*— if it be not Bran, it is Bran's brother; if it be not a shooting star proper that Homer means, he means what is only a variety of the same phenomenon. What the grand old bard, who, depend upon it, was not *always* blind, refers to is beyond all question what is known to modern science as an *Aërolite* or *Fireball*, that, as it approaches the earth at a point somewhere within the visible horizon, so frequently explodes into hundreds of brilliant fragments and disappears. Occasionally it begins to emit sparks for a second or two before it is ripe for the act of final disruption—a disruption sometimes accompanied by a noise like thunder "heard remote," or the discharge of a distant park of artillery, the loudness of the noise, or whether it is heard at all, depending on our distance at the moment from the exploding meteor. These exploding, spark-emitting aërolites are not indeed common, but they are of frequent enough occurrence to make us wonder that the many learned commentators on Homer should have so long missed clutching at them with eager grasp as the only possible kind of "star" fit for all the requirements of the passage quoted. And in order to obviate betimes a possible enough objection in the case, it may be stated that these exploding aërolites have been frequently seen in broadest, brightest daylight, as well as at night. The reader will now understand why we so much desired the presence of Professor Blackie the other night, as the *Minervalite*—for so have we determined to call these exploding meteors in all time coming—burst upon our sight, and, after running its swift and fiery course, dissolved into a shower of bright and beautiful miniature stars.

The fireball or aërolite is known to the people of the Highlands as a *Dréag* (*Scot.* Dreg) or *Driug*, a compound term from *Draoidh*, a Druid, and *eug*, death, because in the old Druidical times it was believed that such a meteor was the soul or spirit of one of these philosopher-priests just released from its tenement of clay, and fast urging its flight to the shores of a dim and distant ghost-land, the geography of which was uncertain. Our own researches, however, into the folk-lore of this particular question rather lead us to the conclusion that the *dréag* or meteor was not believed to be itself the visible soul or spirit of the deceased Druid, but only the psychopompal vehicle, the "fiery chariot," in which the spirit was conveyed in fiery splendour into the happiness and "higher life" of a new form of existence. It is to be observed that by the *drèag* proper was always meant the *non*-exploding meteor that rushes athwart the heavens for a few seconds, an intensely luminous globe of fire, and seems to vanish simply by being swallowed up in darkness. The exploding *drèag*, or Minervalite, as we have called it, is known in the Highlands as *drèag-shradagach*, or the *spark-emitting* drèag, and has always been held as a portent not of such a comparatively small matter as the death of any single individual, however exalted, but of some widespread calamity, such as we should call now-a-days a national disaster, always indeed connected with death, but with death on a large scale, and of a violent or sudden nature. Thus, shortly after sunset on the evening of the 15th April 1746, and while it was still daylight, a large fiery meteor passed over Upper Strathspey and Badenoch, its course being from south-east to north-west. It finished its course by exploding into a thousand brilliant sparks, and with loud and terrible detonations, " more awful," said the old man who related to us the tradition as it had been handed down to him—"more awful than any thunder." This meteor was of course intimately associated in the popular superstition with the sad disaster of the following day on the bleak, black moor of Culloden. The same portentous meteor is mentioned in an old poem of the period taken down many years ago from the recitation of a Badenoch man by the late distinguished Gaelic scholar James Munro of Blarour, in Brae-Lochaber, who kindly handed to us the original copy for publication in a work which we meditated at the time, and which may yet see the light. Similarly, some three-and-twenty years ago, as we were informed at the time by some cattle-drovers who had just returned from the island, a brilliant meteor that finished its course by exploding into a shower of fiery stars passed over the island of Barra, one of the Outer Hebrides, and this meteor was by the inhabitants believed to have been portentous of, and specially connected with, the wreck shortly afterwards of a large emigrant ship on Barra Head, with the loss of almost all the passengers and crew. So that it would seem that in the popular superstitions of modern times these brilliant, spark-emitting meteors are held to be still as portentous of disaster to soldiers and sailors as they were in the days of Homer on the shores of the Ægean Sea three thousand years ago. The commoner non-exploding aërolite, too, is still associated, where possible, with the death of some distinguished personage in the district over which it urges its fiery flight. Not many years ago, while the proprietor of a large estate in a neighbouring county, that has been in the possession of the family for at least five centuries, was lying sick unto death, a large and brilliant meteor, the passage of which we ourselves happened to observe, was, by the common consent of more than a thousand people, associated with the death of the "Laird," a most excellent man, although the two events were separated from each other by an interval of several days. When one of these meteors is associated with the death of any particular individual, it is usually in a good sense; the meteor, that is, in most cases, is accepted in its old

Druidical aspect, a true drèag, in short, with which in some mysterious manner the spirit of the departed is associated in its passage to a brighter and better world. If the meteor, however, were to appear synchronously with the death of a man at once "big" and *bad*, of exalted station, but of evil repute, we are not quite so sure but that the meteor would be held as heralding *his* passage to a very different, though still fitting, abode; while in the case of a laird who was a *novus homo*, a man with neither ancestral name nor holding in the Highlands, and who had but recently entered upon this property by purchase, the meaning of a meteor as regards *him*, if indeed he was allowed to be honoured with the attention of a meteor at all, would probably be very much the same as in the case of the man of evil repute aforesaid.

But the reader must not run away with the idea that these superstitions are confined to the Highlands. We have abundance of evidence beside us to prove that they are quite as widespread, and are held quite as firmly, in the southern and midland counties as in the north; only that in the northern counties, perhaps, their existence is acknowledged with less reserve than among the longer-visaged and more puritanical peoples of the old whigamore counties of the south and south-west.

Finally, let us state that the most magnificent display of meteors we ever beheld was that of the 13-14th November 1866, when, from eight or nine o'clock at night until the dawning day, the whole firmament seemed literally on fire with every conceivable kind of luminous meteor-shooting stars, aërolites, and fireballs, exploding and non-exploding, with frequent lightning flashes to intensify the awful magnificence of the scene, the whole, too, projected on a background of weird auroral light, like the glare you have seen and been affrighted at in a madman's eye. As we sat on, hour after hour, watching the really terrible though magnificent spectacle, the like of which we have but little hopes of ever seeing again, more than once we caught ourselves repeating the fine verse of the Apocalypse— "And the stars of heaven fell unto the earth, even as a fig tree casteth her untimely figs when she is shaken of a mighty wind."

CHAPTER XL.

Cold out of Season—Its effects on the Nidification of Birds—The Golden Eagle in the Hebrides and on the Mainland—Letter about Golden Eagle from Kintail—Story of an Eagle from Loch Lomond—Ben Lomond and Ben Nevis—Best View of the latter from Ardgour and Banavie.

HERE, as elsewhere, with a heavy fall of snow and keen frost, winter is again supreme, a state of matters, however, not likely to last long, for within the last few days we have noticed that almost all our winter wild-fowl have left, or are leaving, our inland lochs and estuaries, as if they foresaw the speedy advent of fine weather, and were no longer afraid of facing the unsheltered waters of the open sea. Never before have we seen the country wear so dismal an aspect in the last days of February, an aspect the dismal wintriness of which is only intensified by the altitude and mid-day brilliancy of a sun already fast hastening to the starry borders of primrose-eyed *Aries*. For a whole fortnight up to the 14th the weather with us here was bright and warm, and our wild-birds, true to their instincts, were celebrating St. Valentine-tide with all the love-making and all the song that the many hardships of a winter so exceptional left them capable of, when, all of a sudden, the cold returned with almost all its New-Year time intensity; the snow began to fall in such multitudinous and thick and solid flakes as is rarely seen in the West Highlands, while the north-east wind blew in fierce and fitful gusts, that, as it shrieked adown the glens, and howled over ferry and firth, drove us all, "beast and body," and trembling wee bird, into such shelters, each after his kind, as were readiest at hand, and most suitable in all the circumstances of our hyperborean surroundings. Our poor birds were instantly and of course made dumb and dowie enough, the old mid-winter chirp at once replacing the voice of song, while the love instinct, like a sensitive flower unable to bear the darkness and the cold, was straightway driven into a second hybernation. The old saw that "*Sine Cerere et Baccho frigit Venus*" is, to a certain extent perhaps, physiologically true; but as regards our wild-bird friends, at least, Venus, depend upon it, has no such formidable enemy as cold out of season, cold at once intense and untimeous. Even as we write, however, there are some signs of a coming thaw, and there is no unpardonable daring in the prognostication that we shall have a bright and pleasant spring after all.

We have had some very interesting communications with reference to a paragraph on the golden eagle in one of our recent papers. The noble bird, we are pleased to find, is very far from being extinct in the Highlands, many well authenticated reports having reached us of its recent occurrence in the Hebrides, as well as within the *Garbh-chriochan*, or "rough bounds" of the mainland, and some of these in localities far enough apart to justify us in coming to the conclusion that, on the most moderate computation, there must be at least a dozen pairs of the true *Aquila chryscätos* still in possession of their favourite haunts in the more inaccessible mountain fastnesses of the eastern and midland Highlands, as well as in the north-west. We are very much pleased to find, as the reader may believe, that proprietors everywhere, with hardly an exception, as well as the lessees of grouse moors and deer forests, are beginning to regard the golden eagle with feelings of admiration and respect rather than of hostility, and have in many cases instructed their keepers and *gillies* to abstain from molesting the kingly birds, unless caught in some indefensible act of red-handed raid and onslaught, and in such cases of *furtum grave* as in the interests of fair sport and good neighbourhood cannot in any wise be permitted even in the case of so magnificent a marauder. The following, from a correspondent in Ross-shire, is of sufficient interest to be reproduced here :—

"LOCHALSH, 4th *February* 1879.

" Last autumn, through the kindness of him who is heir to what we in Ross-shire look upon as the classic region of Kintail, the writer was privileged to go at will through its magnificent corries and up to the highest points of its unsurpassed hills—mountains if you like, for Ben Attow is one, and Scourouran is another. One beautiful day, when the sun was bright and there was enough of wind to make things pleasant after a steep brae had been surmounted, as I, accompanied by my old friend Cattanach, the famous deerstalker of Kintail, and Duncan Macrae, the energetic and skilful foxhunter of the same district, was cautiously proceeding through Corra Chat, all of a sudden I was conscious of a considerable shadow appearing very near, but in motion. Looking up from the effect to see the cause, there I saw one of your favourites in all its majesty sailing past, and it certainly was not eighty yards away. It was a grand bird, in fullest plumage, and, with the sun shining so brightly on it, it looked more *golden* than any eagle I ever saw before. I fear you will be ineffably disgusted when I remark that my first thought was how much I should like to knock it over, send it to the sportsman's guide, philosopher, and friend—Mr. Snowie—to be preserved in his admirable way, thence to Mr. Mackenzie, on whose estate it was pursuing its deadly avocation! However, your correspondent is a most miserable shot, and your friend's great strong wings soon took it far from me without smelling powder, or even hearing the report of a gun. *Laus Deo!* you say, no doubt. But I wish you could have seen the bird of Jove so near you, so unconscious of danger to itself, and yet so vengeful in its intentions to others, as it went hunting along close to the ground, ready for action should some of the ptarmigan you value so little in comparison appear. You, who are so distinguished a naturalist, would have enjoyed the opportunity which was vouchsafed me, and you would have been able to do justice to the occasion in that happy manner which is natural to you. As for myself, the destruction to more *useful* birds—pray pardon the vulgar idea, and probably the ignorance—caused by golden eagles would induce me at any time to try my hand as a marksman, for I would rather see them well stuffed than well fed on grouse and ptarmigan!

"On another occasion, when Duncan Macrae, my good friend *Allie Ruadh* (Alex. Maclennan) and I were in the vicinity of 'The Cnap,' we saw another specimen of the same bird performing most extensive evolutions in the air; and what a gathering of grey crows there was in attendance on his majesty! If it had just pounced upon the crows, and broken every bone in their bodies, I think that for the rest of my life my admiration of that feat would induce me to spare the life of any member of their destroyer's family! The golden eagle has better taste, however, for, so far as my information goes, it appreciates *game*, and will not condescend to vermin—crows at all events. Is this not the case?

"Pray pardon the long screed. I fear it is a poor return, indeed, for many a pleasant hour's reading received from 'Nether Lochaber.'

"P. Campbell Ross."

From another correspondent, a lady in Dumbartonshire, we have had a very pleasant letter, from which we are permitted to make the following extract:—

"In 1876, and again in the autumn of last year, a huge bird, which my son, a keen sportsman, and not likely to be deceived in such a matter, felt convinced was a golden eagle, was on several occasions seen about the eastern slopes of Ben Lomond—a finer mountain, by the by, than your Ben Nevis, though not so high, at least to my thinking. As it was crossing the loch (Loch Lomond) at an early hour one morning in 1876, I had an opportunity of looking at it with a good glass, which reduced the height at which it was soaring sufficiently to enable me to notice that its colour was yellowish or yellowish-brown, and in the bright sunlight that at the moment prevailed, I should not have thought any one far wrong that called it *golden*. In a stuffed specimen, however, that has stood for some years in my staircase window, the prevailing colour is a very dark brown, of a slightly lighter shade on the sides of the breast, and for a small space above the folding of the wings at the shoulder."

We are much obliged to our correspondent for her most interesting communication, although she must not be angry if we say that we cannot agree with her that Ben Lomond is in any sense whatever a finer mountain than Ben Nevis. Of its particular type Ben Lomond is doubtless very fine—one of the first, indeed, of Scottish mountains, but it is only *one* mountain, view it from what standpoint you may; while our magnificent Ben Nevis is rather three or four mountains, each equal to Ben Lomond in bulk, and exceeding it in altitude, roughly rolled together into a huge irregular mass, colossal and vast, whose rugged outlines and terrible precipices and headlong steeps impress one with a sense of sublimity and grandeur such as is only partially felt, if felt at all, in the presence of any other mountain in the kingdom. As you make the circuit of its base, a good thirty miles in circumference, and halt to gaze at some selected standpoint in, say, each five miles of the round, the mighty Ben confronts you at each such step under a totally different aspect, and you finish with the impression, which such a circuit left indelibly with ourselves, that Ben Nevis is not a single mountain at all, but a colossal bundle of the hugest of Scotland's mountains rolled into one mighty mass, and surpassing all others even more in mass and magnitude and prodigiousness of bulk than in altitude. It is the Olympus of Britain, on whose summit, if anywhere, all the hidden mysteries of ancient Celtic Baälism and Druidical worship may be supposed still to linger, and in whose mists and clouds, whether rolling a surging sea before the tempest, or in detached masses reposing in the golden calm of evening, the poetical eye may even yet discern the shadowy ghosts of the demigods and heroes of the old Fingalian song! Ben Nevis is in truth the Charlemagne of British mountainland, the loftiest and proudest of his companion Bens—Ben Lomond included—being but his paladins; great, indeed, in themselves, but still only subsidiary and second to *him*, monarch of all he surveys, and every inch a king! No, no! dear Mrs. C——, your Ben Lomond is a "fine" mountain enough, and a beautiful mountain, and you do well to be proud of it, but you really must not compare it with Ben Nevis. Your Loch Lomond, too, is unquestionably a fine sheet of water, but neither must you boast of *it*, a mere skating pond after all, as against us, when we remind you that ours is the matchless Linnhe Loch, with its fitting continuations of Loch Aber and Loch Eil, not to speak of its winding offshoot, our own beautiful Loch Leven, with its magnificent impending mountains, the home of the osprey and the eagle, and its clear and limpid waters, a harbour of refuge to thousands of grateful sea-fowl, a harbour of refuge in every wind that blows.

For the passing tourist, by the way, one of the very finest views of the grand old Ben is to be had from Aryhualan, in Ardgour, on the afternoon, say, and on till the twilight of a day in March or September. If a nearer standpoint be desired, the immediate neighbourhood of the hotel at Banavie is perhaps as good as any for the spectator, who would take in at one long, deep draught, so to speak, an abiding impression of the rugged massiveness and majestic grandeur of our noble mountain.

CHAPTER XLI.

Storm—Stormy Petrel—Rare Birds—Red-necked Phalarope—Wild-Bird Notes from Mull and Stranraer—Antique Silver Brooch found on the top of Benvere, in Appin—Appin an old Hunting-Ground of the Stuart Kings.

RELYING on our wild-bird friends, we predicted that December was likely to be a stormy month, and very stormy it has unquestionably proved. Nor, if we judge correctly, are we by any means quite done with unsettled weather and heavy gales. Ocean and Arctic wild-fowl are at this moment more numerous than ever in all our creeks and bays, and while they remain with us, we may confidently look either for very stormy or for intensely cold weather. Even the stormy petrels, a small flock of which were driven to our shores by the great November storm, may still be seen urging their zig-zag and swallow-like flight over the Linnhe Loch waves, dipping into the hollows and tipping the crests after the fashion so familiar to those whose fortune it has been to go down to the sea in ships, doing business in "great waters;" and very interesting it is to watch the confidence and ease with which these restless little fellows dash into the surge and hurly-burly of the waves when at their worst and wildest. We never before saw these birds on our shores except once, and that was while crossing Corran Ferry on a Sunday morning many years ago. We at that time drew attention to the presence of the stormy petrel in the Linnhe Loch as a rare occurrence, venturing to predict that a great storm, or a succession of great storms, must be close at hand, a prediction fully verified by the event, for, immediately afterwards, we had a full fortnight of the stormiest and wildest weather ever known along the western seaboard. In the way of further weather forecast, suffice it meanwhile to say that, if we interpret our wild-bird friends aright, January, too, will contribute his own full share of heavy gales and wild unsettled weather to the meteorology of a season already so remarkable for the force and fierceness of its eddying winds.

As a consequence of the late storms, we have had several consignments of rare birds for identification, and some very interesting ornithological notes from competent observers in various parts of the country, and on both coasts, from Galloway to Caithness. Our correspondents everywhere have the same story to tell—a large increase over ordinary seasons of wildfowl, Arctic and Pelagic, some of them of extremely rare occurrence in the British Islands. After the great November gale, the shores in many places were strewn with the bodies of dead sea-fowl, that, in spite of web and wing, were utterly helpless in the storm, and so were overwhelmed and drowned by the sheer force and fury of wind and waves. Of the birds sent to us for identification, the rarest, perhaps, is a specimen in excellent plumage of the red-necked phalarope (the *Phalaropus glacialis* of Latham), from the island of Mull. The lady who sends us this bird says in an accompanying note—

"After the hurricane of the 22d November one could pick up any number of all sorts of sea birds along the north-western shores of Mull, and it was probably the same on all our shores. It was not so surprising, perhaps, to find many dead birds of the smaller 'doucker' genus, for once they were caught in the huge rollers within a certain distance of the shore, there was clearly no escape for them; but it was a striking proof of the violence of the tempest to meet with dead gulls, gannets, cormorants, and various species of curlews, that seem to have been dashed upon the rocks and killed, or driven headlong into the sea and drowned, so extraordinary was the fury of the tempest on that dreadful morning. We have been calculating that the sea rose to a height of *eleven feet* higher than it was ever known to reach before in the memory of the 'oldest inhabitant.'"

Another rare bird comes from a gentleman in Sutherlandshire, and its satisfactory identification gave us a good deal of trouble. It was only when a distinguished ornithological friend in the south fully corroborated our own finding that we were satisfied that the bird in hand was none other than the black-tailed godwit (*Limosa melanura*), a rare species of *Tringa*. It was shot while feeding with a flock of redshanks (*Scolopax calidris*) on the sea beach somewhere in the neighbourhood of Helmsdale. A correspondent who lives near Stranraer sends us the following, which we very willingly reproduce, for he is an exceedingly shrewd, intelligent man :—

"The big storm on the 22d November was very violent all along the south coasts; quite as bad, I should think, if not even worse, than with you in the north-west. You ask about the birds. Well, they suffered a great deal, as you may believe, in such a dreadful tempest. A great number were dead on the shores of Loch Ryan—some killed by being dashed by the waves on the shore and rocks, and some, by being unable to fly in the hurricane, were overwhelmed by the 'yeasty waves,' and drowned. The survivors were for some days quite tame; they had been so much frightened by the storm, that they seemed not to be at all afraid of human beings. You could get quite near to them, for they were almost as tame as ducks or hens, until they recovered their strength and courage, and then they began to grow shyer.

"The land birds suffered a great deal too. Thrushes, finches, and robins were found dead in many places. Even hens and ducks, in some cases, were killed by being dashed against walls and fences by the strength of the gale. A very strong and powerful man, and very active, too, told me that when the storm was at the worst he faced it on a piece of level ground, and tried to go against it by bending well down and trying with all his might, but could not advance a single step. I never in all my life before saw Loch Ryan in such a state of wild commotion, The waves were the highest ever seen, and the screaming of the wind was enough to frighten any one. JOHN JAMIESON."

We have succeeded in procuring for our Antiquarian Museum a beautiful and, archæologically, most interesting and valuable specimen of the old mediæval Celtic brooch. It was found in a very curious place and in a very curious way. One day in autumn a shepherd in the opposite district of Appin, while in the honest discharge of his proper duties, happened to sit down to rest himself on the shoulder of the highest peak of Benvere, a mountain overhanging the waters of Loch Leven, and, although not the highest, certainly the most beautiful of Scottish mountains. While resting here at an elevation of more than three thousand feet, the shepherd chanced to poke his stick in an idle sort of way, and quite undesignedly, into the mossy sward at his feet, and in so doing brought up on the point of his crook what, when it came under our inspection, we discovered to be a very beautiful shoulder-brooch of solid silver, exquisitely chased and graved, and archæologically extremely interesting. It is an annular brooch of solid silver, three and a half inches in diameter. The *acus*, or pin, or "tongue" is wanting, the probability being that it was of baser metal than the annulus,—iron, perhaps silver-gilt or bronze, and that it consequently crumbled away from rust and oxidation, while the annulus, or brooch proper, itself remained as fresh and beautiful as it was on the day when it was lost or laid where it was found. It is graven with many beautiful devices in slight *alto relievo*, in the highest style of mediæval Celtic art, and with griffins or other fabulous monsters in attitudes natural or grotesque,—so beautifully executed, even in the minutest details, that one is constrained to wonder if a modern artist could do it better, or do it at all so well. It is by far the most beautiful thing of the kind we have ever had an opportunity of closely studying. The ornamentation of this brooch, in character, order, and style, is in some respects so peculiar that we gave much close study to the devices, alternating in compartments round the face of the annulus, with griffins and other fabulous monsters, in the hope that they might perhaps be symbolical, and have a meaning of their own, which would add largely to the interest and value of the relics if they were found to admit of any plausible interpretation. In this direction, however, we could arrive at nothing satisfactory; and except a well-defined Greek cross at the part of the annulus on which the point of the acus or pin rested, we suspect that the contents of all the other compartments are mere arbitrary ornaments, without any hidden meaning or message admitting of rational interpretation. The brooch, by the way, is to be known henceforward as the *Benvere Brooch*.

A very natural inquiry in connection with this brooch is, how came such an article of personal ornament to be lost on the top of Benvere? The brooch itself bears unmistakeable evidence, in the partial obliteration of the outer and inner edges of some of its ornamentation and otherwise, that it must have lain for a very long time in the spot whence, by the merest accident, it was so strangely recovered. We know that Appin was at one time so famous for its stags and wild-fowl, that two at least of the Stuart kings, James IV. and James V., frequently visited Duncan Stewart, the chief of the clan—*dilectus consanguineus*—our well-beloved blood relation, as in the charters his royal cousins always styled him—in his stronghold of Castle Stalker, for the purpose of hunting the stag and hawking. Eilean-an-Stalcaire, or the Falconer's Island, on which the castle is built, is so called because it was long occupied by a gentleman of the clan, who held what was considered a highly honourable office by the title of *Stalcaire'a Righ*, or the King's Falconer. We may therefore easily fancy a hunting party, consisting of James IV. and something like a score of favourite noblemen, attended by the Chief of Appin and the "duinne wassels" of the Clan, following the stag in Glen-Duror and Glen-a-Chaolais, and the brooch being dropped and lost, as in the evening the party were crossing the mountains homewards from Benbhan and Glen-a-Chaolais to Castle Stalker. The Chief of Appin himself, or one of his "duinne wassels," may have lost the brooch; for it is an article not likely to have belonged to any one of meaner birth, or, for that matter of it, may not this beautiful brooch have adorned the royal shoulder of the king himself? There is nothing outrageous or *prima facie* improbable in such a supposition, and if we believe that it was worn by the gallant king whilst hunting the stag amongst the green hills of Appin, how vividly it recalls that monarch's eventful reign, and the fatal fight of Flodden Field! The Benvere Brooch is, in any case, a most beautiful and interesting relic of old Celtic art of the fourteenth century, and we are glad to say that, by our intermediation, it is now by purchase the property of the Society of Antiquaries of Scotland.

CHAPTER XLII.

Mild Winter—A *Crubhan-Cait*—Wild-Flowers—Birds singing—Bats' abroad —An Egg in a Sparrow's Nest at New-Year Time.

THIS is in very truth an extraordinary winter, with a temperature almost constantly so much above the average, that we question very much if there has been a single daylight hour since this year of grace 1882 came in, in which, even in the open air, anybody, if directly challenged to it, could not make a *crubhan-cait* at will. And what, you will ask, is a *crubhan-cait*? And we reply that a *crubhan-cait*, literally translated, is just a cat's claw. And what, you will wonder, can a cat's claw have to do in this connection; what can the mildness or severity of a winter have to do with a cat's claw, or what, for that matter of it, can a cat's claw have to do with the meteorology of winter? You must know, then, that in the good old Parochial and Society School times the scholars in the winter season sometimes quarrelled amongst themselves as to the order in which, in pairs, or threes, or fours, as there was room for them around the hearth, they were entitled to the privilege of warming themselves for a few minutes close to the school-room fire. The work of the school usually commenced with the "copies" or writing lessons, and a scholar, with fingers benumbed with cold, was, *ipso facto*, it was evident, the least fit to wield a pen with any hope of being able to master the caligraphical niceties of text, half-text, or small hand. The numb-fingered scholar, it was clear, must get his hands thoroughly warmed into flexibility before he could hope to do his "copy" anything like justice, and the teacher, thoughtfully impartial and paternal, gave the privilege of a good warm at the fire first to such scholars as, at the word of command, visibly manifested their inability to do a *crubhan-cait* even when they tried their utmost. To do a *crubhan-cait* is to draw all the fingers and thumb into close contact at their tips, as a cat's claws lie close together when sheathed. If the hand was really numbed with cold, no boy or girl could do this, and their inability to do it was a clear proof that they were really very cold, and that a few minutes' close and kindly benefit of the fire was absolutely necessary before they sat down to their writing lessons. Others might complain of cold, and might, in truth, be cold enough, but while they could do a *crubhan-cait*, while they had the command of their fingers manifested in that act, it was held that as yet they were in a large degree better off than those who had so completely lost all control over the flexor muscles of the hand, that by no exertion of the will could they bring their numbed fingers into *crubhan-cait* form. Some scholars, in their eagerness to get to the fire, might perhaps try to cheat the master into a belief that they were unequal to a *crubhan-cait*, when they really could do it well enough if they liked. These "malingerers," however, to use an army term, hardly ever succeeded in the attempt, for the master's eye was usually sharp enough and practised enough to prevent imposition in such a case. There is a something *sui generis* in the numb and nerveless fingers really incapable of doing a *crubhan-cait*, easily distinguishable from a mere make-believe in such a matter, and scholars attempting to cheat the *dominie* in that direction were almost always detected in the act, and a brisk application of a stout three-tailed *taws* on the palms of the rascally "malingerers" never failed to render them incapable of anything but a very queer *crubhan-cait* for some time afterwards, because of the hot and pungent *dirl* that in such a case ran lightning-like along and into the tips of every individual digit. It will thus be understood what we mean by a *crubhan-cait*, a digital conformation perfectly possible, from the mildness of the season, for every one on each and every day of the last three months, but utterly impossible in the cold and frost of ordinary winters to people who have been for any length of time in the open air. The next time the reader is willing to persuade himself that he is very, very cold, let him try a *crubhan-cait*. If he cannot do it, his hands are really cold and numb, and by brisk rubbing or stout clapping of them *sub axillis*, an immediate effort should be made to restore the circulation; but if he finds that he can still gather together his fingers into the *crubhan-cait* form, he is as yet fairly well off, and has no great reason to complain.

But our present winter is not only remarkable for its mildness as tested by the *crubhan-cait* performance; its exceptional mildness is also very markedly manifested in other directions. Daisies, primroses, and other wild-flowers are at this moment as common on bank and brae, and almost as full blown and beautiful as one expects to find them in the early April of ordinary seasons. And what is perhaps more surprising still, some of our hardier, early breeding wild-birds have already built nests, and, in some cases at least, these nests have eggs in them. We know an old thorn tree in a neighbouring copse, in the bushy, well-fenced heart of which a pair of blackbirds had in the early days of last week almost finished a carefully constructed nest of the usual well-rounded coffee-cup-like pattern, and by this time, although we have not had an opportunity of going to look at them, we have no doubt at all that it contains its proper complement of beautiful greyish-green eggs, so charmingly mottled and marbled with pale liver and ferruginous brown. On Monday evening last, noticing the liveliness and activity of our own particular colony of sparrows, we climbed a ladder in order to look into a sparrow's nest in a clump of ivy that grows luxuriantly—so luxuriantly that we have to be constantly pruning it —along the south-eastern corner of our humble hermitage, and there, sure enough, were two eggs of a quartz whiteness, spotted as if from a pepper-box containing a mixture of ordinary pepper and cayenne, one of which we took away and pierced and "blew," in order to test its freshness. It was just possible, observe, that it might be a deserted nest of last season with two unhatched eggs still surviving, because so snugly domiciled in the cosy depths of a feather-lined structure so dry and comfortable. The egg, however, proved perfectly fresh and sweet, and there could be no doubt at all that it was laid by some precocious lady-sparrow during the week immediately preceding Handsel Monday. That same evening bats were flying and fluttering about in abrupt zig-zags and lively merry-go-rounds, as brisk and busy as ever we saw them, when performing at their best in warmest, stillest, gloaming of mildest Beltane-tide. Hens are "clocking" in all directions, and almost every hamlet can already boast of its brood or broods of January chickens, all of which, please to observe, have come into existence, not by the assistance of any cunning extraneous aid, or in any way at all artificially, but in the most matter of fact and rational way possible, so that this year, instead of eating our spring chickens in early summer, we may very confidently look forward to eating our winter chickens in early spring. For some days past the song-thrush, blackbird, hedge accentor, robin, wren, and chaffinch have been delighting us all, evening and morning, with their song. Privet and quickset hedges, gooseberry and currant bushes, blackthorn, birch, and wild brier, are already rich with a marvellous opulence of living buds swollen to the bursting, and of the most delicate and beautiful green. Grass, too, exhibits an active vitality and upward rush that is simply wonderful at this season; meadows, woodland glades, and sheltered brae faces being in many places richer and greener now, in mid-January, than in ordinary seasons you expect to find them in mid-April. What it is all to come to we do not know. The probability, however, is that a period of cold, with much genuine winter weather *en attendant*, must come our way ere long, and with an anti-*crubhan-cait* severity that shall make us shiver in our shoes once and again ere yet the Ides of March have come and gone. And in this case, all our pretty little wild-flowers, so sweetly beautiful and fragrant, must shrivel up and die; and if the present exceptionally mild weather only lasts for another fortnight, there will be callow young in many a wild-bird nest—downy little gapers, always painfully naked, as you may have observed, about the lower part of the neck in their first stage of blind helplessness, and these poor little things, in the face of even a single day of intense frost or sleet and snow, must also shiver miserably, and drop and dwine and die. Winter in mid-spring, according to the Gaelic adage, throws summer into the lap of autumn. In any case, our present winter is meteorologically the most extraordinary that has come about since meteorology first formally assumed the functions and designation of a regular science; and whatever are to be the results, pastorally, agriculturally, and otherwise, of a season so abnormal, there can be no doubt that the readings, barometrically and thermometrically, of 1881-82 will, in some six months hence, be well worth the most careful and attentive perusal, with a view to the intelligent recognition of the lessons which they shall be found to teach. And this is, perhaps, the proper time and place to repeat with some emphasis what we said for the first time some five-and-twenty years ago —that meteorology, in order to attain to something like assured success in the direction of weather prognostics, must closely ally itself with living, practical natural history, and more especially with botany and littoral ornithology.

CHAPTER XLIII.

The Cuckoo on February 10th—Willie Drummond, Pearl Fisher and Herbalist.

WE met a man the other day whom we have known for many years as an herbalist or culler of simples, an avocation which he varies in the proper season by doing a little pearl fishing in the deep and almost currentless reaches of many of our rivers near their sources in the mossy solitudes of the distant uplands, and he assured us very solemnly that on the previous day—10th February—about eleven o'clock in the forenoon, he heard the cuckoo, and afterwards saw the bird itself winging its hawk-like flight from one birch-wood clump to another, just as he had descended the last steps of the Devil's Staircase, on his way from the Moor of Rannoch to Kinlochleven. Was he telling the truth? We believe he was, for he is an intelligent, and, so far as we have been able to appraise his character, a respectable man; and in this case our cunningest cross-examination failed to lead him into self-contradiction in the slightest degree, or to make him vary his account of that particular morning's adventures, even in their minutest particulars, by a hair's-breadth. Nor, startling as it seems at first sight, is there after all much to wonder at such an encounter in a season otherwise so exceptional. The cuckoo may well have come, and already given utterance to its minor third melody, so easy of execution, when many of our native wild-birds are already in full song, and others well advanced with the labours of incubation, and when in our walks abroad we find the flowers of April and early May already plentiful on bank and brae. When butterflies, too, are on the wing, and humble-bees already humming their vernal song, it is not so much a wonder, when you come to think of it, that the cuckoo should also be seen and heard in the well-sheltered birchen solitudes, which, on its first arrival in our country, it so loves to haunt, and so enlivens with its song that the wilderness and solitary place are glad for it, and straightway the desert, with its thousand wild-flowers, is made to rejoice and blossom as the rose. We have since noticed in the newspapers that the cuckoo has also been heard in the south of Scotland, which makes it all the more likely that "Willie Drummond," the herbalist, may have seen and heard it at Kinlochleven. Meteorologists will, perhaps, tell us that there have been instances of quite as mild and warm and open winters as this has been, even within the memory of living men, but we do not suppose that any one will venture to say that until 1882 the cuckoo was ever heard before in early February on the skirts of the Grampians.

Willie Drummond, pearl fisher and herbalist, represents a class of peripatetic philosophers, with whom, under circumstances otherwise favourable, we dearly love to have a confidential roadside crack, all about their solitary wanderings in odd and out-of-the-way places, when for days and days together they have no other companions than the *feræ naturæ* proper to the locality whose stream is being duly fished for the pearl-bearing mussel, and whose remotest nook and cranny is being closely searched for some rare plant whose leaves or root, duly prepared, is in certain ailments believed to be potent for good in the form of embrocation, draught, or salve. It is curious that, even if you try your best, you will find it a very difficult matter to discover the particular town, village, or parish to which one of this peripatetic fraternity really belongs. Ask Willie Drummond, for example, where he belongs to, and the reply is never more definite or precise than that he belongs " doon Dundee way ;" while in reply to the same query last autumn, another man of this class, a dealer in the rarer kinds of ferns, would come no nearer the mark than to say that his proper home was " awa' Dumfriesshire way." Willie Drummond does not pretend to be an herb-doctor himself; all he does is to gather the herbs most in request in their proper localities, at the proper season, and these he conveys in assorted bundles to the herb-doctors proper, who duly prepare them in various ways for ready administration to their patients, in the form that may be judged best for any particular ailment. Willie assures us that within his own circuit there is no town of any consequence without its herb-doctor; and sometimes, in the larger manufacturing towns, there will be as many as five or six herb-doctors, all in busy and fairly well-paying practice from year's end to year's end. Willie frequently gets as much as £5 for a month's successful herb-gathering; and of the herbs most in request he gave us a list, which on many accounts is extremely interesting. Willie visits, when his stock of herbs is abundant, some of the manufacturing towns of the north of England, where he has never any difficulty in disposing at a good price of as many herbs "of the right sort," to use his own phrase, as he can carry in the huge waterproof bolster-slip-like bag which serves him for wallet, wardrobe, and general storehouse. Willie is upwards of sixty years of age, and under the middle height, but as active as a weasel and as tough as a bit of ash tree root. Except for a couple of months in summer, he constantly wears two suits of clothes, one over the other, and a short waterproof cape over all. When amongst the upland wilds he sleeps in the best shelter he can find—on the lee of a large boulder, in the cleft of a rock, within the walls of a sheep-fank or deserted bothy—anywhere! and he never has rheumatism, or toothache, or neuralgia, or a cold or cough, or anything of that sort. Never even a headache, he assured us with a chuckle, except sometimes of a morning, after realising handsomely on his herb sales in some large town in the south, when he invites his patrons, the herb-doctors, and a few of his more intimate friends to a supper and *gaudeamus*. When expostulated with for spending his earnings so foolishly, he replied that it couldn't be avoided; that it was the custom of the herb trade, and that he must be like other people. In reply to our inquiry as to how he managed for food in his wanderings amongst the solitudes of the thinly peopled uplands, Willie assured us that, in the matter of food, he was much better off than we might suppose. When he leaves the beaten track and takes to the mountains, he carries a large flask of cold tea, which he can always make hot when he wants it. He has in his wallet a small supply of bread, cold boiled sausage, cheese, and "a bit butter," he added, "when I can get it fresh and good; for I canna thole the butter sold in the shop now-a-days; it's no butter ava." He gratefully acknowledges that he is always well treated in the houses of the foresters, shepherds, and herdsmen of the uplands. "I whiles bring them a dozen or twa o' guid burn trout, for which, in mony ways, they pay me ten times over; and, trout or no trout, I am always sure o' my share o' what's going." Willie Drummond is a bachelor, having no particular home anywhere, living a strange, nomadic life, harming nobody, and harmed by none; and from year's end to year's end probably enjoying quite as much genuine happiness in his own way as is arrogated to themselves by the thousands who, if they noticed him at all, would only notice him as something to be greatly pitied—a waif, a wanderer upon the earth. Little as one would think it, Willie is a philanthropist in his way; not, indeed, in his character of herb-gatherer, for that is simply his profession—a matter of pounds, shillings, and pence —but in another and rather curious direction. It has been finely said that the man who, by his forethought and industry, causes two blades of grass to grow where only one grew before, is a benefactor to his species; and if the multiplication of trees is to be taken as a step in the same direction, and therefore also commendable, then is our friend Willie, waif as he may seem, beyond all doubt a benefactor to his kind. One afternoon, many years ago, Willie was sitting on a brae face in Glen-Ogle, munching a large and rosy-cheeked apple, of which he happened to have some in his wallet. When he came to the core, and saw the dark-brown pips snugly nestling in their cells, he recollected, for the first time in his life, he said, what they meant and were intended for, and looking about him for suitable and sheltered spots, he scraped a bed for the seeds, and covering them in with earth, he marked the spot with a little cairn, so that if he came the way again he might easily find it, and have a look at the buried seeds, if they were dead, or had made a start with the intention of growing into actual trees. It was some two or three years afterwards before Willie had an opportunity of revisiting the spot, and he was delighted beyond measure to find two pretty little plants, very juvenile apple trees, that had grown from the pips in a sheltered spot where they were likely to do well. Always since then Willie has been quietly planting apple, pear, cherry, and other trees from the seeds in odd and out-of-the-way places, and he is delighted on revisiting these localities to find that even a few out of the many put into the ground have germinated and begun to show signs of lusty vitality and general well-doing. Upon the whole, one cannot help looking upon Willie with respect. He gathers herbs to be used in the alleviation of human sufferings and the cure of human ailments. He fishes pearls for the delectation and adornment of beauty, and he plants the seeds of trees of all kinds because it affords him real pleasure to see these seeds germinate into all the promise of a growth that shall at once be ornamental and useful. This tree-planting trait in Willie Drummond's character we thought it proper to mention as something very much in his favour, but mainly because it is well to leave on record the fact itself, in order that the botanist of a future generation may be saved from utter bewilderment when he may come to wonder how certain trees could possibly get a footing in localities so unlikely, so far removed from human dwellings and the usual aboricultural amenities and surroundings.

To no other living man, perhaps, is the topography of Scotland so minutely known as to Willie. The topography, that is, of the mainland, for Willie has never been in the Hebrides. Away from the beaten tracks, he knows every inch of the country in its remotest and least frequented nooks and corners as familiarly as a shepherd who has been years in the same employment knows his own particular beat. He has for years been gathering officinal herbs in the loneliest solitudes of remotest glen and mountain, from Duncansbay Head to the Mull of Galloway, while with the sources, as well as with the many windings of every river and stream and "burn" of any consequence north of the Tweed, he is as familiar as we are with the source and windings of the purling streamlet that waters our own glebe. His description of the upland solitudes which he visits so often, and of which he speaks as if in some mysterious way they were his own property, and in a sense in which they could belong to nobody else, always reminds us of the "Polyolbion" of Michael Drayton. Even Drayton's enthusiasm is tepid, and his praise of Charnwood Forest tame, when compared with Willie's glowing description of the summer and autumnal delights of the mountain solitudes of Braemar, Badenoch, and Breadalbane. As may readily be believed, Willie has had some curious adventures in his many perigrinations amongst the upland wilds. Meanwhile, we may state that a very respectable man told us on Saturday that he, too, had heard the cuckoo in Lettermore of Appin on the 11th February, which goes so far to buttress Willie Drummond's assertion that he heard and saw it on the 10th.

CHAPTER XLIV.

April Drought—Early Nesting Birds—Survival of the Fittest—Rival Song Thrushes singing at Midnight—Ian Mac Roanuill Oig of Glencoe—Singing Mice.

IT is not easy pleasing people in matters meteorological. We were all agrowl with the exceeding wetness of March, and now we are even more querulously agrowl with the exceeding dryness of April. (*N.B.*—Written before the storm of Saturday-Monday.) It is perfectly true that all over the West Highlands March was exceedingly wet, as well as persistently stormy, having given us more rain, perhaps, and soaking sleet, than any other March for upwards of twenty years past; and it is not the less true that April has up to this date been much too parchingly dry—a bright, burning sun overhead by day, a touch of frost by night, with a keen north-east wind constantly blowing across the Grampians, sharp of edge and biting as a newly honed razor—a fierce euroclydon that makes it uncomfortable all round, although favourable enough for such agricultural operations as were simply impossible during the wet and storm of March. Fortunately, however, cattle and sheep are in first-rate condition, owing to the exceptionally mild and open character of the winter, while provender is sufficiently abundant to last until genial rain, succeeding this parching drought, make the grass of early

May to spring up with a rush that shall straightway afford a full and succulent mouthful to the ruminants that then, with paunch abulge, shall low with very gladness in their pastures, as if in acknowledgment of the bounteous care and goodness of Him whose are the cattle upon a thousand hills. Adverse also to our wild-bird friends, and unkindly throughout as was the month of March, they battled it out bravely. Our early nesting birds, many of whom had already hatched out their first broods whilst it was yet February, got through it all much better than could have been expected, for the number of young now on the wing seems to indicate that only the weaklings of these early broods succumbed to the wet and cold of March. And here it is worth observing, what seems to have escaped the notice of most ornithologists, that, in one particular at least, it is precisely the same with our wild-birds as with our domestic poultry. In every brood there is a weakling, a chick weaklier from the first, and less robust than its fellows—a "shott" bird, to use a pastoral term—which under sufficiently favourable circumstances may live and thrive after a sort, but which in an unkindly season of cold and scarcity is pretty sure to dwine and die, even when the rest do fairly well and thrive—a very practical illustration, by the way, of the doctrine of the survival of the fittest, of which the student of wild-bird life may find abundant verification if he only looks close enough into the economics and vital statistics of our feathered favourites, year after year, as the breeding season comes round. All our best feathered musicians are now in full song; their every note at its perfectest and purest, without hitch or halt in strophe or antistrophe, and thrown off apparently with so little of effort or premeditation, that to sing seems as easy to them as to breathe. Having occasion to be abroad at a late hour on Sunday last, we were a good deal surprised, and not a little pleased, to find that in a thickly wooded dell, near which we had to pass on our way home, a pair of rival song-thrushes were in loud and fluent song, when it must have been within less than half an hour of midnight, for Jupiter had long since set, and Arcturus was almost in the zenith. They sang splendidly under the brilliant starlight, the noise of a distant waterfall, as it rose and fell in varying cadence on the breeze, blending not inharmoniously with the midnight melody of the competing songsters in the dell. At this season of the year, indeed, and under favourable circumstances, the song-thrush, with but a very short interval of silence just before the dawn, and for half an hour perhaps about noon, may be said to sing all the day through and all the night long—a fact, by the way, which did not escape the attention of a seventeenth century Gaelic bard of some note in his day, Ian Mac Raonuill Oig, of the Glencoe Macdonalds, who, in a very sweet pastoral, apostrophising the *smeorach* or mavis, says—

"'S binn leam an smeorach a sheinneas,
Gu loinneil 'an coille ran crann ;
Smeorach a bhroillich bhric, riabhaich,
'S mil air ghob dhi 'n àm 'fiachain nan rann ;
'S math a sheinnneas i òran
'N àm do 'n ghréin a bhi g' òradh nam beann,
'Sann 's an oidhche cha stad i
'Chuir nan smuid dhi feadh bhadan nan gleann !"

("Delightful to me the mavis that sings
  Her sweetly musical lay in the multitudinous wood;
  The mavis, with its brown and speckled breast,
  And with honey on his bill what time it lists it to sing!
  Full well can it trill forth its lay,
  What time the sun is bathing the uplands with gold,
  *Nor will she even in the night-time
  Cease to sing in the wooded glenlets amongst the hills.*")

Ian Mac Raonuill Oig, the author of the really beautiful pastoral from which the above is quoted, and which has never been printed, was an old man at the time of the massacre in 1692, from which, after beholding some of its horrors, he only escaped by the gallantry of his only son, who, folding the old man in his plaid, carried him on his back, as the pious Æneas of old did Anchises, until by a difficult and round-about way they reached a boat on the beach of Loch Leven, in which they crossed to their cousins at Callart, where they found friendly shelter, until the departure of the Government troops from the district made it safe for them to return to their ruined and blood-stained home at Achtriachtan. Farther on in the season, the whitethroat, too, and hedge accentor and reed wren, may frequently be heard singing at midnight, when the weather is fine, and the nights are dewy and still. These last, however, always in a subdued tone, tremulous and broken, as if they were singing in their sleep, which not improbably may really be the case; whereas the song-thrush, when he sings, be it morning, noon, or midnight, always seems to sing with all his might his beautiful melody, so mellifluously sweet, and rich, and round.

From singing birds, by the way, to singing mice, the

transition is easy. The singing, so called, of a mouse is due to a kind of bronchial disease, to which the little rodent seems to be more liable than any of its congeners—a disease of the same nature as the "whistling" of a broken-winded horse, and the wheezing of asthma in the human subject. The "singing" of a mouse, in short, is caused by a contracted state of the bronchial tubes in a paroxysm of asthma, and usually ceases, as do the gasping and wheezing in the case of the human subject, when for the time the paroxysm is over. If a singing mouse is caught alive and unhurt, as by means of the "Mouse Lobster Trap," for example, it will be seen to be breathing rapidly and spasmodically, with half-open mouth, and when after a time the paroxysm returns, the cheeping, musical notes called its singing are sure to recur, the little sufferer in such a case usually assuming a couchant position, and with dilated eyes almost bursting from their sockets, and a rapid heaving of the flanks, exhibiting all the signs of extreme suffering and distress. The kindest thing to do with a singing mouse, therefore, is to trap and kill it, for when caught it is usually a mere skeleton, and must lead a very miserable life. It has been noticed that singing mice are commoner in meal and flour stores than anywhere else—than, for instance, in grain, cheese, or bacon stores, the reason probably being that their constant breathing of the finely comminuted and almost impalpable dust of such places brings on the asthmatic ailment, which in its paroxysms gives rise to the stridulous cheepings and quasi-musical notes, whence the term "singing" mouse. Singing, as a rule, implies a sense of joy, realised or expectant, in the singer, or it may be the expression and outcome of self-conscious pride and rivalry in love. The so-called singing of a mouse, on the contrary, is always to be interpreted as an expression for the moment of intense suffering and pain on the part of the poor little panting rodent.

CHAPTER XLV.

Heavy Snowfall in April—Snow at Culloden Moor on the day of the Battle, 16th April 1746—Flora Macdonald.

SNOW-SHOWERS in mid-April are not uncommon, but such a prodigious fall of snow as that of Sunday, the 16th inst., is a phenomenon so rare, that one of the oldest and most intelligent men in our parish solemnly assured us the other day that, in a vivid retrospect of the seasons, extending over half a century at least, he has no recollection of such a fall of snow—*aig am breth nan uan*, as he phrased it; that is, in the lambing season. Fortunately, here, as elsewhere, the fall, though universal, and quite as heavy in the valleys and by the sea-shore as upon the mountains, was a most gentle fall throughout, unaccompanied by a breath of wind of sufficient energy to deflect from a plumb descent the multitudinous flakes by an hand's-breadth. There was consequently no drifting, each individual flake seeming to come direct and undeflected from the zenith, in order to rest itself, as if awearied with its wanderings in space, on the bosom of a world attractive to the chilled and homeless wanderer, by reason of its vernal greenery and wealth of vernal flowers. The snow commenced to fall at seven o'clock on Sunday morning, and on our return from church in the afternoon we found that on a field in our own glebe, and but a few feet above the level of the sea, the depth already was as nearly as possible *fourteen* inches. Had such a prodigious fall of snow at this season of the year been accompanied by the wild, wayward winds so frequently attendant on such phenomena, the consequences to sheep-farmers everywhere must have been disastrous; nor less so if a sudden frost supervening had bound down for a time the vast mass of snow that for the moment covered the face of the country to such a depth. Fortunately, however, as has been said, there was no drift, nor did frost supervene. After the snow ceased falling, a quiet, steady thaw set in, and by the following morning the low-lying lands were clear of it, and under a bright warm sun even the uplands had by the early afternoon parted with their unseasonable burden. On Wednesday heavy westerly rains set in, which soon washed away the snow, even from the mountain heights, so that under the bright sun and cloudless skies of Thursday morning very little snow was to be seen, except the usual corrie and gorge wreaths, which year after year are there in any case, seldom disappearing entirely before midsummer. It was, in fact, a big snowfall, that, if it came unseasonably and unexpectedly, departed quickly and quietly, as if ashamed of itself, and without doing the slightest harm either to animal or vegetable life. The lambing season, shepherds assure us, goes on famously, and none the worse perhaps because of the seasonable moisture supplied to the thirsty uplands by the snowfall that melted so opportunely. Wild-birds are singing merrily in bosque and brake, while of wild-flowers the name is legion, and bright, blooming, and fragrant as the most passionate lover of floral beauty could desire. We would, by the way, call the reader's attention to the fact that our big snow-storm day of 1882 was the 16th of April, the anniversary of the battle of Culloden; and it is interesting to know that on that memorable day, one hundred and thirty-six years ago, heavy snow-showers from the north-west swept over Drumossie Moor, largely interfering at the most critical moment with the evolutions of the Highland army. When the most important charge of the day took place, the Highlanders in their advance were so blinded and impeded by a swirling snow-shower, that they were put to great disadvantage in attacking the enemy. Our knowledge of this fact is not due to any contemporary meteorological record, nor to any of the many histories of the '45 that have been published, but to an old Gaelic song. One of the combatants who was severely wounded, but who escaped, and survived to sing his *coronach* or lament over the deaths and disasters of that fateful day, gives the blinding snow-showers as one of the many reasons why the Highlanders were less successful at Culloden than at Prestonpans and Falkirk. It will often be found that a careful study of the popular poetry, the songs and ballads of any particular era in our annals, will in many directions afford us valuable information not to be gathered from any other source, and information, too, so far as it goes, almost always to be depended upon for its accuracy.

The story of the amiable and gallant Flora Macdonald, by the late Rev. Alexander Macgregor, Inverness, is "a plain, unvarnished tale," stripped of every shred of sensational fiction, and yet more interesting to the thoughtful reader, and even more genuinely romantic as a simple narrative of well authenticated facts, than if presented to our attention with all the embellishments of ballad poetry and romance. Flora was in truth neither more or less than a young lady, very fair to look upon, with a wise head and warm heart, rather small in stature, of quiet and self-possessed yet pleasing manners, who from youth to old age, as maid, wife, and mother, conducted herself so properly, and discharged all the duties of her station so admirably, that she was constantly looked up to for kindly guidance and advice, and greatly respected and beloved by all who knew her. She was the daughter of highly respectable parents, and connected more or less directly with all the best families of the Outer Hebrides and of Skye. Although it is beyond question that the unfortunate Charles Edward owed his life to her marvellous courage and devotion, their acquaintance was much briefer and less intimate than is generally supposed. They met for the first time in the Long Island on the 26th of June 1746, and parted at Portree, in Skye, on the 30th of the same month; nor during the few days and nights they were thus more or less in company were they once, even for a single moment, *solus cum sola*, alone together. There was in truth not a particle of love, in the romantic sense of the term, in the connection. She was as pure and modest as she was brave and true, and in all she did actuated solely by loyalty to the Prince whom she believed to be the rightful heir to the throne of his ancestors. He was to her—as in truth he really was *de jure*—the Prince of Wales; by the demission of his brother, and on the death of his father, whenever that event should happen, the only rightful heir to what may be called the triple crown of James the First. She resolved to save him, when, without her aid, and with a price of £30,000 set upon his head by a Government whom, with a handful of Highlanders, he had frightened out of its senses, his capture and execution were almost matters of certainty. She resolved to save him, and she did save him, counting the captivity and sufferings to which she was subjected in consequence as but of little moment compared with the approbation of her own heart, and the consciousness of having performed a duty the most sacred in such a way as to secure for herself the respect and admiration of the friends of legitimacy, loyalty, and right throughout the world. Many years ago the late Angus Macdonell of Insh, in Brae-Lochaber, a genuine Highlander, and one of the best sennachies of his day, told us of an affecting little incident in the life of Flora Macdonald; and we have often thought that, in the hands of a competent artist, it might be made the subject-matter of an admirable picture. Shortly after her release from imprisonment, and on the eve of her marriage, Flora, while on a visit to some friends near Inverness, went to Strathglass in order to see a Father James Cameron, a priest, who was distantly related to her. Father Cameron, who had been many years abroad, was now a very old man, and so frail and feeble as to be unable to move from his arm-chair without assistance. He had never seen Flora before, although the story of her undaunted courage and devotion in the cause of the Prince was well known to him. After a long confidential interview, Flora rose to depart, when Father Cameron, out of respect for her, made an effort to rise from his chair in order to bid her a becoming farewell. Taking her hand in his, he kissed it fervently, then, solemnly blessing her, the venerable old man dismissed her with these words, *"Benedicta tu inter mulieres; et quòd hæc fecisti beatam te prædicabunt omnes ætates"* ("Blessed art thou among women; and because of the things that thou hast done, all generations shall call thee blessed"). Mr. Macdonell added that his grandaunt, who was present at this meeting between Flora and Father Cameron, used to talk of it in long after years as altogether one of the most solemn and affecting scenes she had ever witnessed.

CHAPTER XLVI.

Sailing on Loch Leven—Mackerel—Porpoises—*Argus* in the *Odyssey*—
"*Lassie*"—Age of Dogs—Dame Juliana Berners—Lassie's Grave.

WHILE sailing up Loch Leven the other day, we saw a very pretty sight, and so uncommon as to be worth the chronicling. It was a bright afternoon, with just enough of wind over the quarter to set our lugsail well abulge, and make our little "Penguin" dance merrily over the rippling wavelets. When just entering the narrows of Ballachulish, the sea right ahead of us became suddenly aboil with the frolicsome play to the surface of quite a shoal of mackerel. It was only for a minute or so, for the surface play of mackerel is always of the briefest, but it was a minute into which was crowded a great deal that was interesting and beautiful. The shoal, which must have numbered many thousands, was in liveliest action, leaping about and dashing along the surface with a splash and incessant flap of fin and tail that might have been heard a quarter of a mile away, the beautiful iridescent hues and metallic lustre of the dancing scombers forming in the brilliant sunshine a play of prismatic colours that was gorgeously splendid. It was at times as if a score of tiny rainbows of the most brilliant hues were being rapidly interwoven, only to be instantly untwisted again, in order to be rewoven into a newer and still brighter pattern, in and over an acre of sea, all abubble and aboil with the gambols of the frolicsome shoal. We have hinted that, when thus leaping bodily out of the water, and wildly gambolling, the mackerel must have been in frolicsome mood; and that fish do frequently leap in the air, and dash along the surface of the water all in frolic and play, is unquestionable; but on this particular occasion the lively action of the shoal may have been owing to terror rather than to exuberance of joy. As we were returning by the same spot shortly afterwards, we noticed a troop of porpoises tumbling outwards with the first of ebb, and *they*, perhaps in their eagerness for a mackerel supper, may very possibly have been at the bottom of all the liveliness of action and sunlit splendour of iridescence in the shoal which, not dreaming of the true state of matters, had so delighted us only half an hour before. Be this, however, as it may, what we wish to impress upon the tourist is, that if he is thoroughly to appreciate and enjoy the West Highlands, he must, if he is wise, be frequently afloat, paddling his own canoe, or having somebody else paddling it for him. The studies of sea-bird life and motion that come under one's notice in such circumstances are alone worth all the trouble and expense attendant on an occasional afternoon's boating on as many of our beautiful western lochs as the intelligent tourist may find time to visit. Our own favourite lochs are the Linnhe Loch and Loch Leven; but the tourist can hardly go wrong, or be much disappointed whithersoever he turns his face, for *all* our western lochs are beautiful exceedingly, and their beauty is never so striking and impressive as when quietly studied from a boat, which, whether moving by force of oars or sails, is constantly changing one's point of view.

Beautiful and touching as is the story of Argus in the *Odyssey*, captious critics have long since been pointing to it as an episode in which honest Homer nods in assigning to a dog too great an age. The reader will remember how, after an interval of twenty years, Argus recognises his long absent master. Pope's translation of the passage is excellent, and not too long to quote at length. The disguised Ulysses and Eumæus are at the palace gates :—

> " Thus, near the gates, conferring as they drew,
> Argus, the dog, his ancient master knew ;
> He, not unconscious of the voice and tread,
> Lifts to the sound his ear, and rears his head :
> Bred by Ulysses, nourished at his board,
> But ah ! not fated long to please his lord !
> To him, his swiftness and his strength were vain ;
> The voice of glory called him o'er the main.
> Till then in every sylvan chase renown'd
> With Argus, Argus ! rung the woods around ;
> With him the youth pursued the goat or fawn,
> Or traced the mazy leveret o'er the lawn.
>
> " Now left to man's ingratitude he lay,
> Unhoused, neglected in the public way,
> And where on heaps the rich manure was spread,
> Obscene with reptiles, took his sordid bed.
>
> " He knew his lord ; he knew and strove to meet ;
> In vain he strove to crawl and kiss his feet ;
> Yet (all he could) his tail, his ears, his eyes,
> Salute his master, and confess his joys.
> Soft pity touched the mighty master's soul,
> Adown his cheek a tear unbidden stole—
> Stole unperceived ; he turned his head and dried
> The drop humane : then thus impassioned cried—

"' What noble beast in this abandoned state,
Lies here all helpless at Ulysses' gate?
His bulk and beauty speak no vulgar praise;
If, as he seems, he was in better days,
Some care his age deserves; or was he prized
For worthless beauty? therefore now despised!
Such dogs, and men, there are, mere things of state,
And always cherished by their friends, the great.'

"' Not, Argus, so (Eumæus thus rejoined);
But served a master of a nobler kind,
Who never, never shall behold him more,
Long, long since perished on a distant shore!
O, had you seen him, vigorous, bold, and young,
Swift as a stag, and as a lion strong!
Him no fell savage on the plain withstood,
None 'scaped him, bosom'd in the gloomy wood;
His eyes how piercing, and his scent how true,
To winde the vaypour in the tainted dew!
Such when Ulysses left his natal coast;
Now years unnerve him, and his lord is lost!
The women keep the generous creature bare,
A sleek and idle race is all their care:
The master gone, the servants what restrains?
Or dwells humanity where riot reigns?
Jove fixed it certain, that whatever day
Makes man a slave, takes half his worth away.'
This said, the honest herdsman strode before;
The musing monarch pauses at the door;
The dog whom fate had granted to behold
His lord, *when twenty tedious years had roll'd*,
Takes a last look, and having seen him, dies;
So closed for ever faithful Argus' eyes!"

Dogs, say the objectors, do not attain to twenty years of age; their allotted span of life is considerably less than *that*, and Homer therefore is wrong. But, curiously enough, it seems to have escaped the notice of the critics that a close study of the text leads inevitably to the conclusion that Argus, at the time of his death, must have been not twenty, but at the least five-and-twenty years of age, so that the objection as usually stated is in truth less forcible than it might easily be made on a full and fair interpretation of the narrative as written. Ulysses was absent twenty years, but to this has to be added the age attained by Argus *before* his master's departure from Ithaca for Troy. He cannot have been a mere pup, or even a very young dog at the time of Ulysses' departure, for he had proved himself a right good dog, swift and valiant in the chase, whilst also in him all the canine faculties had already reached their full development and strength, as is abundantly evidenced by his retentive memory and sagacity in so quickly, after a twenty years' interval, recognising his master even in his beggar's disguise. An old forester and gamekeeper of much experience with dogs, and great love for all the canine race, told us last night that, in his opinion, a sporting dog, duly broken to his work, and under proper management and mastery, was at its best when about four years old; and if we admit that Argus had attained this age before the departure of Ulysses for Troy, his age when he died, under circumstances so affecting, cannot, on a fair interpretation of the text, be put down at less than four-and-twenty, or even five-and-twenty years; and it is simply the truth to say, even if Homer should suffer by the confession, that not one dog in ten thousand attains to such a lengthened age. A dog at twenty years of age is relatively about as old as a man at one hundred, and we know how extremely rare are well authenticated instances of that age among human beings. But when we gather from the text, not indeed directly, but clearly enough notwithstanding, that Argus attained to the age of four or five-and-twenty years, it is very much the same as if Homer had so distributed events in the history of one of his most prominent characters —of Nestor, for example, or of Ulysses himself—that, putting everything together, he must at his death have attained to the age of something like one hundred and fifteen or one hundred and twenty years; and in such a case we should none of us have any hesitation in saying that although such an age, with intellect still unimpaired, is perhaps possible, and not absolutely incredible, yet it is so extremely improbable as to come within the category of unwarranted exaggerations, even in an epic where supernaturalism and exaggeration are confessedly part and parcel of the plot.

Now, if the reader asks what all this dissertation is *apropos* of, we reply that it has to do in more ways than one with the death of our dear, good, faithful, brown-eyed collie " Lassie," who looked upon us her last loving look of absolute trust and affectionate regard on the morning of Thursday last. Poor " Lassie " has often had " honourable mention " in our Nether Lochaber papers, and, liberal as was our praise of her, she more than deserved it all. She was beyond question one of the truest, steadfastest, and wisest dogs that ever barked at heel; and, what does not always happen either in the case of dogs or men, she was as merry and playful when the game was " romp and run—the ball," as she was honest and earnest, and good and true when serious business claimed her undivided attention. If men and dogs would only take a leaf out of "Lassie's" book in the direction of their intertwisting fun and frolic in fair proportion with the serious business of life, intermingling their *seria cum jocis*, the inevitable gravities and solemnities of life, with a due proportion of "weel-timed daffing," all the chances were in favour of brighter, happier, and longer lives, both for men and dogs, than is at present the rule. Despite and notwithstanding all the intertwisted vitality of his "nine lives," the proverb solemnly assures us, as the result of a careful *post-mortem*, that "care killed the cat," and a truer proverb, whether as regards man, or dog, or cat, never was uttered. "Lassie" was in truth the wisest dog we ever knew, and despite all her wisdom, or rather because of it, she was, as we have said, and almost to the last hour of her life, as fond of a bit of frolic and fun as any six months' old scapegrace pup in the parish; always ready, however, to be serious and staid enough when occasion called. We believe that we are within six months either way of the truth in the matter when we say that she had attained the very great age for a dog of nineteen years, a conclusion that we arrive at in the following way. It was in the summer of 1866—just sixteen years ago—that "Lassie" first found shelter under our roof, during a violent storm of thunder and lightning and heavy rain, which doubtless drove her to seek the readiest refuge from the elemental turmoil available at the moment. She first entered our house, in short, as a stray dog, and never afterwards left us. Whence she came, or who previously owned her, we could never discover, although we made every possible inquiry with a view to her restoration to her proper master if he could be found. She was then decidedly a young dog, as her lithe and graceful form, great speed, and magnificent set of teeth, white as ivory and sharp as darning needles, very abundantly proved; and yet she was not so *very* young but that she had already been taught almost all a well-bred collie's duties in connection with the management, both outfield and infield, of sheep and cattle. We conclude, therefore, that when she first found shelter under our roof she was not less than two, and not more than three years old, which, added to the sixteen years she lived with us, make up what we maintain is a very great age for a dog—nineteen years, with a possible error of not more than six months either way. It will be understood that all the circumstances of her surroundings were in the first degree favourable to long life. She was by her extraordinary sagacity and affectionate disposition a great favourite in the district; everybody knew and spoke a kind word to "Lassie." Never pampered, she was always well fed and thoroughly comfortable, with just enough of work to keep her always in a state of perfect health. We cannot fancy any dog more favourably placed for attaining to a great age, and therefore we have come to the conclusion that from eighteen to twenty years may be confidently set down as about the very greatest age ever attained by a dog, and that even at fifteen years of age a dog may safely be scheduled as already *very* old. The Lady Juliana Berners, Prioress of Sopewell Nunnery, who in the fourteenth century wrote the *Boke of Hawkyng and*

Huntyng, a curious subject, by the way, for a lady in her position to write about, says—

> "The beste dogge that ever bitche hadde,
> At nyne yeres is full badde."

Her reference, of course, being to the sporting dog of the period, and meaning that at nine years of age a sporting dog is well nigh useless. Let sportsmen say whether this holds true of the staghound, greyhound, pointer, setter, and other sporting dogs of our own time. Aristotle affirms that dogs frequently live till they are two-and-twenty years old; but, for our own part, we would rather agree with Pliny, who says of the dogs of Laconia what is probably near the truth as to the age of dogs at all times and in all countries, "*Canes Laconici vivant annis-denis, feminæ duodenis, cætera genera quindecim annos, aliquando viginti*" ("The dogs of Laconia live ten years, the bitches live twelve; other kinds, fifteen years, and sometimes, though rarely, till twenty.")

We dug a grave for poor old "Lassie" beneath a silver birch, beside a pool at which she often slaked her thirst, and left her to sleep under an emerald green coverlet of gowan-besprent sod—the truest, best, and wisest dog that ever erected an intelligent ear to the shout or whistle of him whose slightest behest it was her pride and pleasure, willingly and with all her heart, instantly to obey.

CHAPTER XLVII.

A Visit to the Oval Brochs of the Island of Luing—Their Position and Dimensions—The Hiding Craigs near Easdale.

About this time last year we made a pleasant pilgrimage to the so-called Castle of Tirefoor, on the Island of Lismore, and found it to be, not in truth a castle at all, in any proper sense of that term, but a veritable broch, with its concentric double walls, galleries, and all the other architectural characteristics of such edifices. Our paper on the Tirefoor Broch largely helped to draw intelligent attention to many such old ruins that had hitherto escaped particular notice, chiefly on the islands and along the mainland seaboard of Argyllshire. Our excellent friend Dr. Allan Macnaughton of Bailechuain, near Easdale, on reading about the Tirefoor Broch, instantly wrote us to say that on the Island of Luing—and therefore within the area of his many peregrinations, as medical officer of a very extensive district, insular and peninsular—there were two old ruins, fortified places in their day manifestly, and very possibly brochs, at the same time suggesting that we should come down to have a look at them, and kindly offering us every aid and facility for so doing as pleasantly and comfortably as the circumstances of the case permitted. Before we could accomplish it, however, winter, wild and stormy, was coming on apace, and we decided meanwhile that it was best simply to take a note of the fact that on the Island of Luing there were some ruins which, upon a sufficiently close and careful examination, might prove interesting, postponing our visit of exploration to the island until we were joined by our archæological friends from the south here in autumn. It was not until last week, therefore, that we could make up a sufficiently formidable broch-hunting party to go to Luing with. We left Ballachulish Pier by the "Iona," and after a swift and pleasant run, reached our port of disembarkation, which was Black Mill Bay, in Luing, before it was yet ten o'clock in the day. We had telegraphed to Dr. Macnaughton that we were coming, and he having joined us at Easdale Pier, we landed in Luing, a party now augmented to five in number, Dr. Macnaughton straightway assuming his proper position as guide and leader of our expedition over ground with which all the rest of us were utterly unacquainted, but with which he was sufficiently familiar. A walk of something over half an hour along a rough, undulating ridge, which may be called the backbone of the island, brought us to the first or southern ruin. Although in a state of extreme dilapidation, most of its best and biggest stones having been taken away, and probably long ago, to build a march dyke between the lands of two neighbouring farms, enough remains to prove that this, if not actually a broch proper, was at all events a broch-like structure of commanding position and great strength. What startled us all exceedingly, and puzzled us not a little, was to find that, instead of being circular, this broch (if broch it really ought to be called) was in truth very much of an oval, measuring 63 feet along its longer, and 36 feet along its shorter axis; or, adding a thickness of wall of about 12 feet, its dimensions may be set down at 75 feet by 48 feet. Double walls, gallery, scarcement, and other characteristics of a genuine broch were in parts easily enough traceable, and we, for our own part, had very little hesitation in boldly announcing our belief, then and there, that the structure was indeed and veritably a broch, though of a form hitherto unrecognised by Scottish archæologists —an *oval* broch. It is proper to state, however, that our companions were more cautious and guarded in coming to any very definite verdict in the matter, although they were willing enough to agree with us that, meanwhile, to call it an oval broch, and to speak of it as an oval broch, was in no sense to misname it. When we had very closely and carefully examined the southern fort, we started for the northern fort, already visible through our glasses on the top of a conical knoll at the extreme end of the ridge on which we stood, and some two miles away. As we were progressing *en zig-zag* along the ridge, Mr. Willison of Ardlarach House, whom we had already met when landing from the steamer in the morning, made his appearance in the pretty grass-green valley below, and shouted to us to descend for a moment. It was now high noon of a bright, hot day, and when we descended half-way down the steep, Mr. Willison conducted us to a little moss-lipped well of delightfully cool and clear water, of which we drank abundantly. The little nameless well round which we sat is constantly supplied from a crevice in the rock above, the water falling in a silvery thread, with pleasant and perennial trickle, into a partly natural and partly artificial rock basin. It is situated at the foot of the steep, some three hundred yards in a direction north-north-west of the broch; and of its limpid waters the old, bare-legged brochmen of the island, quite a thousand years ago, have doubtless often drank gladly and abundantly. Happening to be the first to bend down and drink largely from its basin with cunningly contracted and hollowed palm, for we were much athirst, Dr. Macnaughton did us the honour to call it "Nether Lochaber's Well," a name which we hope will make its waters none the less palatable and refreshing to the naturalist and archæologist in the West Highlands.

The northern fort—nameless, like the other—is in a state of extreme dilapidation, even more so than its southern fellow, although there is fortunately enough of it still remaining *in proprio sitû* to show that it was a fortified place of precisely the same style as the other, almost certainly of the same age, built for the same purpose, and by the same people. On the same *data* as in the case of the other, we pronounced this, too, to have been an oval broch of immense strength and great size, the thickness of the walls being, approximately, some 15 feet, and the dimensions internally 96 feet by 56 feet, or, including thickness of wall, something like 110 feet by 70 feet over all. Whether we are right as to their being brochs can only be decided *with certainty* by the clearing away of tons upon tons of fallen stones and *débris,* and such excavations in various directions as must entail a considerable expenditure of time and intelligent labour. We have long had a habit of jumping instantly and instinctively, so to speak, to conclusions in such matters, even when to others the immediately come-at-able *data* seemed insufficient to warrant our verdict. A very unscientific thing, doubtless, to do; but still we have done it so often, and, upon the whole, with so large a share of success, that here again we are content to stake any little archæological reputation that may be ours on the ultimate truth or otherwise, as evidenced by intelligent excavation, of our conclusion that these Luing forts are in truth brochs, and of a kind new to Scottish archæology—oval brochs —whether of a date anterior or slightly posterior to the age of the better known circular broch proper, it would in the meantime be rash to say. The surface of Luing over all may be described as strongly undulated, with a main ridge or backbone, frequently springing into knolls of considerable altitude; and on the two highest of these knolls, some four hundred feet above the level of the sea, the forts are placed, the southern one commanding a wide and beautiful view of the Scarban archipelago, with its many isles and islets, all the way to Colonsay in the one direction, and to the westernmost promontories of Mull in the other, while the northern fort has an equally commanding view of the narrows and channels dividing the islands of Seil, Luing, Torsay, and Shuna from each other, and in many a sinuous, river-like curve and bend from the mainland of Craignish, Melfort, and Nether Lorne. Neither friend nor enemy could approach Luing except by boat, and no boat could approach its shores without being seen from one or other of these forts, if only the watchmen were keen-eyed enough and faithful to their duty. Broch towers, oval or circular, an interesting inquiry concerning them, a question not easily answered, is who built them? They are manifestly places of defence, admirably constructed after their kind; but erected by whom? against what enemy? in what age? An attempt to find a satisfactory reply to these queries has given rise to much interesting and learned discussion amongst archæologists. The only thing freely admitted on all hands is that they are not prehistoric, as was for a long time supposed, but of the time of the Norsemen in Scotland; all of them were built some time during the five hundred years between the fifth and eleventh centuries. Dr. Ferguson, the distinguished writer on architecture, and a very competent authority in a matter of this kind, is convinced that they were built by the Norsemen, "by a people possessing command of the sea, to hold a conquered country against the restlessness of its imperfectly subdued aboriginal inhabitants." This view of the origin of brochs Dr. Ferguson advances and upholds with much ingenuity of learning. Dr. Joseph Anderson, of our Antiquarian Society, will have it, on the contrary, that the brochs were built, *not* by the Norsemen, but by the aboriginal Celts, as places of refuge and defence against the frequent invasions of the marauding Vikings, a theory which, upon the whole, seems to us the most likely to be true, although there remains, when all is said, one strong objection to it extremely difficult to get over. If the broch was built by the people of its district as a place of refuge and defence, how comes it that they are so small as to be incapable of accommodating only some thirty or forty individuals, and even then only for a short time, and in a condition very "cabin'd, cribb'd, confined," indeed? These two Luing brochs, for example (if brochs they shall be proved to be), might have temporarily and very uncomfortably accommodated some hundred or hundred and twenty individuals, but the population of the island must have been at least double, or even triple, that number; and how were those who could not find refuge in the brochs to escape the sword of the invader? If they were partly a pastoral and partly a piscatorial people, as they most probably were, even if it be insisted on that the brochs could contain them at all, they were in any case too small to afford shelter to their boats or to their cattle; and if these were left outside for the invader to do with as he pleased, the broch refugees must have been reduced to utter want, even if they managed somehow to sustain life within their brochs until the invader had departed from the island. This seems to us a formidable objection to Dr. Anderson's contention that the brochs were built as places of refuge by the aboriginal Brochland Celts, an objection which, until it is met more satisfactorily than it has yet been, will always give Dr. Ferguson a large and influential following in his counter-contention that the brochs were erected, not by the Celts, but by the Norsemen, for the accommodation of their scattered garrisons, in order to keep in subjection a people ready at any moment to rise against the tyranny of their oppressors. From the northern fort we made for the Ferry of Cuan or Kilbrandon Sound, and, once across, were soon under Dr. Macnaughton's hospitable roof at Bailechuain.

We had still two miles to walk, in order to meet the "Iona" at Easdale, and Dr. Macnaughton took us along the sea-shore, which here, at a distance well back from the present high-water mark, rises into beetling precipices, frequently of great height and grandeur. Our main object, however, in going this way rather than by the road was to examine two curious "hiding cliffs" or "hiding craigs," of a kind not uncommon along the shores of the Hebrides and Western Mainland. These are usually high, and flat or slightly hollow-topped cliffs, inaccessible as to their summits except by one approach, and that as a rule very steep and difficult of ascent, and not readily noticed by a stranger to the locality. The flat summit is usually surrounded by a rough rampart or wall, never so high as to attract attention from below, and merely erected, as it should seem (always a little inwards from the actual face of the rock), as a sort of parapet or safety fence to those who might be obliged to temporarily occupy the place. These refuge rocks are beyond all question as old at least as the time of the brochs. When a hostile galley was seen approaching the land, the women and children probably, and more valuable portable goods of the community, were placed out of sight, and out of any immediate danger, on these hiding craigs; while the men either offered battle to the invaders, or, scattering over the country inlands, hid themselves and their flocks as best they could, until the enemy set sail and steered for some other island. A refuge rock of this kind was appropriately termed by the native Celts a *Creag Falaich*, or hiding craig; and we find occasional mention made of them in old

Gaelic songs and *sgeulachdan*, or fireside tales. Thus, in old Mull song, sung by a girl whose misfortune it seems to have been that she loved not wisely but too well, and who, in her state of wretchedness and shame, is cruelly forsaken by her lover, occurs this verse—

> " Ma thréig thu mi, 'leannain, mo thruaighe mi ;
> Mo naire 's mo mhulad mar dh-fhàg thu mi ;
> Nach truagh leat mi, 'leannain, gun dachaidh air thalamh,
> Mur d'théid mi 'n *Chreig Fhalaich* a'm mhàgaran."

(" Since thou hast forsaken me, once fond lover ! sad is my case :
Oh ! the shame and wretchedness to which thou hast brought me !
Do you not pity me, and no home for me now on earth,
Unless, creeping wearily, I betake me to the *Hiding Craig ?*")

The *Creag Falaich* referred to in this song is at Lochbuy, in Mull; and we recollect seeing a very curious old brooch that was found in a crevice of its parapet wall by a sportsman who, whilst bird-nesting amongst the cliffs, chanced accidentally to discover the place. These hiding craigs are, we believe, new to Scottish archæologists, and we beg to draw particular attention to them. The two near Easdale are admirable specimens, and well worth visiting.

CHAPTER XLVIII.

Pied Swallows—1882 remarkable for Albinoism and Abnormal Colouring in Birds—Kestrel neatly plucking a Partridge Poult, that it might be the more easily carried against the wind.

To the ornithologist, this year of grace, 1882, is remarkable for the frequency of albinoism amongst certain species of birds usually given to any very marked aberrations from normal colouring. From a paragraph in a recent *Courier*, we learn that our excellent friends the Messrs Snowie of Inverness have lately had in their hands "a *white* swallow" to stuff and set up *secundum artem*, a bit of really difficult and delicate work, to which we are very confident nobody could do more perfect justice in the way of thoroughly sufficient taxidermical manipulation and accuracy of pose. Here, in our particular section of the West Highlands, white, canary coloured, and pied swallows have been so common this season, as latterly to be seen and passed by with comparative indifference. A score at least of these abnormally coloured birds have been flying about within a radius of a couple of miles from our own residence all summer, while very reliable information has reached us of the occurrence of white swallows also in the neighbouring districts of Appin, Ardgour, and Strontian. When these beautiful birds were first noticed, we caused it to be made known as widely as possible that anybody caught shooting or attempting to shoot them should be held guilty of a mean and cowardly act, which we should be quite prepared to resent by gibbetting the culprit to the execration of all bird-lovers in this column, and otherwise as we might judge it best. These threatenings were, we daresay, quite unnecessary, for an intelligent interest in and love of birds is now very general over the West Highlands. In any case, we are glad to say that, so far as it has come to our knowledge, not a single albino swallow has been shot in this district; and it will be interesting to watch if, on the return of the swallows next year, any of these beautiful albinos have survived to revisit our western shores. Albino sparrows, too, have been comparatively common this season, and we have heard of what we take to have been an albino corn-bunting, while a note reaches us from a trustworthy and keen observer certifying to the existence at this moment of a pure white hoodie, crow, somewhere along the upper reaches of Lochielside. The *cognoscenti* assure us that albinoism is more or less directly the result of disease, and that albinos are sterile—frequently at all events, if not as a rule. If any of our this season's white swallow friends survive to return to us next year, it will be curious to watch their nidification and the result, with a view to the corroboration or otherwise of this the commonly accepted theory of albinoism.

We have the following little story illustrative of the reasoning powers and sagacity of the kestrel hawk from one of the keepers on a nobleman's estate in our neighbourhood. One day in July the keeper in question, happening to be out after vermin with his gun, saw a bird coming his direction, which he knew to be some kind of hawk, but whose manner of flight puzzled him extremely. It was beating up the wind towards him as if with a sorely wounded wing, manifestly impeded in some way that caused it to zig-zag and struggle strangely in its flight. Seeing that if it kept its course it was likely to pass within easy shot, the keeper quietly subsided into a clump of ferns, on one knee, and with his gun ready for action. He had, however, to wait longer than he had bargained for, for the hawk had meanwhile alighted on the top of a large, grey boulder, a hundred yards away, and seemed very busy about something, though what it was the keeper at that distance could not well make out. In some five minutes, however, the hawk took wing again, this time with a much more steady and even flight, and was soon overhead and near enough to drop to the keeper's gun. On going up to his prize, the keeper found that it was indeed a hawk (from his description of it, we should say the pretty little kestrel falcon—*Falco tinnunculus*, Linn.), and beside it was lying a plump partridge poult, well grown, but, to the keeper's surprise, almost altogether denuded of feathers. On examining the boulder on which the kestrel had rested for a while, all the missing feathers of the juvenile partridge were found scattered about, and the very intelligent keeper instantly took in the state of matters from first to last, and explained it thus: the kestrel, having struck down the partridge poult, was carrying the dainty *bonne bouche* to his curve-beaked and greedy fledglings in their nest. The wind, however, was strong and gusty, and, adverse to the kestrel's line of flight and of the wind, the wings and tail, limp and pendent, of the partridge caught so much, that it was only with great difficulty and a constant struggle that for a time the plucky little raptor could make any satisfactory headway. Getting tired of it at last, he must have reasoned with himself somewhat after this fashion.—" My partridge burden is more difficult to get along with than, after all, it really needs be. I am heartily ashamed of myself, acting thus more like a Palmipede booby than the wise little falcon I ought to be, and, when all is said, I really and truly am! I will take a rest on yonder boulder, and pluck away all the wing and tail feathers from my dainty bit of game, an operation which, while it leaves my partridge quite as big and as good to eat as before, will enable me to bear it up and carry it against the wind with comparative ease." In some such a way as this the little kestrel really seems to have thought it out, and in the direction thus resolved upon he was acting when the contents of the keeper's gun so rudely ordered it otherwise, and put an end for ever to all the fights and fancies of one of the most graceful and beautiful of British birds. We endeavoured to persuade the keeper that it was wrong to shoot the kestrel, who in killing the partridge poult was only acting according to his instincts, and who in supplying his young with food was engaged in the discharge of a high and holy duty incumbent upon us all. We furthermore endeavoured to impress upon our gun-carrying friend that the indiscriminate slaughter of birds of prey is a mistake even from a utilitarian point of view, and talked very learnedly and convincingly, as we supposed, of the balance of nature, &c. &c.; but all our preaching in this direction was, we fear, to little good purpose. Gamekeepers, as a rule, only know that birds of prey sometimes destroy game, and that being admitted, birds of prey, they argue, ought to be killed without mercy, on the same principle that poachers are, on conviction, fined and imprisoned—from the keeper's standpoint, far too lenient a sentence for such misdemeanours!

CHAPTER XLIX.

Stormy October—Birds taking shelter—Superstition—The Oxeye Tit a Bird of good omen.

Like other would-be weather-wise people, we sometimes venture, as our readers are aware, on meteorological prognostications, which, instead of being verified, are utterly put to shame by the event. Not only does what is predicted *not* happen, but the very opposite does happen, and in such a case it only remains for us to shrug our shoulders, feel very small, and say as little about it as possible. Sometimes, however, our prognostications turn out creditably enough; and, very curiously, it is almost always when the data for our prognostics are no more than our observations on the increase or decrease of wild-fowl in our estuaries and bays, the predominant species at any particular moment, as well as the movements of our land birds, whether they most frequent the woods or open fields, and whether they seem brisk and cheerful or nervously anxious, with querulous chirp and constant shiftings from copse to copse, and from hedgerow to hedgerow. While it was yet September, we predicted with considerable positiveness our belief that October must turn out a very cold, and probably a very stormy month, our prognostication being founded solely on the fact that all our summer migrants were already off and away, and that our lochs were swarming with wild-fowl, many of them oceanic and Arctic, quite a month earlier than usual, showing that to the north of us, at all events, the cold and storm of winter had already set in, and that similar meteorological conditions were more than probably fast winging their flight to our own shores. And very cold as well as very stormy, it will be confessed, October proved—colder and stormier, indeed, than any other October month within our recollection. Since the dreadful Tay Bridge storm of a couple of years ago, we have had nothing to equal the fierce intensity of the gale of the 13th and 14th October. Fortunately, however, in this last gale the wind was not from the west *upon* our shores, but from the east and north-east off our shores; a big wind battery of largest calibre, that seemed for the nonce to be served by the arch storm-fiend himself from off his thousand stations along the Grampian peaks and the heights of Drumalbin, blowing great guns adown the glens, and over our heads across the Hebrides, south-westerly and seawards. At midnight it was terrific, from the inmates of most dwellings utterly banishing all thoughts of sleep, for, as it swept adown gully and gorge in fitful gusts, the air was filled as if with shrieks of agony, that evermore seemed to be fiercely battling with eldritch laughter wild and weird, and all intensified by the long-drawn wail, and sob, and sigh, and moan of the succeeding lulls. It was the same, or even worse, on to the following mid-day, the Linnhe Loch and our own Loch Leven, usually so placid, presenting a terrible scene of hurrying, hustling waves, and shrieking, swirling spindrift. Nor was it only stormy, but intensely cold as well; the mountains covered with a thick coating of snow almost to their base, followed a few days afterwards by a frost so keen, that on the pools in our immediate neighbourhood, and almost at the level of the sea, ice formed to the thickness of a quarter of an inch. During the many years that we have given some attention to the meteorology of our district, we have no record of a mid-October month so wintry at once and wild.

What that mid-October storm was may be partly understood from the following incident, anything exactly similar to which we do not remember in all our ornithological experience. It was half an hour after midnight, on the morning of the 14th, all our people were in bed except ourselves, and we were busy scribbling, when suddenly at our study window-panes came a rattling and rasping and rustling which we could not understand, and which therefore startled us extremely, for that window, mind you, was not exposed to, but to leeward of the gale. Instantly remembering, however, that that storm, as to us, was altogether abnormal; that instead of blowing somewhat steadily, direct, and horizontal, from any particular quarter, it was oblique, vertical, rotatory, swirling, anyhow, fulfilling all the conditions, and more if possible, of the children's playground rhyme—

> "Here we go with merry shout,
> Up and down and round about,
> And dance a merry-ma-tandy!"

Remembering all this, we thought that a branch of a *Lauristina*, of good tree size, growing quite close by our window, must have snapped in one of the many swirling gusts that shook our humble hermitage, though very substantially built of solid granite, as if it were no more than a wooden shanty; and fearing that the broken branch might in the next gust smash in the window, we determined to venture out in order to cut it altogether away. Armed with a hand-saw, therefore, and with a lantern, we opened our front door, when there was instantly a rushing and a rustling about our ears that astonished us; even when we recognised, as we did at once, that it was owing to a flock of quite a score of birds, that fluttered into the lobby the moment the door was opened, and as we stood there in the midst of so many circling flutterers, we could only compare ourselves to the archæologists who, torch in hand, so frequently encounter flights of bats when exploring the rock tombs and catacombs of the Nile. Instead of fluttering bats, however, in all ages, rightly or wrongly, accounted loathsome and unclean, we were the centre for the moment of a flock of pretty little birds, chaffinches chiefly, with a few sparrows and redbreasts. We had fortunately shut the inner lobby door before opening the main door; and leaving our unexpected midnight visitors to flutter about and perch as they liked, we went to the window, against the panes of which a few chaffinches were still fluttering and scrambling, and these we easily captured, taking them into the lobby and letting them go among their companions. We then locked the front door, and left our fluttering friends prisoners in the lobby till the morning, knowing that in the darkness they would very soon settle down quietly, and satisfied that for the present at least they were safe from all their enemies, and sheltered enough and snug from swirling sleet and storm. In the early morning we gave them their liberty, and a plateful of crumbs for their breakfast, sitting down to our own morning meal immediately afterwards, with all the heartier appetite that we had been able to help, however slightly, the frightened flutterers in their distress, for we remembered that although these birds, in human estimation, may be accounted of so little value, that "five of them are sold for two farthings," yet it is true, on the authority of Him who spake as never man spake, and taught as never man taught, that "*not one of them is forgotten before God.*"

In the superstition of the Highlands, a superstition in many directions rather dormant than dead, and even less dormant, perhaps, than hidden and concealed from sight, because of the sneers and incredulity of philosophical outsiders, the voluntary entrance into human dwellings of finchy warblers or thrushes is always regarded as an omen of good luck. If in a dwelling thus visited there is any one sick, there is instantly entertained by his friends a strong hope of his recovery; or should he die, the sorrowing friends find consolation, in a stronger belief because of the bird visit than could otherwise reasonably be entertained, that he is gone only to enjoy the unutterable felicity of a better and a brighter world. If, however, in the dwelling visited by the bird or birds everybody is in good health, then the voluntary presence of the feathered stranger is held to indicate a bit of good luck in some unknown direction, or of good news at an early date from absent friends. Not many months ago we happened to call upon a respectable old woman, a widow, in a distant part of the parish, and, on inquiring for her daughter "Jean," who was away at service in the south, and from whom nothing had been heard for a long time, the mother answered, "It is nearly two years, sir, since I had her last letter, but I have great confidence that I shall somehow have good tidings of her very soon, or that she will more affectionately make amends for her long silence by coming herself to see me, and that before the lapse of many days." "I am very glad to hear you say so," was our rejoinder; "but what, please tell me, makes you so hopeful in the matter?" "Well, sir," returned the widow, "this morning a bird, a pretty little bird, a *Cailleachay-Ceann-Dubh*, came into the kitchen by the open door, and perched on the cupboard shelf there for a little while, after which it flew out by the open window. It came in again by the window, and after fluttering about the room, flew out by the door; and I cannot but think that according to the wisdom of the *Seann daoine* (the 'old' or wise people of a past age), it bodes me good luck of some kind; and what good luck to an aged, lone widow as I am, like happy tidings of my only child, or better still, a visit from her own self, to bring once again a gleam of sunshine and joy into a cottage that has been dark and joyless enough since she left it." It was worth while going a long way to hear the old woman refer to the incident on which she founded her confident hope of soon getting good news of her absent daughter, in her own beautiful Gaelic, and now and again, as she described the joys and sorrows, the lights and shadows of a long and chequered life, easily rising into a strain of unconscious poetry that was exceeding musical and captivating. The *Cailleachag-Ceann-Dubh* (*lit.* the little old woman with the black hood), the reader must know, is the prettily plumaged little oxeye tit, with its black head and beautiful olive green back, that at certain seasons becomes exceedingly tame, and cheeky enough to enter by open door or window into any dwelling for which he may take a fancy, generally, however, preferring thatched cottages—*pauperum tabernæ*—in the wall crevices, and round the mossy, lichened eaves of which it usually finds its favourite insect food in abundance. We have noticed that it rarely approaches large and slated dwellings, and never enters these even when every facility is afforded in the way of frequently open doors and almost constantly open windows all the summer through. The amusing part of the story is that, having had to pass again by the old lady's cottage on our return home in the evening, we were pleasantly startled by her rushing out in a state of great excitement, jubilant and joyous, with the intimation that she had just received a letter which she was sure *must* contain good tidings, and which she begged we would be good enough to open and read for her. It was in very truth an affectionate letter from her long-silent daughter, satisfactory in every way, and containing a post-office order for a considerable sum, with the promise of an early visit, a promise which has since been fulfilled. "*Nach d'thubhairt mi ribh!*" ("Didn't I tell you!") exclaimed the old lady triumphantly. "*Beannachd Dhia air*

Cailleachag-bheag-a-chinn-duibh, teachdaire an aoibh- neis 'bha tigh'n orm ; *ged 'their sibhse mo lamhsa 'a geall, gur gòrach mi*" ("God's blessing on the black- hooded little old wifie that brought early tidings of the joy that was coming home to me; although you, sir, I warrant it, will only say how foolish I am"). We contented ourselves with heartily congratulating the old lady on her good news, not deeming it incumbent upon us to attempt, by any arguments within our reach, to reason her out of her belief that the occa- sional visits of harmless little birds to her humble dwelling were ominous of some bit of good fortune in store for her. Confident that she was sound enough in the faith otherwise, and knowing her to be of per- fectly blameless life, the reader will possibly agree with us in thinking that this little bit of harmless superstition added to her creed could not do her much harm in the here or hereafter.

CHAPTER L.

Meteorology and Weather Forecasts—Ornithology in aid of.

It was in the middle of October, that, relying on the movements of our wild-bird friends, we predicted the immediate advent on the British shores of a longer or shorter period of cold and storms, and almost thereafter, sure enough, there was a fall of temperature so sudden and abnormal as to astonish and surprise even our oldest meteorologists, a fall of temperature almost instantly followed by disastrous floods and storms of such force and fury as caused much shipwreck and loss of life. The conduct of sea-fowl, when, because of their mysterious prescience of coming storms, they seek the shelter and safety of our western inlets, so admirably barricaded against storm assaults by the friendly intervention of the whole breadth of the mainland, with its lofty mountain chains to the east, and of those great natural breakwaters, the Inner and Outer Hebrides, to the north and west—the conduct, we say, of sea-fowl who have thus run for shelter and safety is a most interesting and curious study to the philosophic naturalist. It is the sense, it may be believed, of a common danger about to fall upon them that causes them to congregate in flocks, and although these flocks may sometimes consist of many species of birds only distantly allied, if allied at all, and differing greatly in disposition and mode of life, it is doubtless the same sense of a common danger close at hand that makes them for the present forget all their jealousies and rivalries, and live together in friendliest companionship, without a thought of assault or injury in any direction, the timidest and weakest for the time paddling alongside and under the wing, so to speak, of the fiercest and strongest. In these circumstances they seem to have forgotten not only all the ferocity, but all the voracity as well, usually so characteristic of sea-birds, being apparently content with very little food, or no food at all, until the expected storm, the mere anticipation of which has so depressed them, having done its worst and wildest athwart their sheltered inlet, has carried its destructive forces fast and far either inland or seaward, and in any case has *quoad* them altogether subsided. Until the storm has come and gone, they maintain a dull and listless attitude, the divers seldom diving, the flyers rarely taking wing, while along the shores the waders, with bent and slightly reverted heads, and often on one leg, are motionless and silent, as if they were carved in stone. If after a storm these wild-bird flocks instantly scatter and disappear, a period of comparatively fine weather, with easterly and southeasterly winds, may very confidently be looked for; but if they merely break up into small parties, paddling along the shore, and still content to fish in sheltered inlets, and manifestly afraid to venture into the open sea, in such a case either another stormy period must be close at hand, or intense cold is about to set in. We have closely studied wild-bird life in connection with weather changes for five-and-thirty years, and the meteorologists must not be angry with us if we say that we have much greater faith in the prescience of our feathered friends as prognosticators of coming storms and cold than in all the wisdom and accumulated statistics of all the meteorologists and meteorological stations from John o' Groat's to Land's End. About the big storms of the last six weeks, for example—some of them storms of the first magnitude, too, be it remembered—our meteorologists, with all their wisdom and acuteness, and all the machinery at their command, were unable to speak a single word of warning. An examination of our western inlets, however, would have shown that whilst it was yet September, and the weather open and mild, large flocks of sea-birds had already arrived on all our shores a full month earlier than they ought to have come, and many of them birds never seen in our waters except as companions or precursors of intense cold or storms of exceeding violence. The thoughtful student of bird-life therefore knew that something exceptional in the way of storms must be close at hand. The meteorologist knew nothing at all about it, and, to do him justice, made no pretension to any forecast in the matter. The truth is, that, *so far as weather forecasts are concerned*, meteorology is at this moment the most inexact and useless of sciences. That it is gradually becoming more exact, extending and strengthening its grasp over the laws of atmospheric perturbations, is true, but its progress is exceedingly slow, and slower than, we think, it need be. A permanent meteorological observatory on the top of Ben Nevis, under the superintendence of our indefatigable and accomplished friend Mr. Wragge, will be an immense step in the right direction, and from which great and important results may very confidently be expected. For the erection and maintenance of such a high level meteorological station as is proposed, and which, when completed and in full working order, will be the most interesting and important thing of the kind in Europe, the Government ought most assuredly to provide the necessary funds; for it is a matter not of individual or local, but of national, importance. If, however, a "liberal" Government prove illiberal, and unwisely economical and stingy *quoad hoc*—if, in a word, the Government will do nothing—let the Scottish Meteorological Society only make a bold appeal to the country at large, and we are confident that the necessary funds for the Ben Nevis Meteorological Observatory will be forthcoming from private sources. Meanwhile, what we are particularly anxious to impress upon the scientific world is the immense importance and value of close and keen zoological observation in the matter of weather forecasts, not as being sufficient *per se*, observe, but as invaluable in constant and close alliance with meteorology proper. An intelligent shepherd will frequently foretell a coming storm, and its probable direction, a day or even days in advance, and this simply from the movement of his flock on their pastures. On the same *data* he will also often predict with absolute certainty a longer or shorter period of heat and drought. What can be done in this direction by a close attention to the habits of birds readers of this column need not now be told. If the observer at every meteorological station in the kingdom would only also become the intelligent zoologist of his district, with a keen eye for the movements of beasts and birds, as well as for the "readings" of his formidable array of instruments, we are persuaded that reliable weather forecasts, for circumscribed areas at least, would very soon become much more the rule, and less the exception, than as matters are at present.

CHAPTER LI.

Cold and Stormy Winter—Transit of Venus—Dr. Tait, Archbishop of Canterbury.

HURRAH for our wild-bird friends as weather prognosticators! On this, as on many previous occasions, our feathered biped friends foretold, after their own fashion, indeed, and in a somewhat roundabout sort of way, but intelligibly enough to the initiated, what their more pretentious brother bipeds in broadcloth and tweeds, with all the machinery and appliances of their boasted meteorological science, were confessedly unable either to foresee or foretell. Nor will it in the least serve the sceptical to say that it was a chance hit, for it was nothing of the kind, our readers themselves bearing witness. In September, and again in October, and a third time in November, we predicted, and with the utmost confidence, it will be remembered, first, that we were going to have storms, and the storms came, and latterly, that an exceptionally severe period of cold—winter with more than its usual inclemency—must be close at hand; and close at hand it assuredly was, for lo! it has come, and in such form from Land's End to Cape Wrath as will cause it to be long remembered as one of the coldest and stormiest winters of our century. Meanwhile, we have only further to observe that there are still daily arrivals of Arctic sea-birds on our shores, which are now swarming with all sorts of web-feet and waders, and it is best to be prepared for a continuance of cold and storm of exceptional severity, during the present month at least, and probably on till Candlemas Day.

Nowhere else could the transit of Venus on the 6th instant be better seen or more satisfactorily than from our little observatory here in Nether Lochaber. After a night of keen frost, the sky from earliest dawn was cold and clear as a sheet of polished steel, and without a shred or filmiest wisp of cloud that the keenest eye could detect in all the vast circumference of illimitable blue. With instruments in thoroughest order and carefully adjusted, it will be believed that we were at our post betimes, so keenly expectant, indeed, of what was coming, that we had the solar disc under closest scrutiny half a dozen times at least, even when we well knew that quite half an hour had yet to elapse ere the computed first moment of external contact could come round. At last, at 2 hours 24 min. 13 sec. local time, as nearly as with the instruments at our command we could make it, came the first faint touch of the planet's overlapment on the sun's eastern limb, or, in astronomical language, the first external contact at ingress, in the shape of an ink-black convex stripe, narrow and thin and elongated, as if a schoolboy, in a moment of carelessness, had laid too much weight on his broad-nibbed pen while describing the left hand limb of his big text O. Slowly, and one fancied as if with difficulty, and somewhat against its will, the planet crept onwards and inwards upon the solar disc, until planet and orb were again edge to edge, and it was the moment of internal contact at ingress, just

19 min. 57 sec. from first external contact; and thus the only two astronomically important phases of the conjunction, as visible in our country, were seen under conditions the most favourable possible, and altogether in a way that could not fail to gratify and delight exceedingly every intelligent observer. Whilst the transit was still in this its second phase, we were joined by our friend Dr. Maccalman of Glencoe, who took his turn at the telescope, and set us at liberty in order to jot down such particulars, meteorological, horal, and spectacular, as we thought most worthy of record. Presently a thin ribbon of brightest light, a mere thread of intensest luminosity, separated the edges of planet and primary, and Venus, round as a cannon ball, and black as ink, was fairly afloat on the *mare magnum* of the broad, bright solar sea. After this our observations were constant and by turns, at intervals of five and ten minutes, until the glorious orb, with its fairest planet, the Star of Evening and of Love, nestling at its heart, a huge resplendent shield of golden light, dipped and disappeared behind Ben-a-Barnich—the *Limpet* Ben—in Mull. With a power of 170 there was not the faintest trace of the appearances supposed to have been seen in former transits of Venus, and familiarly called the "ligature band" and "black drop;" nor was there any trace of a satellite of Venus, which, because of certain perturbations and anomalies in its orbital motion, was at one time suggested as at least a possible explanation of the difficulty. If the planet really had a satellite, it *must* have been seen on this occasion with the power at our command, and under our exceptionally

favourable condition of long, and keen, and careful observation. It may therefore be set down for a certainty that Venus has no satellite. Nor does the splendid planet need a satellite. Whether as the Star of the Evening or of the Morning, and from earliest times the Star of Love, she is bright and beautiful enough without such an attendant, always delighting, not in services rendered to her by subordinates, but in her nearness to and constant service to her magnificently grand and glorious primary. Although for several days immediately preceding the conjunction sun spots were common, and often of great magnitude, it is worth notice that during the transit there was not a vestige of these phenomena, the solar disc presenting a splendid circumference of living light, undimmed and spotless as necessarily, you will believe, was the object-glass of the telescope with which we viewed it. One very curious and pretty appearance, purely accidental of course, attracted the attention of Dr. Maccalman and ourselves during our last, long, lingering look at the solar shield, as the lower limb of the magnificent orb rested for an instant on the conical peak of beautiful Ben-a-Barnich. This was a large St. Andrew's cross, composed of two bright threads of orange-golden cloud, that chanced to meet and assume a form of cross so dear to every Scottish heart, transversely across the solar disc, and having the jet-black body of the transiting planet at the point of intersection of its arms. It was a very pretty and a very striking sight, and not an unfitting *finale* to one of the most interesting and delightful astronomical observations we have ever made. Shortly after the sun went down, the night came on cold and clear, with about as intense and keen a frost as we have ever known in Lochaber, the stars sparkling and burning on the hither shores of the immeasurable, illimitable profound, with a brilliancy that seemed to throb and pulsate with a consciousness of mysterious intelligence and of a higher life than is dreamt of in the philosophy of our mundane sphere. Our instruments being in most perfect possible adjustment, we devoted the night to astronomical observation, finishing off with belted Will Jupiter (you remember "belted Will Howard" of the old border ballad) and his attendant moons on the meridian at one o'clock in the morning, when, although duly muffered and heavily ulstered from the heels to the ears, five consecutive minutes in the open air so benumbed our hands—so keenly did it freeze, and so intense was the cold—that our fingers became "a' thumbs," in Scottish phrase, and we could not hold the pen to make the necessary jottings in our interleaved "Whitaker" until we had drunk off a huge bowl of very hot and very potent tea at a draught, and comfortably, and round and round, warmed ourselves at a fire, the exceeding gas-like clearness of whose flame and white-heat brightness of whose every ember sufficiently attested the keenness of the frost without.

Much has already been written in kindly appraisement of the late Archbishop of Canterbury, a good man, and, from a wordly point of view, an eminently successful man, to whom, for a wonder, nobody begrudged his success. He was essentially a *safe* man, cautious, self-possessed, and calm and prudent;

never in extremes; a most "kindly Scot," and always a "canny" man, in the best Northumbrian sense of that term. The following little story is very characteristic of him, and will be interesting to all who knew him well. Shortly after his election to the Primacy he was in Scotland, and paid a short visit to a West Highland laird, who was distantly related to him. The laird, one of the most hospitable of men, invited the parish minister to meet the Archbishop at a little dinner party, which went off very pleasantly, for "over the walnuts and the wine" the Archbishop, besides saying much that was wise and good, said also a great deal that was keenly humorous and entertaining—all, of course, in a quiet episcopal way. It had been arranged that the minister was to stay all night, and when the proper time came, the laird addressed his clerical guests in some such words as these—" Gentlemen, you are both aware that I have always family worship in my house. Before I ring the bell, I wish you would arrange it between yourselves which of you is to conduct the service this evening. Perhaps the best way will be for one of you to officiate to-night, and the other, God willing, to-morrow morning." "Not so," quietly and at once replied Dr. Tait. "I am Archbishop of Canterbury, our friend the minister here is Bishop of his own parish, and you, sir, are Bishop of your own house and family. Please conduct worship as you are wont to do, just in the usual way, and remember us both in your prayers." The laird having called his household together, read the beautiful fourteenth chapter of the Gospel of St. John, and prayed a short extempore prayer, recommending himself, his household, and his guests to the Divine Protector, and finishing with the Lord's Prayer,—" the prayer of all prayers," as the old divine hath it—" always appropriate, always fitting." The Archbishop, on rising from his knees, shook hands with all in the room, and expressed the pleasure it gave him to be privileged thus to join his Presbyterian friends in their homely and simple act of evening sacrifice to the Most High. On his return south, the Archbishop, when passing through Edinburgh, ordered twenty volumes of well-known and popular *Presbyterian books* to be sent as his gift to the theological section of the parish library.

CHAPTER LII.

Winter in the Country—Wild-Fowl—Flock of "Hooper" Swans (*Anas cygnus*, Linn.)—Wild-Swan Notes—Letter from Perthshire—The Eagle—Fox—Curious Egg—Alpine Hares on the Low Lands a sign of severe Winter.

INTENSELY cold, with frequent alternations of frost, and sleet, and snow, and always more or less of a gale, loud and blustering, or sharp of edge as a scythe's blade, one is fain to confess that it is really winter at last—winter, with a day so short, and eke so dark, and dull, and dim, as to be scarcely day at all, but rather a cold, grey afternoon from pallid dawn till nightfall. At this season of the year the night is, as a rule, much more enjoyable than the day, whether abroad, if need be, under the frosty starlight, or by the fireside in slippered ease, with lamps alit and curtains closely drawn, while without the elemental battle

"Rages loud and long,
And the stormy winds do blow."

Under these latter conditions, with a really good book to read, or one of the monthlies, or even a newspaper, if of the right sort, and well abreast of the stirring topics of the hour, one can get on very comfortably indeed; the howling of the storm without, and the rattle of the multitudinous hail upon the window-panes, only intensifying the delights of the calm, and quiet, and comfort of the bright fireside and all one's cozy surroundings within—

"The storm without might rain and rustle,
Tam didna mind the storm a whistle."

The truth is, that with something to read and a fair share of home comforts, a winter in the country, " far from the madding crowd," is very much more enjoyable than those constantly engulfed in the turmoil of bustling cities will readily believe. That we are to have a winter of more than usual severity, both as to cold and storms, seems certain enough. Our lochs are still swarming with sea-fowl, the flocks everywhere being daily augmented by new arrivals from the north and north-west. On Tuesday last, while driving home from Fort-William, a well-known clang and trumpeting overhead caused us suddenly to pull up, in order the more easily to give all our attention for the moment to an always interesting and beautiful sight. It was a flock of " Hooper " wild swans (*Anas cygnus*, Linn.), eleven in number, rapidly winging their flight from the far north-west, and across Ardgour and Lochaber to the south-east, probably making for the many linns and lakes of Rannoch and Breadalbane. Their flight was in wedge form, as usual, and at a great altitude, some 2000 feet, as we guessed; the leader, a magnificent male, with long neck, stiff and outstretched like the carved tiller of a yacht, and grand spread of wing, trumpetting now and again with loud, clear notes, not unlike the ring of a hammer on a bar of iron as you drive rapidly past a roadside smithy. Whether it was that a sight of Loch Llundavrà was sufficiently attractive to make them think for a moment of honouring it with a visit *en passant*, or in the mere wantonness of conscious power of wing and easy volition, it is impossible to say, but when over the heights of Coruanan and Llundavrà, they suddenly wheeled to the left, and swept round and round in easy circles, as if they meant to alight. In the course of the third wheel, however, the leader trumpeted a loud, decisive note, that seemed to settle the matter; and again the living, beautiful, snow-white wedge was off and away, heading south-eastwards as before, and was soon lost to sight behind the heights of Mamore. It is long since we had occasion to come to the conclusion that, when at this season of the year flocks of our larger wild-birds, web-feet swans, geese, and cormorants, pass high overhead inland, a period of intense cold must be close at hand—intense cold almost sure to be heralded by swirling snow-showers and fierce gales from the north and north-west.

We have received a long and very interesting communication from a large sheep-farmer in the Highlands of Perthshire. We have only room for the following extract :—

"On the 11th inst.," says our correspondent, "one of my shepherds and myself had a close interview with a golden eagle—a splendid bird, I assure you, it was—under the following circumstances :—Having reason to believe that an old hill fox, a very blood-thirsty rascal, and the cunningest of his tribe, was paying frequent visits to his hirsel, the shepherd in charge determined, if possible, to outwit the fox, with all his cunning. For some time he carried a gun, and frequently hid himself in likely places and at likely hours, in order to get a shot at the bushy-tailed evil-doer. In this, however, he failed, and at last he thought it a good plan to try what a well-baited trap would do. A strong spring trap, baited with rabbit, was accordingly placed near a cluster of large rocks and boulders, which was, with good reason, supposed to be the fox's *saobhaidh* or den ; and next day I resolved to accompany the shepherd myself on his visit to the trap. When, after a stiff climb, we came in sight of the trap, there was no fox in it, but, instead of what we wanted, there was in it a large golden eagle, a splendid big bird, squatting, quiet and motionless, as if sitting on eggs. Knowing how strong an eagle is, and how frequently it will fight at close quarters with beak and claws, I took off my coat (neither the shepherd nor myself had a plaid), and made a rush at the eagle, intending to throw my coat over him, and thus, if possible, secure him alive, without any hurt to myself or to him; but when I was within a few yards of him, he suddenly spread his wings, and struggling violently, he got free and flew away! At first my idea was that he must have carried the trap bodily along with him, but the trap, I found, was too firmly attached to a strong peg in the ground by a new dog chain to be carried away even by so strong a bird as an eagle, and the trap itself told how the thing was done. Between the firmly-closed steel teeth I found almost half a toe of the eagle, with its strong, hooked talon more than an inch in the curve, which was all the trap had a hold of him by, and which, in his last violent struggle, as he saw me approach, he broke off and left behind him. On the spring table of the trap there was a little blood—not nearly so much as I should have expected—but there was a touch of frost all the previous night, and the cold may very likely have stopped the bleeding. The amputated toe is, I think, the hind toe, but of this I am not sure. One of the Duke's keepers, however, says that 'it is either the hind toe or one of the fore toes' (!), a very valuable bit of information, no doubt, for which I am obliged to him. Hind toe or fore toe, however, I have sent it to a jeweller to be mounted in gold as a pin, and I hope if you come this way in any of your rambles you will call and see it.

"I may tell you that, although unsuccessful with the fox on this occasion, the thief was shot by the shepherd a few days afterwards, one afternoon as he was slinking home to his den. He proved to be a large dog fox with very black pads. One of his teeth was wanting, and the rest stumpy and yellow to their tips. He had also a good deal of grey about the muzzle. I therefore conclude that he was a very old fox—ten years old, if he was a day. From first to last, I dare say, the rascal must have killed at least a hundred pounds worth of my sheep and lambs. One comfort is that he will kill no more. Dugald (the shepherd who shot him) was as proud of his feat as ever was an Englishman of his first stag, or an Anglo-Indian of his first tiger. Do you think the eagle will be much the worse of the loss of his toe? Like yourself, I have a great respect for eagles, and should be sorry to think that this noble bird should starve and be miserable by reason of his contact with my trap."

We are much obliged to our correspondent, who writes so well, that we hope to hear from him soon again. The eagle is, we dare say, all right again. The loss of a toe in such a case is " rather an inconvenience than a loss." The eagle can doubtless get on without his toe quite as well as many a skilled handicraftsman whom accident at bench or forge has deprived of a finger. It is simply marvellous how nature accommodates herself to such accidents.

We have also received the following note :—

"INVERNESS, 18th November 1882.

"A friend of mine has in his possession a natural curiosity—a very large goose egg, which had outwardly the appearance an egg ought to have, but which, on being broken, was found to contain the usual white and yolk, and *in the centre of the latter another complete egg, shell and all!*

"Double yolks had been seen before, but *this* was rather unusual, so it was resolved to preserve this egg as a curiosity, and the yolk, &c. having been removed, the inner egg within the outer shell was left intact.

"To assure you of the fact, I may mention that the aperture in the outer shell is far too small to allow of the inner egg being *introduced* through it."

Egg monstrosities are exceedingly common, particularly in the case of domestic fowls, though the special form of abnormality referred to by our correspondent is rare—so rare that we ourselves have never met with an instance of it. In the natural history columns, however, of *Land and Water* and *The Field,* instances of precisely the same oological abnormality have often been mentioned. If our correspondent can get his friend to send us the specimen referred to in his note, we should be glad to submit it to a close and careful examination, with a view to treating the subject on some future occasion more at large.

A gamekeeper from one of the neighbouring districts has just been calling upon us, in order to put us in possession of his views, betimes, of the sort of weather likely to prevail for some time to come. He is a man of high intelligence, shrewd and observant, and we have often had occasion to acknowledge his *nous* and keen foresight in matters meteorological. His story is to this effect :—Whilst out shooting hares one afternoon last week, he bagged eleven, of whom no less than seven were Alpine or mountain hares. They were all killed on low, level lands, close by the sea, and in the immediate vicinity of a couple of populous hamlets. The fact of so many Alpine hares being met with so low down, goes, in his opinion, to prove that already on the uplands the weather is very severe, and is likely to be of exceptional severity by the time the day is at its shortest. In his forty years' experience as gamekeeper he has found that the appearance of mountain hares on the low-lying crofters' lands by the sea has invariably been followed by a period of intense cold and storms. The proper home of the Alpine hare, he remarked, is the mountain crest and the wide moorland solitudes of the uplands. Neither dogs nor guns, nor any amount of persecution, will drive them from their beloved haunts amongst the upland wildernesses. Nothing will do this except the hunger and general discomfort attendant on the intense cold of an exceptionally severe winter; and therefore it is that he feels himself justified in predicting a period of intense cold and storms betwixt this and Candlemastide.

www.ingramcontent.com/pod-product-compliance
Lightning Source LLC
Chambersburg PA
CBHW051247300426
44114CB00011B/919